Being-in-America

Ronald Kent Richardson

Being-in-America

White Supremacy and the American Self

PETER LANG
New York · Berlin · Bruxelles · Chennai · Lausanne · Oxford

Library of Congress Cataloging-in-Publication Data

Names: Richardson, Ronald Kent, author.
Title: Being-in-America: White supremacy and the American self / Ronald Kent Richardson.
Description: New York: Peter Lang, [2024] | Includes bibliographical references and index.
Identifiers: LCCN 2023052117 (print) | LCCN 2023052118 (ebook) | ISBN
9781433194146 (hardback) | ISBN 9781433194115 (pdf) | ISBN 9781433194122 (epub) |
ISBN 9781433194139 (mobi)
Subjects: LCSH: Racism—United States. | White people—Race identity—United States. |
White nationalism--United States. | National characteristics, American. | Group identity—
United States.
Classification: LCC E184.A1. R474 2024 (print) | LCC E184.A1 (ebook) |
DDC 305.809/073—dc23/eng/20231207
LC record available at https://lccn.loc.gov/2023052117
LC ebook record available at https://lccn.loc.gov/2023052118
DOI 10.3726/b21456

Bibliographic information published by the Deutsche Nationalbibliothek.
The German National Library lists this publication in the German
National Bibliography; detailed bibliographic data is available
on the Internet at http://dnb.d-nb.de.

Cover design by Peter Lang Group AG

ISBN 9781433194146 (hardback)
ISBN 9781433194115 (ebook)
ISBN 9781433194122 (epub)
DOI 10.3726/b21456

© 2024 Ronald Kent Richardson
Published by Peter Lang Publishing Inc., New York, USA
info@peterlang.com - www.peterlang.com

All rights reserved.
All parts of this publication are protected by copyright.
Any utilization outside the strict limits of the copyright law, without the permission of the
publisher, is forbidden and liable to prosecution.
This applies in particular to reproductions, translations, microfilming, and storage and
processing in electronic retrieval systems.

This publication has been peer reviewed.

For
Khary, Ade, Kartina, and Endria
With Love

CONTENTS

	Acknowledgments	xi
	Introduction	1
Chapter 1	Brief Encounters	5
Chapter 2	Looking in from Outside	9
Chapter 3	The Hidden World	13
Chapter 4	A World of Play	23
Chapter 5	The Witch of Fourth Street	27
Chapter 6	Chestnuts and Cat's Eyes	31
Chapter 7	Girls and Boys	35

CONTENTS

Chapter 8	Play and Becoming	37
Chapter 9	The Stutter	39
Chapter 10	The Periodic Pilgrimage or Graveyard Picnics	45
Chapter 11	Education in Whiteness	49
Chapter 12	Concerning Violence	53
Chapter 13	Home Sweet Home	61
Chapter 14	Materfamilias	71
Chapter 15	Parental Fears	81
Chapter 16	The Root Problem	91
Chapter 17	Alternate Parents or the Silent Counteroffensive	95
Chapter 18	The Eldest Brother	103
Chapter 19	The Call of the Wild	113
Chapter 20	The Value of Willful Unknowing	121
Chapter 21	Poor Jack	125
Chapter 22	Beyond the Far Horizon	127
Chapter 23	Prophecy	137
Chapter 24	Signs and Portents	141
Intermezzo		157
Chapter 25	Who Am I?	159

CONTENTS ix

Chapter 26	A Life in Many Worlds	161
Chapter 27	Audubon	167
Chapter 28	Memory Palace	177
Chapter 29	The Agency of Objects	183
Chapter 30	The White Supremacist Collective Unconscious	191
Chapter 31	The Socially Autonomous Self and Anticipatory Connectivity	219
Chapter 32	Deprivations	227
Chapter 33	Elective Deprivations	235
Chapter 34	Set Being as Foundation for Artificial Intelligence, Or the Object Triumphant	241
Chapter 35	The Übermensch	245
Epilogue		247
	Index	249

ACKNOWLEDGMENTS

As this book is not a traditional academic work, I have few traditional academic acknowledgments to make. They include former chairs of the Department of History at Boston University while this book was being written, Louis Ferleger and Nina Silber who made me feel a genuine member of an intellectual community and stood up for my rights when needed. They are sterling examples of dedicated and socially committed scholars. Stan Sclaroff, Dean of the College of Arts and Sciences supported my creative work and ably led the college through the pandemic. I want to thank my students over several years for their active and helpful engagement with the ideas presented in this book. They do not often believe it when we make the claim but teachers learn a tremendous amount from those they teach. I am grateful to Dani Green and Alison Jefferson at Peter Lang's Editorial office, and Joshua Charles, Charmitha Ashok and the production team for their excellent and diligent work in shepherding this book into publication. Jenna Weathers and the staff of the Interlibrary Loan department at the marvelous Newton Free Library were diligent and amazingly fast in fulfilling my never ending requests. I am grateful to my inspiring, patient and enlightening Japanese teacher Rie Takashima, Rie-sensei, for her excellent pedagogy, and for listening to many of the evolving ideas embodied in this book, during my all too often retreats from the demands of Japanese grammar.

Portions of this book appeared in earlier form in the following journals: "The White Supremacist Collective Unconscious and the Autonomous Self" in Transition Magazine, Issue 130, 2021; "Home Sweet Home" in Litbreak Magazine, November 2, 2020; and "The Agency of Objects" in Epoché, Philosophy Monthly, Issue 34, September 2020. I am grateful to the editors and staff of those journals for offering me an intellectual forum.

I want to thank my sister Anne Marie Nichols for all of our contentious, constructive and loving discussions. She will undoubtedly disagree vocally with much that she finds in this book, which will become the occasion for many more future debates. I thank my Nephew Terry Nichols for our intellectual engagement, his insights and humor, and persistent commitment to his ideas and principles. I am forever grateful to my departed eldest brother Ernest Richardson for his critical mind, irreverence and perception, and his willingness to engage a younger sibling, my "alternate parents" for all that is expressed of them herein, and not least of all, to my parents, Ethel Toussaint and Ernest Wentworth Richardson, who braved white supremacist America with the courage to raise seven relatively sane children, and to all of our ancestors stretching back in unbroken chains into those primordial wilderness ages I've dreamt of all of my life.

Finally, and most importantly, I am immeasurably grateful to my children who listened to their father expound his peculiar notions over many years, and who read chapters from the work in progress, and offered their helpful criticisms; but, much more importantly, who sustained me with their love, patience and forbearance. They have made my life richer than it would ever have been without them. I dedicate this book to them, in the hope that their future, and that of their children and of their children's children will be vastly better than our present precarious times.

Ron Richardson
Newtonville, Massachusetts
August 13, 2023

INTRODUCTION

I have found that I am a rather elastic, blurred and ambiguous being, never fully coming into focus.[1]

We Americans are children of the same god, endowed by our creator with a virtually unalienable *white supremacist collective unconscious*. This god is not Jefferson's supreme being, but a mode of generating and maintaining humanbeing, to which we have surrendered ourselves in the faith that it will bring salvation. It may well be that we will transform this way of being into a supreme governing intelligence by our technological sophistication, at which time the religious history of humanity may have predicted its future demise.

In this work I am attempting an autoontology in the midst of an autoethnography in the context of a white supremacist society of tremendous oppressive and repressive power, and yet of seemingly infinite capacity to adapt to, coopt and defeat varied challenges to its hegemony. Do not be put off by these terms. They sound abstract but they are actually quite simple. Ontology is the term philosophers use to describe the study of the structure of being. That sounds complex too, but all it means is the way we have come to exist, the way we make ourselves what we are. So, autoontology, in the present context, means that I will use the example of how I came to be what I am to explore the way we create selves in America, and the unavoidable role of white supremacy in our self creation.

2   BEING-IN-AMERICA: WHITE SUPREMACY AND THE AMERICAN

Ethnography is the descriptive study of the way of life of particular people, their customs and values, for example. By autoethnography, I intend to use myself, my family, the communities I have lived within, including universities, and my wider experiences in America as part of my evidentiary base for exploring the way we Americans perform humanbeing. In this book humanbeing is used as a noun to indicate human existence, while *humanbeing* in italics is a verb expressing the dynamic performance of selfhood in America; a performance that engages ourselves, other people, objects, and the natural world. I make no claim to lived experience of personhood anywhere else but in my own country.

I describe our way of being in America based on my experience as a participant observer in a society dominated by white people. The notion of white people found in this work does not, cannot, and is not meant to encompass all white people. I know and have known white people who are honest about their privileged position in society and who are struggling to overcome it. But in my experience they are courageous exceptions to the rule.

Much of what I say in this book is based on the realization that in America, the question of who we are comes to be diverted to our race, our ethnicity, our gender and our sexual orientation. These issues, even while they are crucially important, mask questions about what we are as human beings, by which I mean they conceal the particular way of being a person in America which is fundamentally structured by the white supremacy existing within each of us, whether we are white, African American, Native American, Asian American, or some other "other". One may object that the term human being is an empty set, a place holder, a device for ignoring the unpleasant, racially and gender charged predicament we live in, and has no relevant meaning until it is filled in by the details of a particular human being, which includes race, gender and ethnicity. These are the identity resources we normally draw from when we engage questions about who and what we are. This means we are always-already struggling to realize or resist or redefine or recreate or complicate our racial or ethnic or gender identities. These debates and problems become our existential foundation. We choose to persist in them because they support individual autonomy as we imagine and practice it in America. As such they are ontological structures; that is, they help us shape our American way of being autonomous individuals. When I ask what we are as humans, I am concerned to understand how we create and maintain those structures and our intentions in doing so.

This book is divided into two parts. Part I is largely autobiographical. It deals with my early childhood and adolescence. Much of what I relate in this section may seem raceless. But white supremacy and race are located in the fairly ordinary. Very often their ordinariness is what makes them so hard to identify. In describing my path to becoming a person, which in America means, if one is to be considered normal and healthy, an autonomous individual, I am unavoidably describing how I, like all of us, assimilated a white supremacist unconscious that I have been struggling with all of my life, sometimes consciously, but mainly in an unconscious battle that saps my energies and leaves me wondering why I am often depressed and lonely. Of course, there is also much about race in Part I because I am writing about an American youth, and there is no American youth that is not racial. That some are experienced as raceless is an effect of white supremacy.

Part II also includes autobiographical accounts but it is largely devoted to a deeper analysis of what it means to be a self, what memory is, how we attempt to augment our own "agency" by robbing objects of agency, the idea of parallel worlds, the diversionary role of the "diversity and inclusion" movement, the dangers of AI created Super intelligence, and what I call the *white supremacist collective unconscious*.

My purpose in writing this book is to engage the American people over the issues that I raise, issues that will destroy this nation if we continue to ignore them; but they are issues which if faced and surmounted could open the way to a wonderful future for all of us. That we have very often turned away from that confrontation, and thereby foreclosed the beloved community that terrifies us, is the American tragedy.

Notes

1   Chapter 28 Memory Palace, p.178

· 1 ·

BRIEF ENCOUNTERS

I often wonder about the strangers I encounter in my daily rounds, all those many worlds I'll never know. Multiply one person by nearly eight billion and we're dwarfed by the very scale of human interconnections we're mainly unaware of.

One such meeting sticks in my mind after over fifty years. In the early summer of 1973 I was in school at the State University of New York at Binghamton, which has now been given the prosaic name Binghamton University. That summer was focused on learning German and French in preparation for graduate studies in September. I'd been at it eight hours a day seven days a week and needed a break. I decided to catch the Greyhound Bus to NYC, a leisurely walk to Grand Central Station past the sex shops crowding 42nd Street at the time and a commuter train home to Mt. Vernon. I had my flash cards with me to study verbs on the trip.

The bus station in downtown Binghamton was small and functional. I bought my ticket at the counter and was on my way to the platform when I noticed something through the window. Among the scattered travelers, a young black man of twenty odd was talking to a taller black man in a dark raincoat. The door of a waiting bus opened. The driver called the passengers aboard. The taller man said goodbye. The other, full of restless energy, walked

6   BEING-IN-AMERICA: WHITE SUPREMACY AND THE AMERICAN

about the platform, engaging people eager to get away about their business. The last thing I needed was talkative company. Today, a lone black man in a white city would keep to himself. I could wait for my bus contentedly, whispering German in my head. The 1970s public performance of black solidarity has vanished. In those days young black men felt a sort of bond as inmates of America. On that summer day, as I watched the restless young man, I felt a kind of irritation. If I went out to the platform he'd surely strike up a conversation, with brother this and brother that. If I ignored him or discouraged talk, he'd think I was one of those black people we called bougie, arrogant and full of middleclass pretentions. The main thing was to avoid sitting next to him. I wasn't about to waste three good study hours in idle chitchat.

The big silver bus pulled in, the door opened and the passengers emerged rumpled and worn from their cramped journey. It was time to get out there come what may. And up he came at once, greeting me exactly as I had anticipated by the elaborate handshake, the common bond of black men in those days. He was talkative indeed, and as I had observed, full of frenetic energy. "I just got out of the joint", was the first thing he said after greetings had been exchanged. The revelation did not put me off. I'd met a number of ex-offenders in the university's prison program and in Washington, D.C. I thought of myself as progressive, committed to full equality and regarded the prison system as another tool of white tyranny over black people. The Attica prison rebellion and its bloody suppression by New York State law enforcement officers occurred during my first year at Binghamton. We'd read about it and discussed it in depth in a course taught by Floyd McKissick, a former director of the Congress of Racial Equality. I was full of sympathy for the prisoners who'd been ruthlessly attacked by the overwhelming firepower of the State Police, supported by Governor Nelson Rockefeller and Richard Nixon. My new acquaintance immediately told me he'd been in for a four years stretch. So, I asked, you must have experienced the rebellion. Indeed, he had been beaten by the "bulls" in retaliation and suffered a back injury. He'd gotten out some days or weeks before, I'm no longer sure, and went to Buffalo to avoid getting into trouble in NYC. Now, his ailing mother was asking to see him before she died, so he was on his way to the "Big Apple" and her home on Boston Road in the Bronx. Strangely, he asked me how to get from Port Authority to the Boston Road by subway. The question added to the suspicions growing in my mind about this person so ready to confess all to a complete stranger. Four years wouldn't have erased the subway system form his memory. I gave him my best directions. Then he began a harangue about the condition of the black man in America and the need for all of us to unify against "the Man". It struck me as a sales pitch for an undisclosed product. Something about this fellow was decidedly false, like the many tricksters and confidence men I'd met in Washington, D.C., while at Howard University in the 1960s, men whose entire personality could change in an instant from trusted friend, to Artful Dodger, to murderous Bill Sikes. I sensed in him suppressed violence precariously held in check by the most tenuous restraints. There was no way I was going to sit with him for three hours or allow him to know where I was actually going. When he asked, I told him Washington.

The driver opened the door. The passengers began to enter. The young man and I got in line, he ahead of me, as I had wanted. At the last moment, just as he had stepped aboard, I made the excuse of wanting cigarettes, although I'd stopped smoking weeks before, and went into the terminal. To confirm the dodge, I bought a pack of Tareytons from the machine and waited. When I was sure he was onboard, and just before the driver was ready to start, I walked rapidly to the bus and got in. As I had expected he was sitting alone at a window the vacant isle seat waiting for me. He fixed an intense, sly and knowing smile upon me. I smiled back and continued up isle to a seat beside a large sleeping white man. There were no stops between Binghamton and NYC. The white man would stay put. So would the black man from Attica. I could study my verbs in peace and quiet.

When we got to Port Authority, I waited until he exited the bus and watched as he entered the long passageway to 42nd Street. I had planned to walk to Grand Central but something took me to a cab instead. I was being paranoid. It was a paranoid time. I arrived safely in Grand Central and caught the Stanford Local to Mt. Vernon. The young man was gone forever, his face, one among thousands I'd met, was quickly forgotten. Try as I might I cannot summon an image of it today, only the vague outline of a countenance with short beard and moustache and a modest Afro hairdo. Why the encounter occurred I cannot say. I often think about it, crossing a life I was given a very brief but disturbing glimpse of. I wondered what became of him. Did the reunion with his mother go well? How long did she survive? Would he stay out of trouble, meet the conditions of his parole and lead a productive life. It seemed strange I would never know anything more.

How often we have such encounters. I have met many others at bus and train stations, at airports or simply walking down the street, young people at Howard University and Binghamton, whose lives intersected mine briefly and never again. I recall lonely farms passing the window of my train on the way to California, thinking how odd it was the people in those houses were living lives unknown to me, with concerns and expectations as important to them as mine were to me. We'd passed them by, gone forever, miles behind, days behind, they went on as we spanned the continent from coast to coast, living, thriving or dying in complete isolation from my world, untouched by me or anything I thought or did, just as their existence was aloof from mine except in reminiscence. Why then, do I feel forever connected with every person, animal, plant or thing I've ever come across, as if enmeshed in a hidden fabric weaving itself to some vast scheme, incomprehensible to human consciousness bound by time and space?

· 2 ·

LOOKING IN FROM OUTSIDE

It appears in mind's eye, the Train Cake baked for the second birthday, the engine with its blue boiler and pink wheels, a vague figure kneeling beside the oval track of my elder brothers' electric trains, watching the sleek black engine race across the single bent track, once, twice without falling only to derail on the third attempt and frequently thereafter. "Stay on! Stay on!", a wee voice calls as it sweeps across the warp, half knowing wishing could never change the physical world, half hoping the laws of nature *could* be suspended by sufficient conscientious faith.

Other glimpses from those early days. The basketball the 3-year-old allowed the little boy to hold, who ran away and never did come back. The big boys from the Bronx who snatched the canteen from his hands that same summer. Halloween pumpkins eaten by the white rat on the fire escape. The fall from a backyard log into a pool of muddy water drenching the new snowsuit, all summed up in advance by that intrepid engine and faulty track. Somehow, at the very moment of derailment, there was the dreadful intuition life would be forever haunted by imperfections. Things were warped and never would run smooth. Perhaps that recognition made accessible by the train, and not the train itself, had evoked the earliest recollection. Yet there was, overlaying the intuition of fundamental flaw, the contrary sense of unending presence,

10 BEING-IN-AMERICA: WHITE SUPREMACY AND THE AMERICAN

the ingrained certainty nothing ever went away for good. The basketball, the canteen and the little black engine persisted somewhere hidden, redeemable, if one knew where and how to look. Once old enough to recognize its absence there was the search for that engine in repeated expeditions among the boxes and clutter of the long kitchen closet, the wilderness habitat of mice the father hunted to keep the family safe. The engine is there, somewhere, looking hard enough will find it, perhaps hereafter.

Language brings the gift of memory driving into headlong allegiance with its world and its works. Little by little, until in a rush, the intervention of that world obliterates all discernable traces of primordial time. We begin memoried life several years after physical birth with absorption into whatever linguistic realm we entered. The first attempts at speech did not communicate needs and desires. That could be left to physical and emotional demonstration, crying, fretting and movement. Babbling was for the pure physical and emotional pleasure of making sounds. Soon words replaced babbling bringing the double happiness of sound wedded to meaning.

At first there was no notion sounds made any particular sense of their own. Speech was another mode of touching them, like being held, the imitation of commonplace words coached and encouraged by parents and older siblings. This was a sort of game whose rewards were not linguistic competence, or the satisfaction of communication but sounding as *they* did. In this early dawn speech was simply one more mode of overwhelming oneness, of obliterating the separateness that ambushes each of us at birth.

There was some time before recognizing speaking could influence people, but by then it was occurring. In a familiar pattern, act always preceded recognition and reflection, qualified and restrained it. From that point on the world began to freeze and harden, stiffen and constrain. There was no resisting this onslaught which came with love and nourishment, kindness and caring in a world that grew increasingly orderly and domesticated. In the beginning there was too much to gain by the extraordinary narrowing that marked the rapid entrance to think of anything left behind, nor was there as yet the sense of past or future, every smile and gesture, each mimicked word brought further entanglement with them, narrowing awareness and choices. Until, all at once, with the emergence of a handful of words, everything balanced precariously between two worlds, the oceanic realm in back and articulation into multiplying assemblage of individual entities, until only vague feelings, distant fears ambiguous regrets remained to mark remote and misty emerging as the backward and behind. Soon all ancestral sensations merged in one incessant undefined and irredeemable absence.

Little by little the habit of assimilating to them became ingrained. Later on I would have to struggle against it to clear the cobwebs from my eyes and reopen the world I'd closed to be with them.

· 3 ·

THE HIDDEN WORLD

I must have been three or four, too young for school, living in a very small world enclosed within the boundaries of our third floor apartment, the front and back yards and the little block we shared with friendly and congenial neighbors. On a clear day, if you sat on the window seat in the "front room" and peered into the distance, you'd see the needlepoint of the Empire State Building away off in New York City. That spire marked the ends of the earth for me. I knew, of course, there must be more. I'd seen it in my favorite picture book *Little Folk of Many Lands*. A Siamese boy sat on a water buffalo. A Japanese girl held an umbrella against the sun. A little Dutch boy skated across a frozen canal. It was an extraordinary, magical book for when I looked into its pages the Dutch boy skated, the water buffalo moved, the Japanese girl twirled the umbrella making the pictures on it whirl by. They were real living people somewhere out there. One day I would visit them on an airplane or a great steamship. Until then I was content with my very small world and all the people in it.

My mother and my father were the center of my world, the foundation of my security and my insecurity, fosterers of hopes and architects of their frustration, alternately illuminating and darkening the landscape. They were mommy and daddy to all of us, never ever Mom and Dad, terms that make

14   BEING-IN-AMERICA: WHITE SUPREMACY AND THE AMERICAN

me cringe whenever I hear their glistening white normality. Early home life centered around my mother, always there, organizing, supervising, cooking, cleaning, correcting, instructing and inspiring. It is impossible to imagine that world without her. She ran the household, made the major decisions, paid the bills, prepared the accounts and saved. Until I was three or four my mother dressed me, squeezed me into the old fashioned snowsuit, girdled so stiffly you could barely move, buckled the hat tightly beneath my chin, her rough knuckles scratching, the snap frequently catching flesh. She'd call from time to time from the back bedroom window to check I was alright, and fetch me in when I'd had enough airing for the time being.

When my younger brother was born mommy took us with her shopping on Fourth Avenue, always it seemed in the depth of winter or the hottest days of summer, dragging us in and out of overheated stores, while we whined and sometimes cried at the unbearable, constraining tediousness of it all. The cold of winter, the parching thirst of summer were leavened by the sights and smells of early 1950s shopping, sensory riches and surprises vanished with the numbing, uniform artlessness of plastic wrappers, standard packaging, retail stores homogenized to oppressive sameness and online marketplaces deprived of all humanity. One could not shop in one place. If it was inconvenient to move from store to store it was comforting and connecting as well. For vegetables and dry goods we went to a greengrocer. There were two on Fourth Avenue. My mother's favorite was run by an ancient Italian man with wrinkled face and big mustache. He wore a striped apron and spoke like a foreigner. I never understood a word he said and could only smile when he greeted me, but he and my mother were good friends who spoke knowingly to each other as they haggled over prices. The store was closed on three sides, entirely open at front during business hours and shut at closing by a corrugated iron wall he pulled down with a loud and familiar sound. The floor was covered in sawdust and giant cheeses hung from the ceiling. Big barrels stuffed with salted codfish, still and fragrant, stood in corners. Boxes of cereal and "provisions" climbed all three walls. It was a wonderful place, steeped in the mingled smell of cheeses and salt fish and fresh vegetables waiting in open cardboard crates for customers to take them home.

My mother was exceptionally well organized and did everything methodically, shopping in geographical and temporal order, starting from the perimeter and working her way homewards. Sometimes, she'd alter our itinerary to visit the Jewish Bakery adjacent the firehouse, where the firemen had put me in the driver's seat of the hook and ladder truck one day when I was 3. We'd each get half of a day old raisin bun and once in a long while a fresh black and white cookie. She never bought the delicious looking cheese Danish or chocolate layer cakes with chocolate sprinkles on the top shelf of the glass case. Her "budget", which she never wandered from, forbid extravagance. All of her cakes were made "from scratch", though one could never get enough with nine people eating.

On meat days we'd go to Nana's, another Italian, whose butcher's shop was on the way home. Nana wore a white apron stained with blood and lived behind a tall glass case filled with meat. Whenever we came in he would let us take a "pinch" of the raw chopped beef we called hamburger meat. In those days you could eat a "pinch" without ending up in the hospital. I've never had the courage to try it since. It feels barbaric just to think of but when my brother and I were little savages eating raw meat was just the thing. Beef was cheaper than chicken so my mother often bought chuck steak, the cheapest cut. It was tough and chewy. At meal times my father cut our portions into little pieces on our plates. My brother and I would chew on and on, with my father coaching us, in his West Indian accent, to "crush him, mash him up", all the while gritting his teeth, as if we were lions devouring a live gazelle we'd run down and hamstrung. We'd end up extracting the juices, our jaws aching, and spitting out the pulp. I don't think I swallowed one piece of chuck steak in my entire youth. My father ate everything on his plate, while lecturing us on the sinfulness of wasting food when people were going hungry, not just in Africa but in the land of opportunity. He'd sometimes come home after working late to find my mother had made hamburgers and French fries with corn on the cob as a treat for the children, hardly West Indian cuisine. "Back home we give this to animals", he'd complain about the corn, and make the best of it, stirring the discretely separated items into the semblance of a Caribbean dish, complaining "I'm starving. I'm in America and I'm starving." I thought it very humorous and clever. He liked meat with bones. Whenever we had chicken or turkey, he'd eat every discernable bit of flesh, then carefully chew the bones with great concentration, his forehead wet with perspiration, crushing and sucking them to extract the marrow as if he were a Paleolithic hunter. All that remained on his plate was a pile of crushed and drained bones like the middens archaeologists sift to study prehistoric people. His bone piles beckoned to a half savage past somewhere close at hand, a primordial force and power so intense he seemed never to be completely fixed, but hovered precariously on the gossamer border between human and animal. It was easy to imagine him shifting into a savage creature in the blink of an eye, an aura

BEING-IN-AMERICA: WHITE SUPREMACY AND THE AMERICAN

frightening and reassuring. To be with him at his best was to feel completely safe. To come within his ken when at his worst was like standing on an active geologic fault.

My parents had two boys and two girls followed by eleven years when no pregnancy occurred. Then, at age of 38, in a rather late life pregnancy for the times, my mother gave birth to me. My eldest brother was eighteen when I was born, the youngest sister eleven. I entered an already established family unit that seemed especially formed to receive me. For nearly two years I had them all to myself, a novelty for them and a perpetual source of entertainment and solicitation for me. I have no conscious memories of those two years aside from the fragment of second birthday cake. Then my younger brother arrived, a playmate ever ready to hand. Three years later a sister emerged to be treated with far greater care and solicitation than either boy. From the way they spoke it was clear she was a fragile creature whose gender, blessing my parent's late middle age, guaranteed her special treatment. Never, while we grew up was she made to do a single chore. We two boys largely ignored her in those early days. I have no early memories of her aside from her first few days home from the hospital when a series of relatives trooped by her crib conveying admiration.

My little realm was extended to the corner store two short blocks away, Fourth Avenue a bit further, and St. Clement's Church further still where we worshiped on Sundays. Named after the first Apostolic Father and fourth Bishop of Rome, St. Clement's was a black Episcopal congregation, formed I suppose by Negroes who thought themselves too proper and cultivated for the Baptist Church. To my child's eyes, it was full of middle-aged and older women with enormous bosoms who smelt strongly of sweet perfume and wore reddish makeup on their cheeks. When the spirit got hold of them it could be quite scary to a little boy. They did not shout or faint on the floor, like Baptist women sometimes did, but they grew intense and wet with perspiration and charged with emotion that could engulf anyone standing nearby, like lightening leaping from one to another caught beneath a tree. If you got too close to one of them after church let out and your mother introduced you and you had to bow as we were taught, you ran the risk of being hugged and kissed, pressed into those soft bosoms, engulfed in a thick cloud of perfume and emotion. Though I did not then know the term, I certainly felt something vaguely erotic about those women. I tried my best to keep far away but they were unavoidable, while at the same time guiltily longing for that soft embrace.

We children would laugh and clown during the service drawing scoldings and reproachful glances from adults. In those days adults were everywhere,

THE HIDDEN WORLD 17

always watching. A perfect stranger could reprimand a child and felt obliged to do so: "I know your mother raised you better than that" or "Just wait, I'm gonna call your mother soon as I get home." There was no escape from their unwanted supervision. They were omnipresent on Sundays, Gods eyes and ears.

The best part of church was the breakfasts we sometimes had in the common room downstairs, complete with donuts or cookies, sometimes, especially on holidays, sweet potato pies the women had baked. There was a great deal of talk about God and how he loved us so much he'd nailed his only son to a cross on our behalf and sent him to hell for three days. I looked very hard but I never saw him anywhere in church. He lived in the depths of the giant stained glass window over the altar which glowed and shone like Heaven when morning sunlight struck it. Whenever the priest raised the communion chalice to that shimmering crystal ocean, summoning him to appear, I hid my face in my hands pretending to pray. He must have been very angry because he never came out. I was grateful for his consideration. It would have been terrifying had he emerged with hellfire and damnation and shed his grace on us. A great being who'd killed his own son in such an awful way would certainly do something terrible to naughty children. I was also grateful I was too young to drink from the communion cup not having had something done to me called confirmation. We children had to kneel before the alter so the priest could lay his hands on our heads. The first time I expected a kind of electric shock when the Holy Ghost passed from Father Carbon's hands into my brain, and was quite disappointed when nothing happened. Once I caught a glimpse of the cloth he wiped the chalice with after a fashionable lady had sipped. To my disgust, it was smeared with red lipstick. I couldn't imagine how any adult could drink from a cup with people they were not related to. Adults were very peculiar and often did things that made no sense.

After church, when we did not have breakfast in common, my mother would prepare a minor feast, complete with eggs, waffles or pancakes, bacon and sausages. On special occasions she'd make good rich popovers. I was too young for coffee but the strong smell of it was an essential part of the meal. I can recollect its odor as I write. Once in a while I'd get a sip. I've never tasted better to this day. Everything back then was better, fresher, original. I suppose because I was. The more I wear away the more the world grows weary and tarnished.

About this time I made a remarkable discovery quite by accident. I don't know why I hadn't noticed it before or why I came upon it when I did. It

18 BEING-IN-AMERICA: WHITE SUPREMACY AND THE AMERICAN

was not as if something suddenly appeared like the hierophanies in the Bible. Rather, the intuition of an absence cracked a door ajar in a most prosaic way. I was sitting on the toilet. Our bathroom was the warmest place in the apartment. On winter days, I'd linger as my mind drifted into reverie lulled by the steady hiss of the stream radiator. The floor was finished in commonplace octagonal ceramic tiles you'd have to pay a lot to duplicate today. One day, as I sat with my legs dangling over the toilet, too short to reach the floor, I noticed that if I stared with concentrated attention at the geometric design the tiles would rise in an eerie pattern above the floor, so that there was an original set of tiles, and their ghostly duplicate hovering above it. If I concentrated long enough I'd drift into a meditative trance. A gentle humming started in my ears as my body lightened. I would remain in this state, lingering on a familiar threshold, until the sense of drifting off intensified and I rose towards a ghostly original world from which this solid world had descended. At once something cautioning broke the spell. After this occurred several times I decided to avoid the tiles whenever I used the bathroom but sooner or later I'd return to the patterns and whatever beckoned me. It was a tantalizing game, playing peek-a-boo with a face that appeared from nowhere, lingered a moment then vanished into nothingness with neither the assurance of a return nor the conviction of its continued existence unseen. Peek-a-boo's a child's initiation into faith, the hoped for, unexplained, reappearance of the familiar and the apprehension it might never return leaving something strange and uncanny in its place.

Anything strange frightened me. All my photographs from this time show an apprehensive child perpetually worried about anything out of place. Strangeness could reveal itself anywhere, at any time, like the unexpected manifestation of the divine in a banal bush. Kierkegaard speaks of the demonic as "inclosing reserve" sealed into itself, giving no hint of its presence until it appears as if from nowhere as "the sudden".[1] That is exactly what I felt. I never knew when the strange would set upon me because the world was not a solid stable entity but a porous wood through which all manner of things could penetrate. Once, during those early days, my aunt took me to visit her husband's grandparents who were in their late 80s. I had few memories of my own grandmother who died when I was 4. She was predominantly German, with some Native and African American ancestry. She looked distinctly white. My maternal grandfather died long before my birth as did my father's parents in the West Indies. There were no old people in my family or in the neighborhood. My aunt's aging in-laws were born and raised in Carolina. When I met

THE HIDDEN WORLD

them, they lived in what we called the "projects", in those days clean and safe without the smell of urine in the elevators. The old folks had a small, very neat apartment with heavy oak furniture. After I got over the strangeness they became Grandpa and Grandma to me. He was a keen fisherman who entertained me with stories of fishing trips from Sheep's Head Bay in Brooklyn. He used old fashioned cane fishing poles for freshwater angling and kept half a dozen of them in the corner by the buffet, a solid piece of furniture concealing pretzel sticks and peppermint candy behind its wooden doors carved with the image of a brace of ducks. Grandpa had what Auntie called "the sugar" and I connected it with the peppermint beyond the guardian ducks. We became great friends. I'd often walk the few blocks to their building and shout up to him from the little grassy area below. Grandpa would throw down a peppermint wrapped in a napkin together with an eagle headed quarter and off I'd go to the corner candy store. On that first visit all I could see was strangeness. I'd never been around anyone of so great age. Their dark skin and wrinkled hands with knotted veins made me instantly wary. To my dismay Auntie accepted their invitation to dinner. I must have shown my unease, because she asked me what was wrong. When I said I didn't want to eat old people's food, loudly enough for everyone to hear, they all had a good laugh. "Old people are the best cooks in the world", Grandma told me, and sure enough I had the best dinner I'd ever eaten, stewed tomatoes, mashed potatoes and veal cutlet, followed by apple pie with vanilla ice cream. Strangeness would not enter the world through them.

I approached most new things in the same cautious manner tentatively probing to test whether they were solid or might give way to something threatening beneath. The problem was my constitutional inability to take the world as given. Some of this was due to my father's emotional explosions. Perhaps his outbreaks confirmed a native intuition that anything could change in the twinkling of an eye.

When I was a very small boy we'd picnic on Glen Island Lagoon in New Rochelle. In those days it wasn't skirted by the concrete walkway and modernized marina of more recent times. There was a wooded glen that verged onto the dark lagoon down a sloping bulwark of rocks and boulders. A grassy picnic area had been laid out beside an old boarded up castle with turrets. The castle was a wonderful place for children to play about and an invitation to romantic fantasies of knights on horseback at an age when imagination was sufficient history. On weekends in the early 1950s, families spread blankets on the grass and spent wonderful afternoons enjoying one another and nature's beauties, spiced with the seasoning fragrance of salt water and seaweed. The picnic blanket with its family group, mother and father, older brothers and sisters and baby brother, our wirehaired terrier, occasional cousins with their husbands in tow and always abundant food and drink, provided a stable base from which to sally forth, like those knights of old in search of adventure. My adventures were to the edge of the lagoon or with older brothers or cousins to the beach on the Long Island Sound side of the island. Mainly I fished the lagoon with a hand line and earthworms, my dread of wriggling fish half hoping nothing would bite. When something did it was a fish marked by prior struggles with a gaping hole in its side. I dropped the line, fearful of the damaged thing and ran back to the safety of the picnic blanket. From that secure vantage I once saw an old Italian man fishing enormous eels from the dark waters, pulling them from their salty home, while I watched cautiously from a safe distance as he prized the hook from a thick black one, its mouth opening and closing spasmodically, its sharp white teeth snapping as it struggled to strain oxygen from air. It wrapped itself convulsively around the man's arm thrashing and writhing in agony. Its deep red blood ran down onto his grey khaki trousers like the ones my father wore at work. My 4-year-old mind was entranced and deeply saddened by the pathetic scene, frightened by the advent of this alien from the watery world, depressed by the pathos revealing a hidden flaw at the center of existence and irritated its suffering had forced these thoughts upon me. I suppose white people feel similar revulsion to blacks who intrude their misery into public consciousness. I was unaware of such problems in those days, what disturbed me was the manifestation of strangeness.

There were mice in the house we moved to when I was 6, an old house with many nooks and crannies where mice or ghosts could quietly disappear and suddenly emerge. I dreaded the little creatures without knowing why. My ignorance magnified my fear until it seemed a creature itself possessing me in league with the tiny rodents, a power they exercised, the way a snake holds a bird frozen in its gaze before it strikes. Perhaps it was their quick flexibility flattening them beneath doors and squeezing through the smallest cracks that made me shiver. The old house was full of them, colonies and nations of tiny fearless mice. You'd hear them in the kitchen when the lights were out, squeaking and scurrying about, knocking into pots and pans as if celebrating their liberation, or playing tag the way squirrels or chipmunks chased about the yard.

A particularly evil mouse lived below my bedroom adjacent to the kitchen. While his brethren kept up a racket on the stove, he would enter

THE HIDDEN WORLD

where the radiator pipe came through the floor and sit contentedly on the little wheel that regulated the steam, quite pleased with himself. Night after night he'd appear just as I was about to fall to sleep and stare at me mockingly. His uncommon brown and white fur made him stranger still, as if a pony or a small dog had shrunk to mouse size. He sat and gazed and refused to move. No matter what I did, no matter how loudly I clapped my hands, no matter what I threw at him he stuck with me. I took to stockpiling an armory of shoes, building blocks, crayons and hurling them one by one at my nocturnal visitor. He'd quickly vanish down the pipe. I'd rest my head against the pillow and back he'd come with a squeak of triumph. I was sure that if I fell asleep he'd creep into my bed and nibble on my toes. The only defense was unwavering vigilance night after harried night. How I ever slept is a mystery but inevitably morning would prove I had.

The evil mouse existed on his own terms independent of me and my world. He could retreat within the walls and lurk beneath the floorboards, safely out of sight like a sounding whale. I wondered, if he could squeeze himself beneath doors and between the steam pipes, could he not slip into other worlds unknown and undetected by human beings? Like those sleek black eels and bathroom tiles of younger years the mouse was a species of signs and portents of a hidden world existing side by side with our own. His persistent reappearance demonstrated its ineradicable presence. My fear was the apprehension of being drawn into the inner regions of that world, sucked into the minimal space between the radiator pipe and the floorboards, as if it were a monstrous black hole from which I could never escape, and there transformed into something other than I was. My younger brother and sister had no dread of mice. When my sister took over the room the mouse seldom appeared. Whenever it did she ignored it, turned over and went to sleep. Neither of them felt the call of the wild. Of course my physical body was never at risk. The mouse could hardly injure me, so it was something about me, something that connected me in my mind with my night visitor. Perhaps a part of me remained ajar where things could get in or out, as if a spiritual fontanel had never closed as I grew, leaving me dangerously exposed to whatever was on the other side and this openness had undermined my stability. I must have sensed this when those bathroom tiles rose from the floor taking me with them towards the ceiling. Nothing was what it appeared to be. I hated those Disney movies of the 1950s where people and things changed shape and nature; an army of enchanted brooms drowned a room with buckets of water; wayward boys turned into donkeys and Alice grew and shrank after tumbling down a rabbit hole. For years afterwards, I'd never go near a curb sewer for fear of falling into Wonderland. Looking back, I suspect it was my susceptibility to that wilderness, and the mouse a manifestation of its power, that frightened me. Perhaps, my father's frequent rages had such devastating effects because they prized the aperture further apart, threatening to admit whatever was pressing against the delicate membrane between this world and the other. I understood none of this at the time. There was only the sensation of vulnerability.

Notes

1 Soren Kierkegaard, *The Concept of Anxiety*, ed. and trans. Reidar Thomte (Princeton, NJ: Princeton University Press, 1980), 123, 129.

· 4 ·

A WORLD OF PLAY

Figure 4.1: Little Vester (Sidney), Gregory and me. Photograph by Ernest W. Richardson, Senior.

The 1950s were made for children and there were lots of us, at least two or three in every house on our block. We lived outdoors on the coldest and the hottest days. Outside of the purgatory of school we had about all the freedom we could use. Those were the blessed days before computers and video games, cell phones and tablets, before the routinized and regimented structured life of contemporary children, ferried from soccer field to gymnastics center, to music lessons, math tutorials and other up-building vampires that drain child-hood of its abundant, carefree, self-directed vitality. We lived in a sort of natural democracy, organizing our own society, creating our own adventures, conjuring fun through imagination with little infringement by adults. Left to our own devices we grew independent, resourceful and able to apply the rules of the adult world to our miniature one without prompting.

In the aftermath of the most destructive conflict in human history that claimed the lives of sixty to eighty million people, our favorite outdoor game was "war". We'd divide into armies and fight for hours, until our fingers and toes were numb from winter cold, our throats parched with summer heat. As very small boys on Fourth Street we fought our wars with "dirt bomb"-missiles got by digging up clods of hard packed earth. Etiquette required avoiding stony clumps and under no circumstances were we to aim at an enemy's head. There was, however, one occasion when these rules were broken. Sidney was a very dark and very naughty boy who suffered almost daily beatings. Sidney was very dark at a time when darkness was considered ugly and his complexion seemed to everyone a mark of his naughtiness. He lived in the apartment below ours. Whenever he was punished his terrified screams could be heard inside and out. It seemed to me there was a connection between the corporal punishment he regularly received and Sidney's habit of picking on smaller, weaker boys. My younger brother fit the bill. Fair, with straight hair and a father who never beat us, Sidney resented him although they were otherwise co-conspirators.

In those days the property behind our house belonged to an old Italian man who delivered bread in an ancient truck. A large and legendary white rat lived in a pile of logs in back of the Foster's, one of the few white couples on the block. It was fond of getting at the bread in the ancient truck. The old man waged relentless war on the rodent who proved too wily for his best strata-gems. It was the same rat who'd eaten the pumpkins my mother had left on the fire escape to keep them fresh for Halloween. One morning the pumpkins woke with great gouges in their sides. It was a mystery to us but my mother knew right away. "It's that horrible rat" she told us, introducing a character we'd never heard of before. She described its unusual bulk and glowing white fur in such peculiar tones that the animal assumed a magical aspect, ampli-fied by the fact no one had been able to catch or trap it. Few had even seen it, and then only the fleeting glimpse of a white shadow disappearing in the night. Partly because it lived in her yard and partly by linking like with like, we associated the rat with Mrs. Foster, who unlike her kindly husband, hated children and tried on one occasion to have them banned from the neighborhood. None of us had ever seen the rat, until one afternoon it broke its nocturnal habits to suddenly appear in the midst of our spider hunt. When my brother stumbled and fell as we fled, Sidney took the opportunity of peeing on him. On another occasion Sidney was admiring a flock of robins when my brother frightened them away. Sidney retaliated by striking Gregory on the head with a toy garden hoe, opening a wound requiring several stitches. That evening Sidney's horrible screams filled the air. My brother was unexpectedly sympathetic. None of us kids held with corporal punishment, especially when administered by a loving parent.

Despite our sympathy we all agreed that Sidney had a lesson coming. My brother and I, with three other boys, set an ambush for our wayward friend, armed this time not with harmless dirt bombs but handfuls of driveway gravel of assorted sizes, some large enough to inflict serious injury. This consideration conveniently ignored we secreted ourselves on either side of the front porch and called Sidney out to play. When he appeared, the conspirators sprang from their hiding places and hurled their stony missiles, striking him from head to toe. Sidney cried out in pain, burst into tears and fled the scene. I felt a sudden rush of triumphant glee, instantly subdued by a powerful undertow of guilt. We had done something unusually mean and dangerous. Sidney could have been badly hurt, possibly lost an eye. Perhaps he had. Everyone realized that punishment would follow swiftly. The day past in trepidation. Then the next. And the next. Nothing happened. Fearing another beating Sidney never reported the attack.

In a peculiar manner the troubles with Sidney, his trials and tribulations, seemed connected with the illusive rodent, as if it were a harbinger of how his life would go, the punishments his blackness would draw upon him, and the vengeance he might wreak upon innocent others in misdirected retaliation for a life derailed. From its first appearance the rat made a habit of running through the backyard or up the side alley just as we were at play, showing off its streaming whiteness, not so much the pure alabaster of legend, but a disappointingly dirty, faded greyish shade. It appeared at different times and locations, disrupting the self-forgetfulness of play essential to its work of replicating society's way of being in young minds, making us more like watchful adults than carefree children. It seemed to me that its arrival marked a certain ambiguous milestone. Possessed by the imperative of communal self-defense we set about devising traps for our white tormentor, driving stakes into the ground four or five feet apart with string stretched between them to trip the rat

26   BEING-IN-AMERICA: WHITE SUPREMACY AND THE AMERICAN

as it raced past, while we waited with heavy rocks to crush it once it stumbled. To our unsophisticated minds we seemed stone age humans defending against the saber toothed tiger. Several days of watchful waiting gained us nothing but aching arms and boredom. We set out bread smeared with wild cherry leaves from the tree that grew in the Foster's front yard. The bread disappeared over night but the toxic leaves claimed no victims. Mrs. Foster accused us of terrorizing the neighborhood and insisted our parents lock us up inside. We heroically persisted but nothing in our constant warfare discouraged the creature, until one day, like a vision retreating from sight, it simply disappeared. Even then it remained so deeply embedded in the collective unconscious of childhood that none of us could quite relax again. Years later I realized how the might of that rodent grew as I grew until it had assumed monstrous spectral proportions. Even now, in weariness and tribulation, I sometimes come upon it waiting for me to fall asleep, a gigantic whitened replica of the bedtime mouse of long ago, insinuating itself into my dreams, replacing restful slumber with vigilant defense.

When my family moved to nearly all white First Avenue war became an organized and regimented game of guns and snowballs, divided into rival armies, usually Germans or Japanese against the Americans, replete with hierarchies of command that had been absent on Fourth Street. On weekends and all summer long, in good weather or bad, armies of boys roamed the neighborhood hunting the enemy. War was the most enjoyable boyhood game combining the excitement of the hunt with the solidarity of a sacred union. Like real war it had rules. And like real war they were routinely violated depending on the relative strength and weakness of the combatants. When an enemy was shot he was to fall down and leave the game until it began again. As this was on the honor system great rows ensued. A snowball strike was clear, undeniable, dramatic so winter wars were more realistic. When snow fell deep enough we built forts to defend against opposing armies. The metal lids of iron garbage cans provided admirable shields against attacking snowballs. The same lids became bucklers when we switched to knights on horseback.

· 5 ·

THE WITCH OF FOURTH STREET

Being naughty is one of the joys of childhood, particularly if it can be directed at an irritable misanthropic adult, whose existence compels and justifies whatever mischief is played. The Fosters were one of the few white families on Fourth Street. I say family but it was only Mr. Foster and his hostile and angry wife. We had no quarrels with Mr. Foster, who never uttered a harsh word. His wife was a different matter. They were childless, either by fate or choice. She could not abide children and went out of her way to be mean to us. I do not know what Mr. Foster thought of this. Nothing his wife did or complained of changed the kindly way he interacted with us. We concluded he must be pleased by his wife's discomfiture, secretly gloating at her pain and anger. Living with the likes of Mrs. Foster could not have been pleasant.

By the time I was old enough to play outside on my own Mrs. Foster had become the witch next door. Through our child's eyes she resembled The Wicked Witch of the West from *The Wizard of Oz*. When she was angry it seemed to us her face took on a greenish tinge just like her movie counterpart. We suspected she caught unsuspecting children, cooked and ate them while her husband was at work. It was lovely having a real life villain about whom we could speculate and spin tales whenever we had nothing better to do.

28   BEING-IN-AMERICA: WHITE SUPREMACY AND THE AMERICAN

My 4-year-old brother and his unpredictable pal Sidney, were digging worms in Mrs. Foster's rock garden one day, when my bosom buddy Vincent and I set off on one of our adventures. Her tidy little garden had become for me a symbol of something I felt was wrong but could not quite grasp. The opportunity was too good to waste. I told the boys that if they wanted to they could remove all of the rocks from the garden and pile them on the sidewalk. I did not consciously think of this act as retaliation for the way Mrs. Foster treated us. I did not know much about race in those days, but I was always aware that whites looked down on us and I resented it. Held at the back of my mind was the eager notion that Mrs. Foster should be taught a lesson. It was the kind of act one engages in complete bad faith by the dodge of not actually soiling one's hands in the deed or commanding another to do it. Like Henry II instigating his knights to kill Beckett I was guiltless because my brother and Sidney were free to act or not to act. At six I had already assimilated the fundamentals of American individualism. All the same, I had to suppress a twinge of conscience as we set out, holding off the recognition that I was, in fact, making use of the younger boys' awe of their seniors and ignorance of the dire consequences of destroying Mrs. Foster's garden. It is the kind of self-deceiving tactic sometimes used by "people of color" the world over against white supremacy's insidious aggressions, even when, as is often the case with crime, we are not fully aware of what we're striking out against or why. Thus, I learned the American art of self-deceit by employing it to express a sense of outrage I did not comprehend or understand.

Vincent and I returned about an hour later to an enormous row. My mother, joined by Sidney's and Vincent's were on our front porch shouting across at Mrs. Foster, who was furiously denouncing their children as juvenile delinquents, while Gregory and Sidney crowded behind the matriarchs in defensive silence. Mrs. Foster was getting the worst of it. Not only had her garden been ruined but the entire neighborhood, white and black, was up in arms against her. The consensus was that she deserved whatever she got at the hands of the children she hated. Looking back on the episode, I realize that it was a sort of popular rising, uniting blacks and whites of good will against a misanthropic, undoubtedly racist individual bent on imposing her hateful vision of life on all of us.

Vincent and I slipped quietly into the house, surprised we weren't questioned. Our absence had provided alibis. No punishments were meted out. The matriarchs decided Sidney and my brother were too young to understand what they were doing. The truth remained untold. Yet they hadn't made the least effort to ferret it out. Justice had been done. An important lesson had been conveyed that remained etched in my mind. All in all it was a fine day.

It may have been my imagination, or the conveniently distorting mechanism of memory, but Mrs. Foster seemed a good deal quieter from then on. Certainly, she took care not to say or do anything mean to any of us. Those three mothers were formidable opponents, more than a match for the witch of Fourth Street, with or without her rat.

· 6 ·

CHESTNUTS AND CAT'S EYES

Our play marched in rhythm with the seasons as generations of ancestors going back to the beginning of time had lived in tempo with the sun. Today's children, imprisoned in cyber space, are increasingly alienated from earth, moon, sun and stars. I wonder what this distancing will mean for the future of a species famously vulnerable to hubris and unable resist the lure of convenience.

As the days shortened and the leaves turned crimson and gold the air took on a comfortable chill. By September chestnuts were ripening in the trees. Chestnut gathering began in late September and early October when bands of boys roamed throughout the city in search of trees. Each of us carried a chestnut sack for our accumulating finds. Early on the treasured nuts could be picked up where they had fallen. Once the ground was scoured clean it was time to address the trees themselves. By now the best pods grew near the treetops and you'd have to knock them down by hurling a stick accurately enough to shake them free without hitting nearby houses or striking unwary passersby. And the goal of this autumn hunting ritual was simply to smash them to bits, taking turns suspending our chestnuts on shoestrings to be struck by our opponent's. Perhaps it was a silly and destructive game. Yet, it seems to me, the main attraction was the collecting process itself, always done in groups, as if we were prehistoric nomadic foragers in search of precious life sustaining resources. The joy we experienced on discovering an untouched tree laden with fruit harkened back to our forebears' delight in coming upon a virgin patch of blueberries or walnuts, a natural apple orchard, or a thick colony of muscles clinging to a rocky shore. The chestnuts themselves, with their dark radiance suggesting magical depths we could marvel at but never plumb, were worth possessing even if they never saw combat. I had bags full of them by mid October. They'd soon grow moldy, ending in the trash as chestnut season faded and we hoped for early snow.

In winter sledding was our favorite occupation whenever sufficient snow fell. You could sled almost anywhere but our main attraction was Snake Hill a few blocks from my home. Here a narrow path wound steeply down through a woodlot for a hundred yards. The hill was risky as it was, with precipitous drops and hairpin turns. We made it more challenging by building up "jumps" with mounds of snow. When the temperature plunged, and the path had been well sledded, it became hardpacked, glazed and extremely slippery. Turning sharp corners became openly dangerous. This, of course, was exactly what we wanted. Each of us had a single passenger sled called Flexible Flyer, a small wooden platform atop steel runners with a steering arm in front. You'd sit or lie on it and down you went. Sitting was an invitation to disaster on Snake Hill. You were bound to fly off into the trees at the first turn so most of us navigated prone. This too was hazardous. You could easily bounce above the sled, come down hard on it and rupture your liver. An unfortunate boy could end up in the hospital.

My younger brother was always a daredevil, fearless in matters large and small. Late one afternoon he decided to race down the sledding trail despite it having iced overnight. This was carrying courage to the limit. As his older brother I made the necessary protests but did nothing to stop him. We all wanted to see the results. To our astonishment he made it through the first three turns. At the fourth the sled refused his direction and went directly into the trees. Gregory smashed head first into a big beech and lay completely still. I was terrified. We rushed down the slope expecting to see his head split open with his brains pouring out. What a relief to find no blood, but he remained motionless and only recovered consciousness after a bit of shaking. Reporting the accident might mean the end of Snake Hill, but even small boys sometimes recognize limits to selfishness. X-rays revealed no fractures but he had sustained a concussion. Surprisingly, we

CHESTNUTS AND CAT'S EYES

were not banned from the hill, only enjoined to greater care in the future. Undeterred, my brother went on to even greater sledding feats. There seemed no limits to his courage.

Unless we had abundant snow winter hung on forever cold and gray. Then one magical day it succumbed to blessed springtime. As soon as the air was warm enough, the ground soft and dry enough, we took to marbles. It's strange to think how excited we could become about those tiny glass balls with colored slips of plastic inside. We called them cat's eyes. To us they were treasures. Opaque solid colored marbles were valued as "shooters" for their seeming hardness, while the occasional oversized ones called "bowlers", for their ability to knock multiple marbles out of the pot at one shot, were less easy to come by. It is a characteristic of small boys arbitrarily to change the rules of any game going the other way, so we sometimes decided in the middle of a marble shoot to ban bowlers. Success in this maneuver rather depended on the relative size of the winners and losers. Size and strength carried great weight among boys. As we matured we transferred that lesson to power and influence.

Marbles were mysterious. Whether transparent or opaque, there was an intangible quality about a glass marble that pointed beyond itself to something wonderful. I spent many afternoons watching my little band, washing them, and counting them off as I returned them to their shoebox. Of course the game was part of it, each of us staking our marbles in a "pot" drawn in a circle in the dirt, taking turns shooting at them to keep whatever we knocked out. Yet even without the game those little glass idols were worth having, fingering like prayer beads and preserving for posterity. I kept mine for decades, well into adulthood in a large glass jar for all to see, until one day they inexplicably joined the sleek black engine, the errant basketball and my army canteen, things I look forward to finding again on the other side.

Chestnuts, marbles and guns were a kind of nonlethal warfare waged by boys, or perhaps a kind of pre-lethal one. As harmless as they seemed and felt, I wonder did they prepare some of us for actual combat by portraying the world as a Hobbesian jungle marked by tribal warfare. Some of my childhood playmates ended up in Vietnam, a few by their own volition, one who replied when I asked, "I wouldn't have missed it for the world." He had always been a callous, aggressive boy. Did the games we played, their rules, the way they habituated us to strife, the expectation of winners and losers, most of all the unspoken, mainly unthought taboo against questioning the competitive premise of our childhood vocations, of transgressing boundaries, deflecting any possible notion we might share our marbles, equitably distribute chestnuts without smashing their heads in, abolish war in favor of cooperative pursuits, did all of this prepare many for the slaughter, and many more for the immoral status of bystander? It is an unpleasant thought, and one I normally avoid. Only, sometimes, when I search for that missing glass jar, I find faces I've long since forgotten, ghosts of possibilities sacrificed for the sake of the game.

· 7 ·

GIRLS AND BOYS

A good deal of our play was peaceful and gender neutral. Some 1950s TV programs depict boys as normally hating girls, their play completely gender segregated. In reality, except for war and Jacks much of our play included girls and boys. The boys I knew, black and white, liked to be around girls, play games with them and looked forward to dating them when we were old enough. I do not recall one boy expressing dislike of girls or feeling "creepy" around them. That notion is a myth created by all white male TV producers and writers for reasons I cannot fathom, but whose effect was to reinforce sexism in the context of white supremacy, for shows like the exceedingly misogynistic *Leave it to Beaver* television series were also aggressively anti-black. The seemingly innocuous family show, which dramatized some excellent values, was nevertheless clearly white supremacist, for although black people were abundant and highly visible in the late 1950s when the show first aired, and making headlines with the Civil Rights Movement, they were redacted from the world of the series, until at the very end they turned up in menial positions. The normal that *Leave it to Beaver* presented, and therefore defended, was a world without black people.

What I know is that on long summer days fleets of girls and boys roller skated up and down the block, rode their bikes to destinations near and far or

36 BEING-IN-AMERICA: WHITE SUPREMACY AND THE AMERICAN

played red light, green light, giant step, baby step, or some made up game. We'd play hide and seek on hot summer nights, disappearing into the shadows. How we could turn those shadows into horror stories. I can still feel the disappointment at being counted out and forced into a July evening's doldrums. It was as if you'd passed through death to purgatory. A barrier descended between you and all those living screaming ecstatic boys and girls still in the game. I often think of death that way, as a very long out, sitting and watching helplessly from the sidelines as the game plays on until the final trump, and we choose up sides again, in the biggest choosing up of all times.

There was nothing like play, the more absorbing and carefree the better. Its intensity kept you fixed in the exact present and simultaneously carried you off to a world of continuous wonder where you'd remain as long as the spell held. And when it broke, because it was time to go to bed, or you finally had to complete the chores you'd fled from out of doors, there was the distant intuition that such coming downs were going to be a pattern in life, so that gradually one came to accept them, the way the characters in a play accept the Given Circumstances of their dramatic world over which they have no control. In those enchanted days all of that was away off in adulthood with an eternity of time between.

· 8 ·

PLAY AND BECOMING

Like all the fun and pain of childhood play was a mode of self-discovery and assimilation to our *American way of being*. Whether with a crowd of children on the block, a brother and sister at home or imaginary companions, play allowed us to call forth and actualize those felt, anticipated, but unknown aspects and possibilities of ourselves we'd not yet found or failed to recognized. The games we played, always modeled on the adult world we expected to enter, pressed each of us to draw out and test intuited talents and forces we'd need to survive and flourish, provoked not by discourse or precept but through active engagement with the group, responding to its rules, searching ourselves for the powers and aptitudes for relating successfully to others, to things and to ourselves. That is why all of our games were completely consistent with the culture, reinforced and affirmed it, drew out its implications, inculcated and justified its rules and regulations, its rewards and punishments, and rarely, if ever, went against the grain or offered even a mild critique. They taught us to accept the Given Circumstances without complaint, to embrace the parameters of the adult world we were eager to enter and demonstrate how like them we were. Our play trained us in how to excel within those horizons. It was through them that we discovered who we were and what we might become, to recognize the extent and the acceptable limits of humanbeing, what we might seek to uncover and what was better left concealed. Encouraged, chastened and censored by the group we were guided, willfully and by example, to the abundant riches or poverty within, opening and closing, narrowing and pruning what had been an expansive untamed wilderness. We soon discovered if we had the wherewithal to lead, the urge to create, the tendency to analyze, the patience to wait, the tenacity to endure, the courage to resist and prevail, the determination to follow, the burdensome gift of "normality" or the liberating curse of "strangeness". Play joined sensual pleasure with knowledge, the juncture infants make when they put everything into their mouths. It is no accident that children play intensively for the first twelve years or more, for play is the most profound and productive tool of world discovery and self making that we have, far more enlightening than almost all the edification that follows, because by the time it does we've already been tightly circumscribed for good or ill. Adults lose the capacity for spontaneous, unselfconscious play, because it demands an openness they've closed in defense of a settled *way of being* that lets them get on with life, and fear the unsettling consequences of further revelations.

· 9 ·

THE STUTTER

As I grew towards adolescence my imaginative bent deepened and a latent seclusiveness manifested itself. Those looking for a psychological explanation for this retreat could probably find it in the persistent stutter that seized me suddenly when I was three and held on until my sophomore year in college. Even now I hesitate in awkward silence before certain words, phrases and thoughts. And, as Americans abhor the absence of speech, my interlocutor rushes in to close the gap, invariably with the wrong word, phrase or thought. Such misapprehensions of what I would have said were misapprehensions of who I was, or would have been at the precise moment. For white people being black is a kind of stutter. You are forever completing our thoughts with your own meanings, some of them deadly, in which you would imprison us were we not perpetually fighting back, a self-defense you distort as a perpetual surly and antagonistic disposition. I experienced this white tendency while I was a doctoral candidate at the State University of New York at Binghamton, where over a two year period I was rejected from every job I applied for. Finally, I was the unanimous choice of the search committee for a professional position. The committee insisted on my appointment despite the opposition of the Vice President. He called me to his office to explain that I had been rejected from all the other jobs because I was a Marxist and Black nationalist. He was going to take a chance on me but I had better be on my best behavior. Then he made it a condition of my employment that I complete my dissertation within the first year on the job, a deadline he had no right to impose and which he doubtless believed I would fail to meet. The dissertation was completed on time. I was also required to endure a lecture by the Associate Dean. For three hours this white woman tested me on my alleged predisposition to convert students to Black Nationalism. They would be watching, she warned, to ensure I promoted "western civilization", the actual words she used. I had two children and could not afford to tell her or the vice president to go to hell. Neither accusation was true. I had never been a Marxist or a Black Nationalist. It was probably unconstitutional and discriminatory to use such grounds to deny anyone employment. That hardly mattered. They were protecting white civilization against the barbarian hordes. This white man and white woman had completed my thoughts, anticipated my actions and subjected me to speech therapy, as if my entire being was a fantastic stutter threatening to overwhelm and divert their way of being to some dark satanic purpose. Over the next several decades I was to experience many such oppressions, as when I was pointedly asked, during an interview at Pratt Institute in New York City, if I could teach the history of slavery objectively. Then there was the dean at a University of Rhode Island college who told me the director of African American Studies was only employed because he was black, and was outraged when as her assistant dean I hired an African American male student in the university's ex-offender program. These incidents and many more represent the great white habit of supplying their versions of our identities in place of our own.

Today we seek physical causes for everything. This is partly a result of our loss of faith in transcendental foundations. If there are no gods or hidden worlds to ground existence in there is at least the undeniable presence of the body which can be objectified, modified, perhaps immortalized by science and technology. We live in the distant hope of achieving complete control of that vessel and worry complete control would abolish meaning in any form. Modern neuroscience theorizes that stuttering is a genetically based, "multifactorial" condition, involving a problem of hyperactivity in one area of the brain and problematic communication between hemispheres that 80% of childhood stutterers outgrow.[1] I certainly felt the presence of an internal enemy waiting to ambush every verbal gesture. It was clear to me my stutter had nothing to do with nervousness, the prevailing explanation when I was a boy. "Don't get excited. Slow down. Take your time" my father would say.

THE STUTTER   41

I suppose the staccato ejaculations of a stutterer might sound excited, but though I was naturally energetic I never felt agitated until the words refused to pass my lips whole. The nervousness came with the injunctions which missed the point. The problem was something resisting beyond control that willfully seized my own intent and directed it elsewhere. All the calmness in the world would never avail while the invisible saboteur was at lodge. It lay in wait to derail not only my speech but my thoughts as well. My inability to articulate many things I understood or felt was a mode of stuttering. Often my best efforts, when I should have been in masterful self-control were subverted. At thirteen I was an infallible expert in Semaphore. I never made a misstep, until the Boy Scout Jamboree. Then, before hundreds of jeering boys, I froze, inexplicably, unable to send the simplest signal, derided and disgraced by my persistent internal enemy who seemed intent on sabotaging memory as well as speech. Once again, my visible, audible, appearance diverged from my "true" self.

In this way I came to know viscerally what others might never perceive or glimpse distantly with intellect alone. There was more to me than me, a vast trackless wilderness within that stuttering revealed as the Caribou had lured my Native ancestors into a new world. Whatever the mechanism, stuttering was a form of self repression, or self retention, or repossession, an autonomic restructuring and holding back, perhaps in anticipation of rejection, exercised by a self, concealed within the recesses of my being, an ambivalent self-censorship that fragmented and fractured rather than abolished communication.[2] It was a frustrating ambuscade, like an autoimmune disease operating to hidden ends of its own. I doubt most people think of stuttering as the expression of purpose, the revelation of an alien intent brooding over its host like Conrad's "implacable force."[3] To those afflicted, stuttering is a frustrating and embarrassing obstacle to communication. Only lately did I begin to suspect its purposeful design and think I could read my life as one deciphered an ancient riddle. It was when I came to see what each of us calls our self as a profoundly unknown, perhaps unknowable mystery, that I started to reflect on the flaws, the errors and imperfections of my life as holding greater clues to what I might be than the successes. Success is passage from intent to accomplishment similar to unimpeded speech, but like the latter points largely to the surface leaving the depths unsounded. Failure invites us to plumb them, to discover what went wrong, how to rectify our errors and amend our ways. To our great impoverishment we seldom heed the call.

42   BEING-IN-AMERICA: WHITE SUPREMACY AND THE AMERICAN

I had, and still have, a sense of unwilling and unwitting complicity with an unknown infernal project, as if I had signed a pact with a devil and willfully forgotten its existence and content. I never spoke, nor do I speak now, directly into the world. There was always a moment of doubt, an unavoidable hesitation, while the inveterate censor driven by fear of ridicule, tested the words and phrases I was about to utter, weighed their vulnerabilities, their many potential conflicting meanings, struggled to find the right ones to truthfully convey what I meant, always aware that whatever I said would instantly misrepresent all I felt, narrow it to a fixed significance, deplete its fullness, render one-dimensional the inherently shifting, ambiguous and bottomless. Then the utterance, invariably garbled and distorted in collision with a world that acted like the nozzle of a garden hose, and the gauntlet of the body that reduced its strength and vitality to a pale shadow of its original self. What emerged was abridged and stunted, making me appear less than what I sensed or imagined I was. This was the painful experience of being misunderstood, perpetually underestimated and dismissed. For when you cannot speak coherently, and in America when you do not speak promptly, you are not entirely human.

Knowing I was infinitely more than what I was taken to be stuttering made me constantly and acutely aware of what I took to be myself, a doubling of that double-consciousness Du Bois described as the psychological condition of the American Negro.[4] It seemed reasonable to suppose that what was true of me, marked by my stutter, must be true to some degree of the vast majority who free of my impediment had no way to bring the realization home. In this way my stutter illuminated the world. There was more here than met the eye. I knew this was true, because there was more of me than could be heard in my speech. In a circuitous way stuttering conveyed upon me the gift of an enduring faith in myself. I do not mean self-confidence, for that is a different matter and comes of success in the world. My belief was based on the experience of being always more than my words could tell, even to myself, and being me differently than they suggested. For I could sense that the speaking, feeling, thinking me was the uncertain interpretive translator of a vast wilderness extending from the borders of the me who spoke and thought and felt into the infinite unknown of which I had inklings but no sure knowledge.

Of course we're all vastly more than words suggest. At one time or another everyone experiences a gap between what they mean and what they say. But for those who are accepted as "one of us" the gap's diminished by the willing and determined intuition we are actually all alike, a perception that can be easily *held-off* when needed, an especially useful white supremacist weapon. The occasional lapse of verbal clarity hardly weakens that judgment. Acceptance encourages complacency, diminishing, even eliminating, the need for self-questioning, particularly in the case of whiteness, as illustrated by the followers of Donald Trump ignoring his aggressively antidemocratic, authoritarian and demagogic behavior.[5] Indeed, any hint at genuine introspection may bring one's soundness into question. My omissions and elisions were constant and habitual marking me as distinctly different, which encouraged others to fabricate a distorted image of me, punctuated by persistent underestimation of my intellectual abilities and exaggeration of my emotional constitution, in order to confirm the individual and collective identities they had staked themselves on. Stuttering sounded chaotic, as if I were possessed by a riotous superabundance of primitive emotion robbing me of coherence and threatening to leap from me to anyone in earshot, as spiritual power circulated in a holiness church, undermining and weakening their defenses against the inner wilderness their collective denial kept at bay. This dreadful surmise was accompanied by the suspicion of a congenital flaw in my makeup that had disabled a similar defense mechanism in me. I knew the inside and the outside stories and the dissonance between them. There was a world of people who knew a me that was not me, even my own family, so that I was a stranger at home and abroad. At times it was easier to live the external image, abandon insistence on being a self whose unitary solidity appeared less and less certain and accept the compassionate forbearance of those my sacrifice would release from the risks of self-questioning. For how could they admit their flawed understanding of me without calling into question their understanding of themselves? How could they do any of this without unsettling their entire sense of being? It seemed selfish to insist on me at their expense. Yet even while I entertained these noble sentiments, I suspected myself of conjuring selflessness in justification of a desired performance. Living the image became my way into the group. Living the image was playing a part and in taking this path of least resistance I became an accomplished actor. As with all actors there was a part of me aware of the performance usually with sad regret and anxious anticipation. To suppress what I was condemned me to living a series of escalating artifices. To emerge from behind the persona risked rejection by the local societies I lived within and condemnation by the larger world imprisoning us all. A great tension took hold of me that has never released its grip though it has weakened over the years.

Notes

1 Pierpaolo Busan, Nicole E. Neef, Maja Rogić Vidaković, Piero Paolo Battaglini, and Martin Sommer, "The Neurophysiology of Developmental Stuttering: Unraveling the Mysteries of Fluency," in *Frontiers in Human Neuroscience*, Published online 2022 Jan 27. doi: 10.3389/fnhum.2021.833870. Accessed on 8/9/2023 at 7:04 pm; see also Anne Smith and Christine Weber, "Childhood Stuttering—Where Are We and Where Are We Going?" *Semin Speech Lang.* 2016 Nov; 37, no. 4: 291–97. Published online October 4, 2016. doi: 10.1055/s-0036-1587703. Accessed on 8-9-2023 at 7:13 pm.

2 By the term autonomic I mean to posit a seemingly involuntary mental and emotional reflex, which, in fact, is culturally and psychologically set through our socialization in white supremacist America, to function as if it operated independently of human will, similarly to the autonomic nervous system. This idea is elaborated in Chapter 32 "Deprivations", and Chapter 33 "Set Being as Foundation for Artificial Intelligence".

3 Joseph Conrad, *Heart of Darkness* (Mineola, NY: Dover Publications, 1990), 30.

4 In 1897 Du Bois wrote:

> "It is a peculiar sensation, this double-consciousness, this sense of always looking at one's self through the eyes of others, of measuring one's soul by the tape of a world that looks on in amused contempt and pity. One feels his two-ness,—an American, a Negro; two souls, two thoughts, two unreconciled strivings; two warring ideals in one dark body, whose dogged strength alone keeps it from being torn asunder. The history of the American Negro is the history of this strife,—this longing to attain self-conscious manhood, to merge his double self into a better and truer self." W. E. B. Du Bois, "Strivings of the Negro People", *The Atlantic*, August, 1897.

5 On the strategic role of whiteness in obviating the need for self and collective criticism among whites see Chapter 30 "The White Supremacist Collective Unconscious".

· 1 0 ·

THE PERIODIC PILGRIMAGE OR GRAVEYARD PICNICS

For some years after my grandmother died, my mother and the train cake aunt made periodic pilgrimages to her grave. From the time I was eight my younger brother and I were impressed into these unpleasant excursions to Beechwood cemetery, a place we preferred to keep at a distance. We were assisted in this ambition by the zoning laws that placed the cemetery in a remote corner of the town near the railroad and the interstate, as if those earthly highways were meant to symbolize the soul's journey to other worlds. The graveyard was further marked off by a high iron fence running all round it that kept the realm of the departed from encroaching on the world of the living. The foreboding silence of the place was punctuated by the occasional New Haven Railroad train roaring past the back fence on its way to Boston, its noisy intrusion confirming the continued existence of the world we'd left behind and were eager to rejoin.

Cemeteries had their own rules and regulations not dissimilar to those in the outside world but more solemn. There were proscriptions and taboos one had to heed or suffer terrible bad luck. Among these the most disrespectful infringement was to walk on someone's grave, which was a kind of sanctified private property. To heed that injunction, you had to walk gingerly in a rectangular pattern, trying to estimate exactly the parameters of each grave from

46   BEING-IN-AMERICA: WHITE SUPREMACY AND THE AMERICAN

the location of its headstone and go around it, taking care not to lose your balance and tread on its neighbor, a daunting task since the cemetery was old and the graves as crowded together as sunbathers at a public beach. It was impossible not to edge a grave or two. Whenever we did our humble apologies would follow quickly, explaining that we were only children who knew no better. For all of the trouble the apprehension caused, it was comforting to think that even in the other world we continued as discrete individuals whose private spaces, as ambiguous and often coterminous as they might be, particularly with ancient graves that had shifted over time mixing the contents of one with its neighbor, must somehow be vigilantly respected and defended, even if that meant inventing artificial borders that in the course of time would gradually disappear from the earth and human memory. Knowing where one soul ended and another began was a calculated estimate approved by community consensus, if not by the cemetery's plot map. In my naiveté, I sometimes imagined that a like ambiguity applied to living people, and that the limits of one and the beginnings of another were similarly matters of custom and consensus. Putting such discomposing considerations aside we were free to walk wherever we wished provided we did not violate the personal territory of each underground resident. Thus the cemetery became an object lesson in John Stuart Mill's philosophy of liberty, which I had got the essence of before I'd learnt the word or ever heard of Mill, just by existing in America. At the same time, and in a contrary and undercutting direction, we were deeply impressed by the continued presence of ancestral spirits, so that while our graveyard excursions reassuringly confirmed the solidity and naturalness of an individual autonomy that endured even after death, they subverted the notion that we existed in one world only.

After the daughters had planted new flowers by the headstone, and we'd prayed with our eyes closed and heads bowed, my mother and my aunt would give us a picnic lunch on a blanket spread on higher ground. Neither Gregory nor I enjoyed picnicking among the dead in a place that should have been kept strictly apart from the living world. Eating in a graveyard gave us the unsettled feeling of transgressing sacred boundaries. The immediate presence of death drew the taste from our mouths, even from the sandwich cookies for desert. All we wanted was to get back home to play in the clear July air and lose the moldy memory of death, but the dutiful daughters lingered, talking about old times or spent hours looking for the lost headstones of relatives, like Uncle Joe or Auntie something or other, who we'd never heard of and had no interest in finding. Eventually we'd leave, careful not to look back as we made the long hot walk to the bus stop and home.

For me those visits provoked the unwanted intuition of interpermeable worlds, which suggested that the one we lived in our waking hours was not the only one, nor as solid as we might hope. There was the vast realm of the dead, which continually and geometrically augmented and increased, dwarfed the world we knew and clung to. I was grateful for the isolation of burial grounds from the rest of life, marking an abrupt discontinuity, the way wakefulness deprives us of troubling dreams. And yet, the periodic pilgrimage renewed the connection and kept it present, as the tendency to reverie kept the dream world close at hand.

· 1 1 ·

EDUCATION IN WHITENESS

The Mt. Vernon of 1953 was overwhelmingly white but things were reversed on Fourth Street. There, what we were taught to call Negroes, with a sense of pride, predominated. I didn't see them as Negroes, only my kind of people, genuine, dependable, kind and protecting. Nor did I know anything about race, except that white people were not like my people. They were not kind or genuine or dependable, and certainly not protecting. It was clear even to my five year old brain that white people thought a great deal more of themselves than they did of us. They felt and acted superior. It didn't matter as long as we lived on Fourth Street and only encountered whites when we shopped or at the beach. On those occasions the adults would speak with the shopkeepers or the people selling refreshments at the concession stands on Glen Island. We children had no reason to interact with white people at all. We were protected from their prejudices and cruelties by our parents and other adults.

All of that changed with school. My birthday was in February so I started school on a cold and blustery day in midwinter. On the fateful morning I stood in my underwear, my hands in a basin of hot water contentedly absorbing the soothing warmth. I wanted nothing more than to remain in my domestic sanctuary forever following the same daily routine I'd known all of my life. A great sadness descended rooting me to the spot. My mother had to call me

50   BEING-IN-AMERICA: WHITE SUPREMACY AND THE AMERICAN

several times and finally roust me from the bathroom and out of our secure little apartment into the strange and alien world of school.

School was a hostile environment dominated and controlled by white people. Most of the Children and all of the teachers and administrators were white. They rarely said anything one could call racist. Their superiority was conveyed by the tone of their voices, the cast of their faces and the gestures they made. Most of all the order they established in the classroom. All the children selected for special distinction as monitors, to clean erasers or distribute the readers and other material were white. White children were complimented on their verbal contributions ours were passed over in silence. Where race featured powerfully was in pedagogy itself. All of the readers pictured middleclass white children and adults enjoying themselves in one occupation or another, like going on the vacations or other family outings which we never experienced. Learning to read from *Fun With Dick and Jane* was learning to think and feel inherently inferior to white people. The series began publication in the 1930s featuring a white family of Mother, Father, Dick, Jane and Sally. The only color was provided by dog spot and Tim the teddy bear. The text employed an effective repetitive rhythm: "Run Sally run. Run Sally run run run." "Look at Dick go. Look at Dick go go go." The world of Dick and Jane was uniformly and unalterably Caucasian. Thus the normal world was white. Our absence from the book suggested that our presence in the real world was an aberration we should not draw attention to by making too much of ourselves. If white people were clean and tidy, black people must be dirty and messy. Since none of the black people I knew were dirty or messy my conclusion was they must be closer to whites than blacks. In this way a simple reader fomented division among black people. Whites were worthy enough to represent and model the language we were to learn to think and speak in. The more we spoke and thought like them, the more authentic we would become. Without knowing the implications of my ambition, I was eager to do so, and excelled at it which was a source of great satisfaction and pride. At age six I was unaware of the subliminal message concealed in the pedagogy that only white people counted. Their concerns were real concerns. Their lives were real lives worthy of depiction and emulation. Most destructive of all their looks were good looks, normal looks, the beautiful, the gold standard. All of this was vividly reinforced on TV where everyone was white except for the buffoonery of the all black *Amos n Andy*. The heroes of Children's programs, mainly westerns like *The Range Rider, Annie Oakley, Hopalong Cassidy, The Adventures of Wild Bill Hickok*, were white, except for The Lone

EDUCATION IN WHITENESS

Ranger's faithful "Indian" companion Tonto, played by Native American Jay Silverheels. The powerful negative impact of school and TV was amplified by our obliviousness to what was being done to our young minds by the repetitive reinforcement of whiteness as the normative, the excellent, the ideal all the more devastating because it was unobtainable for any Negro who did not look white. No matter what one did, or how hard one worked or studied or wished one could never become white. I was left with the feeling that there was something inappropriate about me in an unspecified but fundamental way. Our classroom, pedagogy and curriculum gave every white person the advantage of presumed rightness and all of us the disadvantage of assumed wrongness simply by being who we were.

If *Fun With Dick and Jane* and *Leave it to Beaver*, were acts of covert white supremacy, in which the authors who knew black people existed in large numbers in America, decided to leave them out, the supplementary reader we were assigned in the first grade was glaringly racist, so much so that even at six years old I recognized the outrage. One morning one of the white monitors distributed a new book to read aloud from. On the cover of *Little Black Sambo* was the picture of a coal black boy with thick red lips, woolly hair and gleaming white teeth, that immediately summoned the image of Lucius Allblack of my mother's stories.[1] The original Sambo published in Great Britain in 1899 was written by Helen Bannerman featuring an East Indian boy named Sambo, his mother Black Mumbo and father Black Jumbo. He was jet black but did not have what were then called Negro features. The book's popularity led to unauthorized American editions introducing the panoply of vintage black stereotypes. Those were the texts we read in my school. The book was certainly interesting. One story told how Sambo outwitted a group of tigers he met while out walking. To persuade them not to eat him, clever Sambo gave them his colorful clothing and umbrella, whereupon the jealous Tigers chased each other around a tree melting into a pool of butter that Sambo used on his mother's pancakes. Tiger butter sounded delicious and I felt guilty enjoying a story that I recognized was derogatory to any Negro from any nation. Race was here to stay, although I felt it not as race but as an ever present sense of being culpable for something I knew nothing of, an intimation of unworthiness that connected to my sense of derailment. Perhaps the little black engine that couldn't was a projection of what American racism had instilled in my psyche.

Notes

1 See below, chapter 14 Materfamilias

· 1 2 ·

CONCERNING VIOLENCE

Whatever the agonies of school, at the end of each day I returned home to Fourth Street where all was sweetness and light. On Sundays there was Church, reassuring and solid, a community of unquestioned dependability, love and support. Suddenly all of that changed. My father had hit the numbers big enough to afford a down payment on a three family home in a lower middle class neighborhood. Rental income would help pay the mortgage. My parents did not involve the younger children in their planning. We had no idea they were searching for a new home until one day my mother told us we were moving. The news was exciting. We had never lived in a house before. There would be new and interesting things to learn and do. By the middle of January we'd all moved in.

There is nothing a child loves more than being surrounded by family all of the time. I had felt completely secure living in our little apartment with my parents and my six brothers and sisters, all crowded into three small bedrooms. Now, we were all together in a much larger home but I was seldom happy in that new world. As the years past I became increasingly unhappy. Today we'd call it depression. In those days we did not know of such things. My parents would have felt it shameful if any of us had been diagnosed with mental or emotional problems. It would have been regarded as a mark of weakness, a

54   BEING-IN-AMERICA: WHITE SUPREMACY AND THE AMERICAN

character flaw that one should remove through right thinking, willpower and prayer. In any event they would likely have seen the mitigation of my problems as beyond their control, for their source was the outside world I was thrown into without warning, or preparation by any of the adults around me, and my parents own demons. The idea of changing that world in order to produce mentally and emotionally healthy individuals lay beyond the creative horizons of most Americans in the 1950s. Failure to adapt was regarded as a personal problem, a judgment that obfuscated the need for and the possibility of social change, until the Civil Rights Movement showed how possible and needed it could be.

Moving to the new house meant leaving the beloved community and the boys and girls I'd played with for as long as I could remember. We moved in the depth of winter and its frozen reaches never seemed to thaw with the changing seasons. It was a world of arctic whiteness bereft of human warmth. I felt completely alone. There were no black children in the new neighborhood and very few at school. Robert Fulton was a decent enough elementary school as far as it went. I cannot recall any overt racial incidents, although it was even whiter than my old school. Like the other the classroom was structured around whiteness. The walls of the school were adorned with huge murals depicting scenes from American history, all uniformly white, except for a few "Indian" "savages" sitting at the feet of their civilized conquerors. I certainly did not think in such terms then. Rather, I felt an intensified sense of lacking some essential quality others possessed. The feeling of myself that I had learned in early childhood deepened into a colder and more isolated aloneness. More and more I sought refuge in my sanctuary. This was not one particular place or way of being but a congeries of acts, willings and defenses united by imagination and always encompassed by wilderness.

I cannot recall being in one fight on Fourth Street. Yet, after a year in our new neighborhood, I began to pick fights regularly. They were always with white boys. Not just any white boys, for all of my friends were white, but they were uniformly from the working or lower middle classes and even as children we shared a sort of rudimentary class consciousness. When we went on our frequent fishing expeditions to Twin Lakes in New Rochelle we entered upper middleclass areas we derisively described as *Leave it to Beaver* neighborhoods. It was obvious to our young minds that they were different worlds from ours. My fights were always with solidly middleclass white kids who struck me as stuck up. I was always ready to fight anyone who showed any disposition to look down on me, and as the best justification for brawling was retaliation against the hurled curse "Nigger"! I sometimes tried to goad my adversary into losing his temper and shouting it. This was a very easy task, for the kinds of kids I detested, already detested me precisely because I was black. The word was on the tips of their tongues. My resentment sprang from my attunement to their true feelings. That attunement has never left me.

In those days beating up a white racist, though none of us knew the term back then, was pure joy. There was a spoiled white kid who occasionally visited his racist grandfather who lived next door to my best friend, a boy of English ancestry. Whenever he came to visit he would spend considerable time leering at us safe from retaliation in the sheltering arms of his doting grandfather. One day I overheard the old man ask him to go to the local grocery store for something or other. Before he left I got him to shout "nigger" at me several times which led my friends to throw rocks at him. I calmed them and explained my plan. Just about that time his grandfather called him in to give him money and a shopping list. I left my friend's yard, walked up the street and concealed myself behind a tree along the route he would have to follow to the store. I waited in high excitement. When he finally passed by, I jumped out, seized him by the arms, threw him against the tree and pummeled him with a flurry of hard punches to his stomach. He doubled over, gasping for breath, began to cry and ran back to the house. I stayed away from my friend's yard for a day or two. They told me later that his grandfather came out looking for me, threatening to go to my parents, but when my friends explained what his darling boy had called me he lost his nerve and gave up. He had no claim to the moral high ground. If he had complained to my parents my mother would have given him a well deserved dressing down. If he'd been unlucky enough to find my father at home he might have received worse treatment than I had dealt his grandson. I can still feel the sense of freedom, the liberation, the thrill of vindication released in me when my fists connected with his body and he cried out in pain. No doubt my ambush of this symbol of all I had endured provided relief from the pent up anger and frustration I felt but whose sources I could neither identify nor explain. I imagine that it was similar to the psychological therapy Frantz Fanon prescribed for colonized people through the use of violence.[1]

I hated the oppressions I felt but could not articulate. At 13 I got into a knockdown dragged out fight in the churchyard after a Boy Scout meeting, with a larger light skinned black boy, the toadying favorite of the prejudiced white pastor and his vicious daughter who treated me badly. I hated him for his complicity in concealing their true colors and determined to take my anger out

56 BEING-IN-AMERICA: WHITE SUPREMACY AND THE AMERICAN

on his hide. Moreover, he stuttered even worse than I did so he should have known better. That occasion was memorable for my older sister, Anne Marie, coming to the scene and defending me. She understood my rage and I was not punished. I came home sore and with bruises but a deep sense of the justice of my act. There was a similar incident during boxing night at Scout Camp. I managed to get myself paired in a match with another fair skinned black boy who kissed the asses of the powers that be in our nearly all white church. It didn't help that he went to an exclusive private school, could read Latin and was the most arrogant kid I had ever met, despite the fact that he actually was extremely intelligent and unbearably competent. He looked down on me and all of us, so the match was eagerly awaited by the other boys who encouraged me to knock his block off. He was, perhaps, no pushover, larger than me and for all I knew a good fighter, but I was determined to beat the shit out of him even if I ended up getting the worst of it. We were given boxing gloves and headgear. I noticed that as our match drew near and he witnessed the bloody noses and split lips of other combatants he became increasingly nervous, pulling up clumps of grass and throwing them down. His condition wasn't helped by other boys assuring him that "Richardson's gonna knock you out." I had no confidence I could do anything of the sort. Apparently, he did, and to my great and enduring frustration and disappointment he chickened out, and told the camp counselor in charge of the event that he was feeling ill. No doubt he was telling the truth but that was that. He spent the rest of the evening sitting in the shadows. Despite my disappointment I felt sorry for him and did not join with the others when they taunted him. I asked them to leave him alone. He had backed down. That was punishment enough in the world of boys for whom physical cowardliness is among the cardinal sins.

In all of my early conflicts, my white friends within and without the Boy Scouts were uniformly supportive of my actions. When the white boys at the trailer park at the edge of our scout camp hurled racial slurs at the black scouts, all of our white comrades joined in the ensuing rock fight, and the white scoutmaster did not punish us. We shared a common sense of justice and intolerance of stuck up children or adults and a hatred of bullies. It was a pretty good group. There was little sense of race between us. When it did raise its ugly head, it was invariably introduced by a white parent. I don't mean directly but through their childrearing and prejudiced observations. The degree to which parental racism stuck depended on the sensitivity of the child. It would sometimes come out casually, when a boy would relay, almost as a compliment, his parents' judgment that my family was different than other "colored people".

CONCERNING VIOLENCE

Being the exception to the rule was a common observation about me and my brother. My family were seen as respectable. All children like being special but this kind specialness came with a bitter aftertaste. I had sense enough to recognize that being an exception was a condemnation of the race I belonged to. I don't think I ever argued about it, kids want desperately to get along, but neither did I take it as a compliment. Rather it seemed to contain a hidden caution. I was being warned by their parents not to fall back into the morass out of which we had somehow climbed. Their suspicions suggested the possibility that I too could be found wanting at some point. I can't speak for my younger brother. I'm not sure he was ever told the same thing. Kids generally accepted him as white and simply ignored the fact that I was a different color. There was an odd ambivalence about such situations. I resented others calling me and my family exceptions. Yet I certainly felt that we were and not just my family. All of the Negros, as we were taught to call ourselves, I had known and grown up with in family and church and in the old neighborhood seemed to be exceptional. In what sense this was true I could not say at the time, except that they were for the most part kind, respectable-for even I understood that term-hard working and honest. I had never known any Negroes who were not. Before we left Fourth Street, indeed until I got to junior high school and encountered black boys who were actually bad, I had thought all Negroes were good. For me Italians were the juvenile delinquents and dangerous people because those were the ones who featured in movies and television programs about teenage gangs. Ironically, segregated TV reinforced a positive image of black people in my young mind. It came rather as a shock to learn there were black boys as bad as the white ones on television.

Among our playmates were two undoubted white supremacists even at a young age, though neither of them had any more idea of that term than I did. The elder was about 12 when I was 9. His brother must have been my age. They loved to play war and had realistic looking toy guns that could get a black boy shot by the police if he carried them today. The elder boy, who wore a coonskin cap all winter, looked uncannily like the bully in the movie *A Christmas Story*, and imagined himself a sort of Davy Crockett. He wasn't foolish enough to use the N word or perhaps he had no inclination to do so. He certainly felt superior to any "colored" person and made the sentiment known by his condescending and dismissive attitude towards me and my brother, and the disparaging remarks he made about "colored people" from time to time. He was much too big and strong for me to beat up so I learned to live with him the way we've learned to live with you because you're just too big and too dangerous to confront on a day-to-day basis. The brothers' hubris was in marked distinction to the other kids in the neighborhood who treated each other with respect. Their aunt was our Sunday school teacher who labored to impose white Christian values on us. She resented my critical approach to the gospels, outraged that a stuttering black freak dared open its mouth as if he had as much right as anyone to state his opinion. Once she threatened to sit on me unless I shut up. The idea was so hilarious that all of us kids had a good laugh at her expense. At least once she fled the classroom in tears.

It strikes me as strange today that those boys' parents forbid them candy, sweets and soft drinks. They drank V8 Vegetable juice instead, and relished it. Perhaps it was this early experience that has made me wary of progressive people where race is concerned who are advanced in other areas like animal rights, organic vegetables, gender or sexual preference. I learned early on that good sense in those areas of life did not imply good sense where white supremacy is at stake.

There were a few kids forbidden by their parents from entering our house, though they were allowed to play with us. We were never invited into coonskin's house. In fact, on the entire block, only my English friend's home was open to us. His mother was unfailingly kind, and made me feel completely welcome. White kids visited each other freely. Our friendships were restricted to outside play. My younger brother was invited into several homes because he looked white, but as their parents banned me, my mother decreed that my brother must remain out as well. Thinking back it seems to me race was not much of a problem between children because there was very little at stake. We were too young to date, too young to work and were not yet consumed by ambition. As we grew up race and racism grew with us keeping pace with our awakening intellects and growing ambition, our surging sexual desire and our expanding awareness. Increasingly, many of the friends we played with became my brother's friends, while my friendships dwindled, until by the time I was in high school there was only the boy of English ancestry who I could call a friend. He was a very unusual, sensitive boy and in his own way scarred by the world he lived in. I wonder how many others among those boys managed to hold onto their childhood honesty as they grew into adulthood faced with the inevitable demands for compromise and the powerful temptations and rewards of white privilege.

Notes

1 The allusion is to "Concerning Violence" the famous first chapter of Frantz Fanon's *The Wretched of the Earth* (New York: Grove Press, 1961).

· 1 3 ·

HOME SWEET HOME

The depressing effects of stuttering were compounded by my isolation within the nuclear family. Mercifully my father was home only in the predawn hours and late at night. For the rest of the day we were spared his demons. Most of the time the household consisted of my mother, my younger brother and sister and me. It is in and through the family that white supremacy produces some of its most psychologically devastating effects. The black community has long struggled with color consciousness. Perhaps those concerns have lessened these days, but in my boyhood and adolescence they were alive and active. My mother was fair skinned with wavy hair. People thought she was white. I dreaded her appearances in my classroom when the black kids would tactlessly ask "How come your mother's white?" This was always an acutely embarrassing moment, the presentation of an American racial contradiction impossible for a fourth grader to comprehend or explain. My father, light brown with a long narrow headed reflecting his English and Scottish ancestry, resembled an Englishman who had lived in the tropics. To most whites and blacks my younger brother and younger sister also looked white so similar questions were asked of us routinely. Among my older siblings my eldest brother was what was called "light skinned", could easily be taken for Middle Eastern and bore a striking resemblance to Muammar Gaddafi, not quite white but close enough to merit better treatment. My eldest sister was also fair with straight hair. Many people thought her white as well until she made her identity known in no uncertain terms. The older sister closest to me in age was what we called "brown skinned". But she too had straight hair, an asset at that time among blacks and whites, added to which she had escaped what were derogatively called Negro features. Only my older brother, Charles who was sixteen when I was born was darker than I. There was no mistaking his racial identity. He was dark with "Negro" hair, although it became distinctly wavier as he aged.

By the time I was eight or nine the older siblings were grown and out of the household, so I grew up the darkest person in the family group remaining at home. This was an unspoken oppression for me. I felt distinctly inferior to the rest, palpably different. How could I not when *Fun With Dick and Jane* had reinforced the lessons of TV, billboards, Christmas and Thanksgiving. Everything beautiful, aesthetically pleasing and intelligent was white. As far as I could tell, my mother, brother and sister were white, or at least closer to that ideal than my brown skin and Negro hair, which had enough curl in it to spark my mother's ambition. She spent a good deal of labor trying to brush a sort of waviness into it with the help of Wildroot hair tonic, a practice I adopted once I was old enough to groom myself. On top of this, once we entered school my brother and sister, both smart and diligent in their studies, far excelled me in academic pursuits. I was slow, laborious and hated school. The lesson was right out of my first grade reader.

Although my mother forbid my brother to enter white homes where I was banned she did not forbid him to play with children whose parents shut me out. This was probably only fair. Why punish children for the sins of their parents. Equitable or not the lesson was not lost on me. He was wanted. I was not. I may have felt a good deal better had my parents shown less regard for other children and more for me in this particular respect. I say parents, but it was my mother really. My father was not involved in these day-to-day concerns. Mommy ruled the domestic roost.

HOME SWEET HOME 63

I am certain that neither my mother nor my younger siblings entertained the slightest notion of my discomfiture. There may have been some awareness bred by personal experience among my older siblings. If so they never betrayed it. My eldest brother was an outspoken critic of the color caste, yet he showed no consciousness of how his own fair complexion and devastatingly good looks had advantaged him, particularly with women of all races. I often wonder if his later adoption of a messianic posture was related to a sense of specialness rooted in his physical appearance.

Whatever anyone else did or did not feel, whatever they assumed about my sense of self, whatever they knew or pretended not to know, for as long as I lived in that family I lived as an outsider. Things were not helped by my brother and sister laughing at my stuttering with my mother occasionally joining in. Or their disparagement of my intellectual abilities. My father was fond of ridiculing my younger brother from time to time, accusing him of having a "big head", presumably compared to his own narrow British one, calling him a "little Jew" because he saved his money conscientiously preparing even then for college. In defense my mother normally replied, with a sort of smirk, that at least he didn't get bad grades like Ronald. On these occasions she would paint me as shiftless and irresponsible at the ripe old age of 12 or 13 compared to my brother's uprightness. This delighted my brother and no doubt discomfited my father, but the impact on me was devastating. It was one more indication of how insufficient I was compared to the rest. Not only was the comparison exceedingly harmful but the fact it was made suggested a hierarchy of valued children. He could be elevated at my expense because he was intrinsically worth more than I was. Whether the assault was conscious or not its negative results were lasting and devaluing. Nor was I complimented when she frequently referred to me when angry as "a big ape", but never used that phrase to my brother. I recall the mingled feeling of rage and shame. It was an extraordinarily hurtful epitaph. I lived with a burning sense of the injustice of my situation without any idea of how I might change it. In fact I did not think it could be changed and often thought of running away but that option seemed to offer no real resolution and entailed a lot of discomfort, misery and even danger. As you may gather, in those days I had very little confidence or courage. Sometimes I thought if only I could make my case to an objective outside authority they'd understand and rectify my situation. The absurdity of this wish was not apparent to me at the time. Nearly all authorities were white. They would have rejected my complaint with alacrity and a good deal of scolding. Any possible black authority, such as a minister,

64   BEING-IN-AMERICA: WHITE SUPREMACY AND THE AMERICAN

would have reinforced parental authority and condemned my waywardness. Few black adults would have seen anything remiss in my parents' behavior. Far from it, they would have accused me of ingratitude towards parents who were putting a roof over my head and giving me what my father liked to call "a good foundation."

I was left to struggle on my own. What puzzled my young mind was how my mother could be quite sensitive to the woundings of race, and was what one might call a race conscious black person, while she could become self-deceiving when it came to the oppressions of color. This gave me great insight into how white people are able to willfully unknow so much when it comes to white privilege. She was distinctly unsympathetic whenever her eldest sister, the darkest child among her siblings, complained of her childhood trauma. She seemed not to understand the painful woundings my aunt had sustained when her entirely white looking mother with little or no black ancestry, would never take her out in public, preferring to be seen with my mother. She focused instead on her own innocence as a child rather than admit the privileged position she enjoyed at the expense and pain of her darker sister. Among themselves the other sisters would ridicule my aunt, having judged, without much of a hearing as far as I could determine, that "she ought to get over it." This vintage American reaction, self defensively intensified within the black community where strength and self-reliance are primeval virtues, reminded me of how Irish and Italians reject black demands for compensation by bragging of their own immigrant ancestral triumphs despite discrimination. My aunt was fond of me because I was darker. I understood how she felt but resented the special attention she paid me because it felt like when my mother used me to get at my father. There seemed no escaping race in one form or another, even children were not immune to the transparent machination of adults.

I never mentioned any of this as a child. How could I? I loved my mother and had great sympathy for her because she was mistreated by my father and lived a frustrated life. For all of her woundings she was my North Star, a source of unquestioned stability and self-worth. Though never affectionate she could be supportive by her lights. When my dog died after a horrible bout of distemper and meningitis she slept in my bed all night. Yet she had blamed me for the dog's illness in the first place, though she was unable to explain what I had done wrong. I felt guilty nonetheless. Just as I remained deeply distraught for weeks when she called me a "disgrace to the family" when I was falsely accused of trying to steal a book at the elementary school book fair.

The condemnation resonated powerfully with my already well entrenched feelings of inferiority as a "colored" boy. Because the whole world suspected I was always on the verge of some malfeasance it was hard not to believe they must be right. Despite my own knowledge of my undoubted innocence I could not escape a profound sense of unworthiness. Once again merely being who I was provoked condemnation. Those things stay with a child. The book fair incident has remained with me since the fourth grade. No doubt my mother was driven by the notion of respectability hammered into her by her parents, a sense of propriety meant to arm Negroes for life in a world that cast them as worthless "coloreds". One must not drag the family or the race down by acting like a common lower case negro. In her eyes, that is what I had done. The lessons were too well ingrained for her to recognize how harmfully they were distorting her interaction with her own child or to regard him as an individual worthy of defense against a false charge, no matter the consequences. The imputation of misconduct was equivalent to a guilty verdict. If I had been arrested for stealing I would have been cast into the outer darkness as a lost soul. It is ironic, but in respect of race blacks and whites are sometimes very much alike, each living within the narrowness of a horizon we jointly conspire in keeping closed.

There was in all of us an overwhelming tendency to self-deceit where it came to the woundings we experienced at the hands of white society and by my parents' perpetual warfare. The prevailing family ethos taught that only weak and ungrateful people "dwelt" on problems. A lifetime of illusion was preferable to paying serious attention to one's own injuries. This was called being strong, no doubt a learned survival technique passed down through generations of trauma. "She never complains" was the highest tribute one could pay to someone dying of an incurable illness or struggling with honest poverty. It made no sense to me. What was the advantage of silently enduring wracking pain that would only end with death, or hiding the depressing effects of one's destitution? The cult of silent suffering is a way of deflecting consciousness from the inequity of the system we live beneath, while masking this self-deceit as stoic heroism performed in the face of adversity. The uncomplaining are celebrated as model people, exemplars who refuse to impose their suffering on others, thereby forcing them to face unpleasantness whose causes would be difficult and even risky to remove. The silently suffering affirm our fearful wish to be predetermined by something more powerful than ourselves, something we can accede to, bow down to and serve even if it is adversity and disease.

My eldest brother, who'd been drafted into the Korean War as a very young man, was the rare example in my youth of a person who paid serious attention to the psychological wounding of race, family and America, a Job who loudly complained when and where it was necessary, and seemed to delight in calling the white god to account. His breach of faith with the phalanx of silence was dangerous because it threatened the family's collective affirmation of the discontents of life as if they were the Given Circumstances of a play. He was a liberating voice articulating concerns most of us recognize as crucial today but which gained him the reputation of a troublemaking near-do-well back then. He interpreted my father's violence as a reaction to the frustrations of American racism and race-bred self-hatred. It would, he argued, have a negative impact on the younger children. He opposed our going to church and Sunday school where we were being "brainwashed" and taught to feel guilty about normal sexual urges and pleasure of any kind, and he was right. Later, in the 60s, he wore a kind of Afro hairdo and encouraged me to do the same. Like Malcolm X he preached Black liberation by any means necessary. All of this was seen by most of the family as evidence of a problematic character. If he did suffer some congenital flaw his condition was not regarded sympathetically as a problem we should help him resolve by love and nurture. Instead, he became my mother's favorite cautionary tale for what to avoid, the model of an irresponsible and undisciplined person. I was often compared to him in these terms, an analogy I spent years trying to disprove. Worst of all he was sometimes painted as weak, one of the most damning accusations in my family. In this we were quite typical of Negroes. The idolization of strength, specifically the ability to overcome obstacles to achieve one's goals or merely to survive is a national cult. America's folk heroes epitomize this value. George Washington, Daniel Boone, Andrew Jackson are remembered for their toughness, relentless determination and physical stamina, not for habits of compassion, charity or intellect. The national fixation on toughness seems natural to Americans. Isn't it strength that allows an individual to keep going despite difficult circumstances, to rise above unfairness, even injustice to build a fulfilling life? We heard a lot in the 60s of the need for strong black men. We hear today of the need for strong black women. On the face of it there seems little to object to. On the contrary it appears laudable to praise models of strength. Black people had to be strong to survive slavery and Jim Crow. They must be strong today to overcome the injustices and barriers in their way. Weak people fall by the wayside and cause problems for their families, friends and communities. Strong people hold things together and put their backs to the

HOME SWEET HOME

wheel of progress. The problem is that all too often the strength we worship comes at the expense of sensitivity to the manifold injuries we suffer through life. This is certainly not always the case. There are plenty of examples of the strongest among us demonstrating the most compassionate understanding of human suffering and the deepest commitment to removing it. Martin Luther King, Jr. is only one among many. But when strength obscures or trivializes those injuries, in order to rise above them, we're apt to forget the injustice of the injuries themselves and regard those who succumb to them, or even take them seriously as weak.

With one or two exceptions my parents and siblings adhered to this national mythology. No doubt, if I'd voiced my feelings of injustice and repression they would have elicited anger, outrage and derision. So I kept my humiliations to myself and lived as a secret stranger in that household. Where early on the family group had facilitated my search for possibilities of myself and encouraged their development it now frustrated and forbid that expedition. Even now I cannot help feeling as if I am betraying something by speaking truthfully. Such is the extraordinary power of white supremacy and the national culture of self repression that it can reach into the privacy of family life, distort and pervert a child's developing sense of identity and leave the adult defenseless against unmerited guilt. Such is our complicity that we willfully ignore the signs of oppression in our own children transmuting them self protectively into character flaws. Perhaps it would have been too much for my parents to recognize behavior they characterized as irresponsible and wayward as reactions to the oppressions of race inside as well as outside of the home. To do so would have questioned the identities they lived in, which despite their severely narrowing effects allowed them to raise a family. They were nothing if not strong.

Like many children, I blamed and punished myself for feeling weak and inadequate. Model building was one of my great passions, always pursued at the risk of being thought impractical and self-indulgent like the eldest brother. He had been a master model airplane builder as an adolescent and was pointed to as the archetype of failure. In fact, modeling was an activity uniting creativity with a kind of practicality. It took patience, skill and determination to build a successful balsa airplane that actually flew.His flew superbly. Mine never flew particularly well. As I got older I turned to model ships. For my fifteenth Christmas I received a model kit of the British clipper ship *Thermopylae*. It was the most complex model I'd attempted involving the antiquing of the hull in stages over several days and threading standing

68   BEING-IN-AMERICA: WHITE SUPREMACY AND THE AMERICAN

and running rigging through tiny blocks and tackles with a pair of tweezers. It took several weeks to complete the project. What I had then was a beautiful piece of craftsmanship which I proudly displayed on the mantelpiece over the artificial fireplace. Some weeks later I was once again the butt of jokes and derision about my artistic, allegedly "happy go lucky" temperament which brought me to tears behind closed doors. In anger and humiliation I smashed my beautiful ship to pieces. It was not the first time I'd responded this way. There was the cutting board made for my mother in woodshop and an earlier model airplane destroyed for similar reasons. I was possessed by a sense of self-loathing that I was too immature and too repressed to understand. I lashed out not at my human provocateurs, who I was constitutionally incapable of confronting, even if I could have understood what was happening to me, but at myself through my own creations. There seemed something at once squalid and treacherous about my feelings. I had been taught not to feel sorry for myself but I could not help doing so. I often secretly cried from some deep wounding I was unable to identify while the sense that the little family were somehow to blame created a deep feeling of guilt. I knew they could not help looking like and being who they were. I felt sorry for them because they too seemed out of place, awkward and deficient in their own ways. I had no idea about anything like emotional honesty and openness. We were trained to believe emotions were dangerous demons to be controlled at all costs, usually at the price of our emotional wellbeing. Talking about emotions empowered their deviousness so I kept doubly quiet. We had no sense of the liberating power of open communication.

In consequence, the family became a form of self-incarceration rather than the liberating community it could have been. By ignoring the unspoken lies supporting the illusion of harmony, we foreclosed the possibility of authentic emotional engagement with one another and imprisoned ourselves within ourselves. Then we concealed our dishonesty behind the mask of familial love and piety. Any attempt to penetrate behind that façade provoked instant condemnation as a disrespectful, selfish, ungrateful and disloyal child. My eldest brother rose to the challenge and earned for his heroic efforts the stigma of being an irresponsible whiner, persistently put before me and Gregory as the example to avoid. My parents were rather austere authority figures whose notion of respectability seemed more important than the emotional stability of their children. All compromise was on our side. They were never granted the blessing of being called to account by any of us, an act that could have loosened the iron restrictions they labored within, while they tore each other apart in reaction to influences they denied existed, but which followed them like shadows. It seemed ironic that my father who frequently called on God for an accounting of his sins never called on us to discover his own. My parents' sins were common to all of us in this land of illusions, the refusal to question the complacent assumptions they based their lives on and the typical American aggressively hostile rejection of any attempt to prod them into doing so. It was an attitude and conviction they learned at the hands of their parents and grandparents. Their particular guilt lay in defending what they had received as if it came from the hand of God. I could never imagine entering into any kind of dialog with them. We never did.

Under the dominance of white supremacy, this is what an American family inflicts upon its loving members; not all, of course, but enough to leave an indelible mark upon the national character. One learns to avoid questions to get along, to ignore contradictions, for it is apparent that to take exception cannot be limited to the case at hand. Inescapably, it will uncover fundamental disagreements and divergences, so one keeps quiet and accedes. With stronger willed and aggressively defensive people one's acquiescence is marked. To them we appear of one mind which makes future objections all the more disruptive as if all along you've baited them towards some final deceitful trap. One gives up trying and adopts the self-serving lie that they're far older and more permanently fixed than anyone ever is. Eventually the claustrophobic absence of authentic communication becomes insuperable. One simply stops talking and accepts whatever explanation for disengagement they choose to select.

In this domestic environment, which really is America in miniature, all that was left to blame was myself. The art and talent, the sensitivity to light and line, the rapture of creation that produced those models, the paintings and sketches that brightened my world were symptoms of what was wrong with me. Smashing my beautiful ship was a spiteful self-punishment for being what I was. Just as I had earlier stopped planting my annual garden for similar reasons, I now abruptly stopped model building. I stopped painting. I stopped writing too, closing off my most immediate routes to the wilderness so vital to my survival. When you come right down to it, I stopped me, for it was a kind of living suicide in which I entombed myself in a sepulcher of my own creating, every bit as life denying as the cemetery that had so depressed me, emerging just long enough to function minimally, before returning like the living dead to my native soil.

· 1 4 ·

MATERFAMILIAS

Unlike my cousins and all of my friends I grew up in a matriarchal household. Having discovered that men tended to be more rigid, less creative and harsher than women I found this situation to my liking, although my mother could be quite inflexible in her own way. It was not that my father had abandoned his family. Despite my fervent wishes that he would do precisely that, daddy persistently returned home every night after long hours at work to resume his marathon jeremiad against God, humankind and his wife. Mommy became the "foundation" he frequently declared he sought to place beneath us but just as frequently demolished. She was the great organizer. She paid the bills, prepared the household accounts and saved. No significant decision could be made without her consent. She supervised the child rearing, including meeting out frequent punishments. My father was never involved, never lectured us and spanked us only once during my entire childhood.

My mother was our great defender from the dangers of the outside world and my father's rages. At age 12, I was brutally and daily bullied by a large 14-year-old boy, who having been left back several times, was put in my seventh grade homeroom for the sole purpose, it seemed, of tormenting me. When the school authorities washed their hands of the matter my mother removed me from school and educated me at home for several months, until for some

72   BEING-IN-AMERICA: WHITE SUPREMACY AND THE AMERICAN

reason the boy dropped out or moved away. I can't think of any father in those days who would have responded with such sensitive imagination. Their normative preachment was to stand up and fight, a prescription that would have escalated the violence, to my detriment. By such motherly interventions we were spared much of the unbending and nearsighted backwardness of patriarchy, only to suffer some of its worst effects in other ways. Though she did her best, not even the most powerful matriarch could shield us from all of the depredations of white supremacy. Ironically, some of its most destructive effects entered our lives in consequence of her determined efforts to keep them out.

She had gone from a family of eight in Mt. Vernon, New York to marriage at nineteen and seven children over the next twenty-three years in the same town. Her childhood seemed the happiest period of her life. As small boys my brother and I adored the bedtime stories she'd tell of Cortlandt Street in the second decade of the twentieth century. She would sit for a while on Gregory's bed, then shift to mine as she recounted the sights and sounds, the neighborhood children, the games they played, so different from our own, and the fun they had, so much better. And with the descriptions came the American racial order with its panoply of anti-black stereotypes. Mommy often told the story of Lucius Allblack, a coal black boy with big eyes, thick red lips and a surname that invited cruelty from blacks as well as whites. On each retelling the image of Little Black Sambo would return from the cover of my first grade reader, with the familiar sense of something wrong I failed to grasp. "Lucius Allblack is all black!" the kids shouted till he chased them. My mother had not joined in the taunting. Her race conscious father would have been appalled if she had, but she would laugh in recollection, quickly adding that it was wrong to belittle Lucius because of his appearance, which suggested, of course, that his looks were somehow aberrant. Yet, as she related the game that must have hurt Lucius deeply, she did not explain the woundings we had sensed in those words but never asked about, or the history that made such childhood assaults permissible and funny. Nor, when relating her entirely white looking mother's disparagement of adult versions of Lucius, did she describe or critique my grandmother's anti-black stereotypes. Her silence, given her centrality to our lives, lent unintentional legitimacy to the humor. Perhaps she was reluctant to expose our young minds to the traumas of race we would soon suffer. If so it was a sheltering defense that left us unarmed and unprepared to fight against what she had allowed to remain concealed. I wondered what became of Lucius and his remarkable blackness but I never asked. Like most children in those days, we'd been conditioned not to inquire about anything left unexplained,

MATERFAMILIAS 73

and therefore presented as beyond question. In this way, without our knowing it, horizons were gradually erected all around us.

Born in 1909, my mother lived with her parents, four sisters and the older brother in a world with few motor cars or airplanes, no electric lights, telephones, radio or TV and no central heating, so they dressed for warmth in cold weather behind the potbellied stove in the kitchen. In the winter, James Oris Powell, Jr., whom the girls called "Brother," would break the overnight ice in the hall toilet before it could be used. The stories she told about those "olden days", as we called them, took us back to a time when horses pulled wagons, the lamplighter lit the gas fueled street lights at dusk and extinguished them at dawn, where the iceman delivered huge chunks of frozen water to cool the icebox and children wore knickers as they roamed the city playing games entirely unknown to us.

The father, James Oris Powell, Sr. was a music teacher and superintendent of the black Baptist Sunday School. Mommy described "Papa" as a very strict man who forbid talking at the dinner table and kept a glass of cold water by his place to dash in the face of offenders. He was born in Petersburg, Virginia a year after the Civil War, and was eleven when Reconstruction was suppressed by a reign of terror unleashed on black southerners by white redeemers with the acquiescence of Northern whites. My mother never spoke about the social conditions of her father's youth. It is likely he never discussed them with his children. The move north to Mt. Vernon meant his eyes were firmly fixed on a better future not the world he had left behind. For him that included the progress of the Negro race, for he was what was then called a "race man", dedicated to the advancement of his people. Determined to instill dignity and racial pride in his children he gave my mother the honorific middle name Toussaint, after Toussaint L' Ouverture the hero of the 1791 revolution that ended slavery in Saint-Domingue and led to the founding of Haiti. Strangely, although she was proud of her name, Ethel Toussaint Richardson never told us about her namesake and his illustrious history, except that he had immense strength of character and will, both of which she had inherited. It was not until I got to Howard University and read C. L. R. James, *The Black Jacobins: Toussaint L'Ouverture and the San. Domingo Revolution* that I learned his story.

The closest I came to my grandfather was the discovery of a speech he had delivered in Mt. Vernon on Memorial Day 1895. The manuscript of "The So-Called Negro Problem" was in an old box of documents at the back of mommy's walk-in closet. She had forgotten about it in the decades since she'd carefully preserved it in cellophane. It was the only contact I ever had with

74   BEING-IN-AMERICA: WHITE SUPREMACY AND THE AMERICAN

the grandfather they say I favored. I felt enormous pride as I read his words and imagined his sonorous voice declaiming that "The So-Called Negro Problem" did not exist and never had. The problem was white racism. To solve their problem, and thus the nation's, white people must live by the Christian morality they professed and act on the principles enshrined in the Declaration of Independence. It struck me as extraordinary that a truth clearly visible in 1895 is still obscured by large sections of white America. It was a courageous and necessary statement. When he delivered his speech blacks were being lynched in large numbers, 113 in 1895 alone, while Congress continued to reject anti-lynching legislation, unwilling to deprive white supremacist terrorists of their most horrific weapon.[1]

My grandfather was an impressive man. Not only did he teach music, but his voice was beautiful enough for Victor Records to offer him a recording contract. A brightening future beckoned the family, but like my little black engine the dream was too good to stay on the rails. In an oft repeated story, my mother told us how he fell ill on the train home from signing the contract and died of pneumonia soon afterwards. He was 51. I don't know if her sequencing was exactly right, but the coupling of success and death was momentous. Mommy was barely eight when he passed away, too young to understand or even recognize the racial political economy that had in all likelihood blunted her father's career prospects and shortened his life. I remember hearing the story as a small boy and thinking that it fit well with the way I felt, reinforcing the intuition of doom waiting for any of us who aspired to American normality. Over nine decades after my grandfather's passing, when I tried to reassure my eldest brother that with proper medical care he could survive his illnesses, he pointed, with a resignation surprising in a man who had always prided himself on his rationality, to our grandfather's death as a harbinger of his own. The story of James Oris Powell, Senior's demise on the threshold of success had become a veiled warning not to hope for too much and was passed on as part of the accumulating cultural trauma handed down from slavery and Jim Crow times. Thus, despite her commitment to racial and individual progress, despite her emphatic assurances that we could accomplish whatever we set our minds to, and her constant injunction to think positively, my mother was haunted by a pervasive dread that something was bound to go wrong at any time, a mood and a sentiment she passed on to her children, driven by her overprotective determination to shelter us from whatever it was that threatened.

What threatened, but was never given a name or a face was white supremacy. The ghostly anonymity of that power was the consequence of what my

MATERFAMILIAS 75

parents called "positive thinking", which led them, and all of the black people I knew growing up, to abhor blaming external conditions or obstacles for problems they regarded as their own responsibility. This false pretense to more agency than they actually possessed, performed in order to create the illusion of strengthening the modest agency they did possess, made it all but impossible to identify and combat the psychological effects of white supremacy in themselves and their children. Unfortunately, those like my eldest brother Ernest, who insisted on exposing and engaging those effects were cast as persistent whiners lacking in moral character. In this stealthy way, the normally unmentioned white supremacist regime we labored beneath, penetrated the sheltering defensive parameters of the family as if it had been designed to do so. Its effects were all the more devastating because none of us children or my parents recognized it or its dangers while it was doing its perniciously destructive work.

My grandmother, Adele Powell was the daughter of a German father and a black and Native American mother. She looked entirely white, and from the stories my mother told she would have been happier growing up in Germany where her father wanted to take her to live. Her mother, Mariah, had other ideas. Without her knowledge or consent she arranged for her to marry James Oris Powel a black man twenty years her senior, an experience mommy described as traumatic. Then, suddenly, at age 31, she found herself facing the daunting responsibility of raising six children alone with no social safety net beneath. Even white Americans had to wait for the New Deal for that, but while they might have savings to draw down or relatives and friends to borrow from before hitting rock bottom, for most black people slavery's brutal generational thefts of the fruits of their labor, compounded by the ravages of Jim Crow, had left them with little or nothing to fall back on except individual and collective sacrifice. My uncle, James Oris Powell, Jr., a remarkable and always kindly man, deferred his dream of becoming a doctor, dropped out of school and went to work to help support the family. He never went back and became an auto mechanic instead. In his later years he owned a service station. Adele Powell worked as a domestic and laundress in the homes of well-off white people. The family survived, and all of my aunts became nurses.

After her first four children were old enough to care for themselves during the day, and we younger three had not yet arrived, mommy served as an administrator at Mt. Vernon's West Side YMCA, developed by the entrepreneurial black Reverend Emmett Lampkin for what were then called Negroes. She flourished in that post until my father decided he didn't want his wife working. My mother had great talent, tremendous self-discipline, impressive organizational skills and a powerful will. She could have become a professional administrator or a successful business woman if given the chance. Perhaps my father feared she'd surpass his achievements or become involved with one of her male colleagues. Whatever his motivation it was painfully unfair to her. Few women today would tolerate such an intrusion. In the late 1940s she complied, but she must have resented the forcible suppression of her budding career. There was an anger that seemed to simmer inside, to boil over in the bitter, and often effective, verbal attacks she launched at her husband during their frequent violent emotional altercations.

The destruction of her career came on top of an earlier frustration She had grown up with a love of literature and the dream of becoming a writer. In the segregated and racially oppressive 1920s and 1930s it was a calling very few black people were able to pursue. There was little prospect of making a living as a writer unless you could support yourself some other way such as teaching. But teaching required a college degree Struggling to make ends meet mommy's family could hardly fund higher education, few Negros could. Deprived of the wherewithal to develop her creativity by centuries of white supremacist oppression, and driven by that same demonic force to seek a safe career my mother chose bookkeeping and homemaking, and excelled at both. Later, for about fifteen years, she cared for foster babies, sometimes taking two at a time. They'd come right from the hospital to our home where mommy and daddy showered them with love and attention. Two stayed for nearly three years before they were adopted. By then it was painful for the children to leave the only home they'd known and heartbreaking for my parents to give them up. Yet, for all of the intrinsic value of this work, and the undoubted fulfillment she gained through it, it was no compensation for the career she should have had.

Of course, mommy never put it that way. In all likelihood she never thought of it that way. Conscious awareness of the great extent and deep psychological damage of white supremacist oppression was *held-off* by my parents and their peers. Becoming conscious of white supremacy's intimate effects on individual and family life would have posed the difficult choice of ignoring those effects in one's self and one's family, re-concealing them and living in selfdeceit, or embarking on the active attempt to imagine a different way of *being-in-America*, with the prospect of a life of struggle against white supremacy, waged in all likelihood without group support. My parents aspired to integrate into American society as it was not to alter or reform it. And because

American society is founded on an extreme version of individual autonomy that supports and is supported by white supremacy, accepting society as it was trapped them within a way of being that was destructively constrictive for themselves and their family as black people. Responding to the promptings of what I described below as the *white supremacist collective unconscious*, both of my parents interpreted that destructiveness as among the unavoidable discontents and imperfections of life that are complained about only by whiners and weaklings.

Sadly, their self defensive hobbling of creative imagination hindered their attempts to find clarity in a white supremacist environment. America as they found it, constituted the horizon within which they were resigned to live their lives. My father persistently railed against that fate but was unable or unwilling to effectively comprehend or critique it. He was quite aware that many of our troubles were what he called "manmade", a term he used very often to deplore avoidable suffering. He had got hold of a powerful transformative notion that could have produced liberating effects in our family, but he did not develop it. White supremacy had denied him the educational training and the institutional support that might have provided the skills and allowed him the time to pursue the implications of his intuitive grasp of the situation he had been thrown into. Instead, his angry ejaculations sounded like the misanthropic pronouncements of a madman unable to apply his random insights to his own situation. With few resources to work with mommy and daddy settled for wanting the same rights as every other inhabitant of the American intrahorizonal world, rather than looking for a way beyond it.[2] Accordingly, without critically examining them, they transformed the oppressions they struggled beneath into the inevitable horizon they must live within. Things might one day be different, but in the meantime they had to work within the Given Circumstances, which seemed to them the best way to gradually change those same circumstances, a notion captured by my father's injunction, a product I suspect of combat fatigue, that "You must join them to beat them", which meant that you'd become them, whereupon you would lose all interest in beating them, while *they* would have been expanded without substantially changing their nature. This is what we now call *diversity and inclusion*, a typically American way of avoiding the fundamental American dynamic of white supremacy by enlarging the problem, the same strategy Donald Rumsfeld and the Neocons recommended be applied in the case of Iraq and terrorism with disastrous results. In my parents view, which was commonly shared within their cohort of family and friends, the best way to gain entrance was to excel

78   BEING-IN-AMERICA: WHITE SUPREMACY AND THE AMERICAN

at whatever one did. This attitude augmented their sense of agency over what they could control, focused their energies on the day-to-day struggle to get ahead, and allowed them to persist in the face of often overwhelming odds and raise a family.

But there are consequences of affirming horizons, whether they consist of the Given Circumstances of one's lifeworld or the cosmic event horizon. In my parents' case, the most significant was that without locating and evaluating the sources and origins of their psychic oppressions, they were unable to trace or address their effects in themselves and their children. Left concealed those influences were misidentified and metamorphosed into the fatalistic mood of mingled apprehension, resignation and occasional despair that permeated our family life, and which neither my mother nor my father could free themselves of because they were unwilling or unable to uncover and confront their sources. Yet, without a supportive *facilitating group*, such as Gregory and I had in the "alternate parents" that I described below, it would have been extraordinarily difficult to do so. Moreover, the groups they lived within were dedicated to keeping horizons closed on behalf of peaceful lives as full-fledged autonomous individuals, not to rocking the boat.

Long before my parents met, my mother put her dreams aside and adapted to the restrictions of white supremacist society, in exchange for making as secure a private world as she could. By example and precept she taught us to do the same, even as she assured us we could achieve whatever we set our minds to, provided our ambitions remained within safe limits. As mine wandered persistently into what she considered the dangerous territories of art, literature and theater we clashed frequently and often angrily. When my tenth grade English teacher, an admirable and progressive young white woman, strongly supported my literary and acting ambitions, my mother went to school and told her not to encourage me in that direction. I was a Negro, she lectured, and could not expect to make a living as a creative artist. Her intervention clearly demonstrated that despite her usual silence on the matter, and her reluctance to name, analyze and confront the culprit, mommy was well aware of white supremacy's destructive power. She never warned me against pursuing a writing career because it was insecure, but only because it would not provide the maximum of financial and job security I would need to survive in America as a Negro. Worried about our economic welfare and safety in racist America, she drilled into our heads her conviction that medicine and law offered the best protection for a black person, as well as being the most honorable professions.

MATERFAMILIAS   79

For all of the negative effects of her narrowing regime, my mother was correctly reading the Given Circumstances of her childhood, youth and early adulthood that were steeply and actively stacked against any black women succeeding as a writer or an artist. Yet those circumstances had changed since she had abandoned her own creative ambitions. Despite the continuing inequalities and oppressions of the American racial order, the Civil Rights Movement and the cultural revolutions preceding, accompanying and following it had opened careers beyond law and medicine, teaching and the ministry. By the time I entered my teenage years in the early 1960s it was possible for a black person to earn a living in literature and the arts, as increasing numbers of African Americans were doing. There was something else, something more damaging at work than mommy's pragmatism, something wounding. She had, as far as I could tell, internalized the brutal lessons racism had inflicted and come to regard creative work itself as the mark of a weak, profligate, self-indulgent character, an occupation of a wholly unproductive order, inferior to the socially highly valued work of the doctor or lawyer. In short, a morally dangerous way of life. In an act of vilifying what she had once loved, as if it had betrayed her for being out of reach, she cut herself off from the healing and liberating power of art, fantasy and speculation, and the critically revealing and constituting power of intellect and imagination, a self-wounding that strengthened white supremacy's grip on her, for it is precisely imagination that is capable of liberating the self from the straightjacket of *white-supremacist-being-in-America*. And its suppression or denigration works to keep us within the ontological horizon of white supremacist individualism.

Mommy's response to oppression by self-censorship, represented to herself and to her children as hardheaded, responsible pragmatism, which indeed it was, encouraged me to suppress my creativity as something unhealthy and aberrant, and to regard the creative me as the lurking enemy within. Like my mother I vilified and demonized it, regarding those who heeded the call of art and literature as self-indulgent decadents. Rooting it out was part of my struggle to reconstruct myself as a "normal" person who would be valued in the family and succeed in society. It was not until I was in my late 40s that I felt secure enough to begin to admit and release my creative energies. And it was only after mommy had passed away that I fully embraced them. This was also the time that I achieved a degree of material security, thanks in no small measure to her emphasis on pragmatism and opposition to creative careers. In my case her strategy for surviving white supremacy worked and she lived long enough to see the success of her wisdom, love and nurture. But it was a product of compromise. Academia offered a middle way between pure creativity and pragmatism which my mother never had. In academia I found a means of expressing my creativity that seemed to me, at a time when I was recovering from my experiments in transcending the culture horizon, that I described below, more grounded and responsible than the free creation of literature and art.[3] This was, of course, a way around my fear of creativity, a desensitization by gradual emersion. Yet, it is indisputable, that in turning against my youthful artistic aspirations I had cut myself off, as my mother had done, from the spiritual springs that could have sustained me through some of the most difficult passages of my life and allowed me to challenge and perhaps transcend the restrictive horizons I have lived within. My younger brother had so effectively hidden his own creative bent, refusing even to read fiction or look at art unless it was required homework, that it was not until he was in graduate school, and I accidentally discovered a rather good short story he'd written, that I had any inkling of his creative talents and interests. The oppressions of white supremacy, which had taught my mother the virtual impossibility, and therefore the inappropriateness, of a Negro living a sustainable creative life, had provoked a self-repressive response in her that she passed along to her children in greater or lesser degree. In this creative desert, my eldest brother Ernest, and my sister Shirley were life sustaining springs. Both were poets and impressive artists. I remember the pride I felt on discovering Shirley's artwork on display in my junior high school ten years after she'd graduated. Sadly, they were labeled dreamers by my mother. While their existence was a lifeline for me, their marked failure to forge successful careers and marriages reinforced her cautionary tales. Art and fantasy were prescriptions for disaster.

Times change and people sometimes change with them. When mommy was in her late 70s, with all of her children grown, and my father had passed away, her creative energies returned, or perhaps she finally felt safe enough to release them. She resumed writing. The local newspaper thought her work good enough to publish her poetry. One wonders how much more fulfilling her life and her children's lives could have been had she not felt compelled to suppress her creativity in order to negotiate white supremacist America.

Notes

1 http://archive.tuskegee.edu/repository/wp-content/uploads/2020/11/Lynchings-Stats-Year-Dates-Causes.pdf, p. 2. Accessed on 8-5-23 at 12:59 am.
2 For my notion of horizon see Chapter 32 "Deprivations".
3 See Chapter 22 "Beyond the Far Horizon".

· 1 5 ·

PARENTAL FEARS

Throughout my childhood and youth my father smoldered in chronic anger that frequently kindled into rage. For the most part his condition was the gift of his immigrant's collision with racist America. Driven by his unrelenting sense of duty to support his wife and seven children, come what may, he repressed his indignation at the daily humiliations and inequities inflicted on him by his employers, their customers and any white person who chose to exercise their privileged position. He controlled himself for forty-two years with the same company.

Self repression came hard to a man of six one who'd been a prize fighter and driven bootleg for Al Capone back in the 20s. That was when he arrived in Chicago from his native West Indian Island full of eager ambition and hope. His father's name was Ishmael, the only one I'd ever known who wasn't in a book. He passed his namesake's disposition to his son. Like Ishmael my father's hypos sometimes got the better of him and since he never had the option of foreign travel or killing whales to vent his spleen he brought his anger home.

Relocated to New York he found employment as an elevator operator in a commercial building at 10 East 39th Street in Manhattan. Twenty years later, when I was born, he had become chief engineer of the same building. The job meant a bit more money, enough so that with the aid of a down payment from a lucky numbers hit my parents were able to purchase their first house when I was 6. The upward move brought increased pressures for a black man who knew his first mistake could easily be his last. For the next twenty years he worked six days a week, often going in on Sundays as well during the winter, always worried something would go wrong and he'd be fired. By 1954 he had seven children, a mortgage and a growing sense of respectability to protect. It took a toll. Every evening he'd return home after hours of overtime exhausted by the daily battle. We could hear his habitual teeth gritting before he opened the door. As a child I didn't think much of his grinding unless he was angry. Then it became loud and menacing. Now I realize the tremendous stress he must have been under to go around constantly gritting his teeth, always ready to defend his dignity, always pushed sternly up against his duty, never letting his guard down or relaxing his conscientious determination. Yet whenever I visited him at work in my teens I was surprised to find how relaxed and contented he appeared. My impression was confirmed by friends and relatives who knew him at work and at home. It seems ironic, but it was not uncommon in those days for black people to find a degree of peace and freedom working at jobs that allowed them a measure of creativity and control no matter how small, despite the racism attendant on it. This is why they could often be the most diligent, productive and cheerful workers, exemplars of what Americans call "a positive attitude" while denying its possession by blacks. The recognition does not lessen or diminish the oppressions of white supremacy. On the contrary, it emphasizes, and makes more laudable, the resilience and relentless determination of people like my father who were able to make meaningful lives even under racist oppression.

Daddy's struggles did not stop with the mortal world. Night after night, like a West Indian Job, he called on god to account for his inscrutably maddening decisions and deceptions, shouting "Why? Why? Why?" to the ceiling, as if someone living upstairs could supply the cosmic answers he sought. Why must innocent children suffer? What was the point of famines and plagues? Why had god caused a world of conflict when he could have made a paradise? Sometimes, he'd suddenly start, utter an agonized moan and command "Down Boy!" to an internal opponent, and I'd wonder if like Luther he'd seen the devil. My mother valiantly defended Jehovah against his frequent attacks with the accusation of free will against humankind. "Why would an omniscient being give free will to creatures whose misdeeds he knew in advance? He must be playing a joke!" he'd respond, I thought brilliantly, promising to "Spit in his eye and kick him in the teeth" as soon as he got the chance. Clearly, daddy's mind was far too honest and sensitive to grasp the mysteries of faith. To him religion, hypocrisy of every species, cruelty, injustice the myriad miseries of life, all of which he felt deeply, were "all manmade", a sentiment that impressed me. It often seemed to me that my mother was less interested in defending the deity she rarely visited in church than in defeating my father.

He was born on the Caribbean island of St. Kitts in 1905 when it was still a British colony. All of his life he proudly called himself a British Subject, even after becoming an American citizen in 1947. As a boy he would swim out with other lads to where British ships swung at their moorings, dive beneath their keels and surface on the other side to a shower of coins from amused sailors. He played in the forests, climbed coconut trees, lived in a big house with a verandah and was escorted to school by a servant. The house belonged to his Dutch grandmother whose Victorian portrait shows a stern woman dressed in black who took him from his parents to raise as her own. He dearly loved Granny as he called her but it could not have been a warm childhood. She seemed an insensitive woman who once locked him in a closet overnight to cure his boyhood fear of the dark. Yet, in the days before he passed away, she came to his bedside with his parents to hurry him on.

For as long as I knew him my father lamented the loss of his relatively privileged life in a colored colonial elite, and reduction to common Negro status, with the rest of the black multitudes he called "Cotton Pickers." He never fully adjusted to America which he disparaged as a country without culture. For him Britain was the epitome of civilization. There was no future in the islands outside of sugarcane, and even less in that backbreaking, thankless toil, so at 17 Ernest Wentworth Richardson left to work on Canadian steamships traveling to Britain and the docks of Ireland where he loaded cargo. He soon joined the West Indian migration to America, making his way to Chicago where his immigrant Uncle Archie took him in. Working days he went to school at night to become an electrician. It was decades before he got to use his skills on something other than manual labor. Those years must have been filled with frustration as he grew older and his dream of becoming an engineer faded, replaced by devotion to his family.

Despite, or perhaps because of that devotion it was impossible to live a normal childhood and adolescence in his presence. One never knew when daddy would insult a friend or curse out loud for no apparent reason, or worse, engage in a life and death battle with one of his older sons, where usually the fault was not all on his side, and the physical provocations came from them.

84   BEING-IN-AMERICA: WHITE SUPREMACY AND THE AMERICAN

He could be particularly rude to anyone with a dark complexion, once complimenting one of my sister's best friends by telling her she'd grown lighter since he'd last seen her. He distinctly favored his fairer grandchildren over the darker ones. When my youngest son stayed with my parents for some months when he was not yet three, my father was fond of affectionately calling him a "little white man", because he took after my mother and was fairer than either of his parents. He had similar sensitivities about my younger brother but picked on him, it may be, for the very fact of looking white. Perhaps Gregory reminded him of his Dutch grandmother who'd locked him in the closet, and which the conflicted bonds of love and authority forbid him from striking back at.

On occasion his anger was justified. Our nearly all white Episcopal Church organized a youth program that I desperately wanted to join. My suspicious father invited the director to our home to explain the purpose of the group. The middle-aged white Christian man visited us one evening to recruit me. Things seemed to be going fairly well. My father had remained calm. Then the man said something my 8-year-old brain did not understand. "We want to keep the boys off the streets so they don't go around stealing and raping." Something snapped in daddy's brain and he literally threw the man out of the house. I was embarrassed and disappointed, even when my mother surprised me by strongly supporting him. She tried in an awkward and incomplete way to explain what the man had said. I remained confused but her attitude reassured me. It seemed there were times when violent outbursts were justified. Years later I would look back at that incident with pride.

There were days when he'd act almost normal, and I'd pray that whatever demon possessed him had tired of the torment and found another host. He could be very affectionate. We received surprise boxes of Fanny Farmer lollypops for no particular reason making the treat all the more enjoyable. Quite often we'd find the chocolate kisses we called Jingle Bells in the deep pockets of his heavy overcoats. Late at night when no one was watching, we'd filch coins from those same pockets that always seemed full of quarters going begging. It was only after he was gone that I realized he'd put them there for us to discover. He was romantic too, far more so than my mother. Not one Valentine's Day passed without a box of chocolates or flowers, when he'd hug her and kiss her on the cheek. She always reacted a bit stiffly I thought, making me uncomfortable.

Late spring and summer were his best seasons. Perhaps they took him back to his youth in the sands of a tropical paradise when life was full of

PARENTAL FEARS

85

promise. Whatever the cause, on hot summer nights we'd sit on the high backed wooden bench beneath the old magnolia tree, I on his lap, with the stubble of his beard rough against my cheek, the pungent smell of larger beer mingled with the scent of magnolia blossoms. He'd let me sip the foam atop his Rheingold, the hat he called it. If I were quick enough, I could get just the slightest taste of beer itself, not bitter not sweet the jingle said. We'd sit, just the two of us, and I'd have the feeling of being special children adore when a parent singles them out for attention. He'd tell stories of the island, so far away, so close, it seemed the place where I should be, among the mango trees, sailing on the warm green sea, chasing lizards in the roots of silk cotton trees, running from the jumbies in the shadows. The great calm descended. Slowly, no matter how hard I tried to stay awake, my eyes would close. I'd rest my head against his chest and hear his heart beating strong and steady, the way it beat all his life, the way it wouldn't stop even when the final cancer had ravaged his body it kept on. That heart, big, open, genuine, proud, tormented was the last bit of life to leave. Then he lay still and rested.

Sooner or later the storm would break, made worse by the intervening sweetness, always without warning, always amidst happy times. A passage of high spirits gone too far towards perfection to endure, summoned the ever watchful furies and he'd erupt like a dormant volcano, shattering unguarded expectations of quietude, spewing out a torrent of profanity, often humorous as well as frightening, a language mercifully alien to my boy's vocabulary, warning my mother she too could "get fired". He seemed always firing someone at work, some laborer who wouldn't apply himself, some poor soul who drank on the job. It never ended there. His heart was bigger than his temper. He'd brood on the man's fate, how his family would fare, how his children would eat. He'd had to do it, gave the fellow many chances. It all came home to us. He terrified me. When I was nine my mother locked him in the basement in self-defense. He hammered on the door while we cowered with her in another room. Then he punched his way out, shattering the door and its frame. I have no memory of what happened next. My younger brother was not to be put off by our father's tantrums. Once, when he was trying to complete his homework with my father ranting and raging, he closed the door to our room. Daddy slammed it open and demanded he leave it so. The closing and opening went on for some time before my father simply ripped the door out of its hinges and carried it to the cellar, my fearless brother following behind with accusations of insanity, and hurled it into the darkened basement. Gregory seemed to have enjoyed the spectacle. I can't think he actually did. He had his own

86 BEING-IN-AMERICA: WHITE SUPREMACY AND THE AMERICAN

way of coping. Once he secretly tape recorded one of daddy's eruptions, hid the recorder, turned the volume to maximum and let it play. My father was furious, but neither then, nor ever did he take it out on me or my brother physically. I felt completely shattered and helpless nonetheless, living in a state of constant anxiety waiting for the night, riddled by fear, dreading that he'd eventually lose his grip and kill my mother. It was not an overreaction. We'd seen him do and say such terrible things. "Whore!" and "whore master!" he'd shout at her. His explosive words striking her small body like a physical assault. Often his anger would erupt from some hidden smoldering magmatic chamber and he'd spit furiously in her face, projecting all of the contempt and hatred bubbling inside as if the velocity of his spittle would demolish her physical, emotional and spiritual being. I can never forget the sickening sight of his thick saliva running down her face, the humiliated and deeply wounded look in her eyes that always reminded me of a hurt and whimpering animal beaten by a cruel and brutal master. I felt the confused flush of profound pity for her, anger at him and helpless fear least he do worse. And he was capable of doing worse. The assaults only confirmed my fears that he could end her life at any moment.

Why she continued to live with him puzzled and frustrated me. Gregory and I begged her to leave or have him committed. She was angry with us for suggesting an action she warned would bring disgrace on the family. Instead, we were made to feel ungrateful and treacherous. Didn't we appreciate how devotedly he was supporting us unlike many men who simply ran off, thus reducing it all to the bottom line, as black people so often did back then, and so often still do. The castigation only added to our already overdeveloped sense of guilt. All of us understood the dynamics of his agonies. I had written a short story about him, a deeply sympathetic treatment of a man tormented by the assaults of race and his own inflexible sense of duty. By posing the alternatives of loyally suffering continued abuse, or selfish betrayal of the breadwinner on behalf of sanity, my mother became complicit in my father's incremental destruction of our fragile emotional health. By instigating guilt in us for desiring normality she undermined our ability to fight back, and because she alone could change an intolerable situation her refusal to leave reinforced our sense of powerlessness. For me, living in that house meant almost perpetual fear, a way of being I never adjusted to. Many nights Gregory and I slept with our Boy Scout hand axes and sheath knives under our pillows, held at the ready should my mother need defending. It may seem strange today, but although we possessed them, it never occurred to either of us that our 22 caliber long rifles or the powerful Winchester model 94, 30–30 might be used in self-defense. We have since declined as a society.

It is a terrible thing to fear for your mother's life. It robs a child of the absolute security innocence deserves, and leaves in its place the enduring and nearly ineradicable conviction that anything could go wrong at any moment. My apprehension was reinforced by the physical fights daddy had with my two older brothers that seemed duels to the death. During one terrible brawl he stabbed my brother-in-law with a screwdriver breaking a rib. Another fight ended with my father going after my eldest brother, who had started the affray, with a hammer, a weapon that could easily have killed him if he had not quickly driven off. Any of these desperate altercations could have ended in death. It seems miraculous none of them did. The fact that they always occurred at family gatherings, in the midst of domestic happiness, when good times were instantly transformed into life and death struggles, left no solid ground to stand on. My mother's underlying mood of dread confirmed my intuition that the world could fly apart at any moment.

The conviction of instability was amplified by daddy's habit of alternating extreme violence with kindness and loving attention. His very goodness signaled the lurking beast in the best of us. It was impossible afterwards to encounter love and nurture without anticipating their sudden metamorphosis into their very opposites. I was caught in an emotional riptide threatening to sweep me out to some vast infernal sea while a great tectonic fault ran beneath the fragile bit of shore I clung to for salvation. It seemed to me astonishing that anyone could live as if things would go on quite well, rather than going off the rails as that little black engine had so long ago. By the time I was seventeen I knew my nerves were ruined for life. It was a prescient intuition. To this day I have never found genuine and unthinking peace, except in rare and suspected moments.

Despite the traumas he had inflicted on all of us, my brothers and sisters continued to interact with daddy as if nothing had happened and our way of being was normal, until normality was interrupted by a sudden explosion that they seemed prepared, even eager, to overlook. After he passed away they were fond of reminiscing nostalgically about his sayings and doings, with no discussion of his depredations, or their role in provoking them. To mention how dangerous he had been drew the defensive reaction that after everything, Ethel and Ernest loved each other and stayed together for over forty years until his death. This construction has always struck me as a willful denial of the actual past to avoid confronting the horror and what it had made of us, a typically American reflex. It struck me as grotesque to think that love could have kept them together at the price of traumatizing their children and themselves. Such persistence would constitute deplorable, rather than admirable behavior. Putting it all down to love, while ignoring the racial and gender political economy my parents lived within and accepted as the Given Circumstances of their lives was always too simplistic. My mother never spoke of love whenever Gregory and I pressed her to leave her husband. When angrily rejecting our pleas she warned that divorce would bring disgrace to the family and to ourselves. She scolded us for not appreciating how diligently our father was supporting us by his labors on our behalf, but never once did she mention her feelings. Of course, she might have thought it inappropriate to talk of her emotions with us, but if so that would have been a misjudgment, and part of the problem. She may have hesitated to tell us that she remained for love at our expense for fear it would have sounded selfish. Perhaps, but in fact, I never heard her speak affectionately about her husband at any time. Where their feelings were concerned, the relationship always seemed one sided, with any sign of affection coming unilaterally from daddy. Mommy always seemed to have the emotional upper hand, even when he was explosive. She could control herself. He could not or would not. I suspect that he longed for her respect and felt he didn't have it.

My mother was a proud woman, every bit as aristocratic in her way as my father. She prized respectability and financial stability, and was mortified by the thought of living a life of hardship marked by the indelible stain of divorce. Gregory and I had no interest in respectability gained at the expense of our emotional health and told her so. At such times, she emphasized the poverty that would result from ending the marriage. The memory of her mother raising six children alone in straitened circumstances must have weighed on her mind. In fact, she had left him once before I was born, and gone to stay with her mother until he came to fetch her home. I wonder, would she would have returned if she'd had an independent income. It was more likely the Given Circumstances of the times, which included white supremacist gender and racial oppression, rather than emotional attachment, that militated against my mother leaving my father. Had she lived in more liberating circumstances, she may have started a new life on her own whether she loved him or not. Perhaps that possibility prompted my father to force her out of the YMCA.

In the end, the fact that my parents did not separate does not prove the strength of their love, nor does the duration of the marriage demonstrate that it should have continued. That conclusion reflects the fatalistic thinking common in our family that what has occurred was meant to happen, as well as an underestimation of our parents' capacity for growth. In all likelihood they remained together because my mother, a black woman without a college degree or professional training, did not see a viable alternative to staying. From this perspective their decades-long marriage was a tragic affair they sometimes made the most of, and sometimes did not. It is no wonder that by the time they were in their 70s they could smile together, as my siblings were fond of saying. By then, they had been through so much pain and tragic loss, that formed a sort of traumatic bond between them, that they were likely resigned to their "fate."

· 1 6 ·

THE ROOT PROBLEM

My parents struggled within the horizon of white supremacist individual autonomy to make a life for their family. In the process they deeply wounded their children and themselves. Operating within the parameters of autonomous individualism, they felt responsible only for what they did to us and to each other by their consciously intended actions, not for the unintended consequences of their behavior or for what they did not do. Therefore, their attention was directed to the love, nurture and support they gave us, not to their omission of any attempt to discuss the impact of their chaotic relationship on us. Faithful to the American tradition of parenting, they wrongly considered their issues and disputes personal matters which were none of our concern. If we had accused them of damaging our mental health by their frequent emotionally violent arguments they would have angrily rejected our complaints as disrespectful. If I had pressed my father to reveal the significance of his oft repeated accusations of "whores and whore masters", it is likely he would have "blown his top", as he liked to put it. Because they existed within the horizon of autonomous individualism they were able to ignore the intimate connections between their selves and our selves that caused their suffering and their actions to produce immediate and long term harmful effects in us. Those of us who claimed not to have suffered adverse effects behaved as if experiencing them was the sign of a weak character. Since I could not help feeling devastated and terrified by my parents' wars, I often felt lacking in moral fiber. Therefore, I was reluctant to ask for help from my parents or siblings or other relatives or the authorities for fear of being cast as weak, abnormal, even immoral and treacherous. When, at age 17, I told my older brother Charles, a medical doctor, that I could no longer stand the emotional violence, suffered constant anxiety in consequence, and thought I would soon break down, all he could think to say was that daddy drank too much beer, yet another denial of reality.

The common debilitating denominator in these painful experiences was the unspoken but omnipresent goal of suffering into the American variety of individual autonomy. Through this mainly insidiously unconscious process any inclinations toward regarding ourselves as deserving the nurture and support of society as a whole, professional counseling services, or even of each other's comfort within the family, were burnt and purged away in the name of character building, which meant producing self-reliant autonomous individuals who did not ask for help. This upbringing was not invented by our parents. Except for eschewing psychological therapy, which my mother thought disgraceful, they were following the normative practices of American culture, and prided themselves on producing fully self-supporting, independent minded adults who fit into society as it was and did not rock the boat. They were largely successful in achieving that goal. Although some of us made waves that occasionally created rough passages, none were disposed to mutiny or even abandon ship. We all aspired to American style individual autonomy founded on successful careers. Our parents' guidance echoed nearly everything we read, or heard, or saw on TV or films, at school or from friends and relatives. Despite the way it went against my nature, I was eager to be "normal" in this sense, and had no inclination to live as a starving artist in a cold, drafty garret in Greenwich Village. My mother's injunctions and stern cautionary tales against creative work, which certainly had a deeply deleterious effect on me, also provided a negative rationale for not throwing caution to the wind and courageously living my art. I could internalize her elder's voice as a horizon I could not and should not get beyond. Of course, I was not consciously aware of my bad faith at the time. If I had been it might not have been effective.

Mommy and daddy's success in giving us what my father called "a foundation", my mother's censoring of creativity, and our own complicity in the project, concealed the tendency of this training to deprive us of the psychic, intellectual and spiritual resources that might have allowed us to envision ourselves, society and our future lives differently, away from the destructive isolation and competition of relentless individualism, and towards a more expansive conception of self capable of transcending *white-supremacist-being-in-America*. Ironically, my mother's older brother had enacted the larger self when he left school to help support the family, just as my parents did through their many sacrifices on our behalf. But they obscured, rather than drew out and developed the implications of those acts of love, construing them within the purview of individualism as responsibilities, what daddy described as "my duty as a father", which for my parents, and for most Americans, in one of the many forestalling contradictions of our way of being, includes the children as extensions of the parental selves, but not the other way round, so that parents rarely have the benefit of critique, guidance and nurturing by their children.

Due, perhaps, to his Caribbean upbringing my father had a more expansive notion of self which was manifested in his openhanded generosity, his proneness to help others, his love of children, and his compassion for suffering humans or animals that prompted his recriminations against God for blaming His own creatures for their failings. He felt sorry for my brother-in-law Skippy because his father had abandoned him and he never had an altercation with him. Unlike my mother, he encouraged creativity, and would frequently ask to have a drawing or painting I had done, which he would hang on the walls of his tiny office. My mother was quite different in this respect, with a rather Protestant self-concept and little evident concern for anyone outside of the extended family. These habits were not hers alone, but reflected the American character.

It is easily missed that our American upbuilding into responsible autonomous adults normally includes the downbuilding of any inclinations towards larger self-identity with other people and other than human beings, outside of the narrow group of those our individual autonomy makes us responsible for as extensions of ourselves, such as our children and our partners. This was the lesson of the stolen canteen and the borrowed basketball. Both incidents had been presented by my worried mother as my fault because I was "too generous and trusting". The unstated but essential qualifier was "for the Hobbesian world of American society", that she feared would overwhelm me. It is essential to emphasize that in acting as they did my parents were not behaving aberrantly, but were acting well within the normative tradition of American parenting, in autonomically diverting our consciousness away from any possible broader self-identities that they regarded as potentially dangerous. We

94   BEING-IN-AMERICA: WHITE SUPREMACY AND THE AMERICAN

were taught to labor and suffer alone, with no gesture toward even the possibility of collective cooperative projects, and were thereby deprived of the chance to become aware of our always-already existing interconnections, wherein lie the possibilities of genuine democracy.

The destructive impact of this deprivation is better appreciated when one considers that all of my siblings and my mother were creatively endowed and inclined, while my father supported and encouraged creative work, but we either suppressed our creative urges for practical reasons, my mother and older brother Charles going so far as to disparage creativity itself, or struggled unsuccessfully to find a means of expressing them. One wonders what possibilities might have been envisioned had our parents encouraged us to pursue our creativity, to celebrate and share it with each other within the family, searching for ways to help one another live creative lives, for creative imagination is the key to transcending horizons and freeing ourselves from our current unsustainable and destructive style of individual autonomy and its political economy. Perhaps an actively creative family life would have allowed my parents to engage with each other and their children constructively. Unimagined vistas of new life might have appeared if we had been invited and empowered to openly discuss the destructive impact of their arguing on all of us, and allowed to share with them our insights into their problems and frustrations. All of us were quite capable of doing that by the time we entered our early teens if not before. Encouraging creativity could have empowered my mother and father to travel beyond conventional notions of respectability and status, respect and disrespect, private and public, parent and child, marriage and divorce, whores and whoremasters, credit and loss, blame and praise, love and hate, betrayal and vengeance and begin new lives, either together with us or separately with us. Tragically, trapped within the horizon of *white-supremacist-individual-autonomy*, and handicapped by their subliminal obscuration of what had trapped them, my parents probably did not feel they had the right to imagine any such possibilities.

· 17 ·

ALTERNATE PARENTS OR THE SILENT COUNTEROFFENSIVE

My boyhood and adolescent traumas were mitigated by the presence of an extraordinary set of siblings and siblings-in-law. Most of all my sister Anne Marie and her husband Skippy were big influences on me and Gregory. When I look back it seems astonishing that a young couple would devote so much of their time and energy to interacting with us, but they did. To a large extent, we enjoyed with our alternate parents and their friends, the kind of open, interactive and discursive relationship we were not allowed to have with our parents.

After their marriage Anne and Skippy lived in a tiny apartment on the second floor of the big house we all shared from the winter of 1954. There, on Saturday mornings, we would watch *Looney Tunes* with Skippy, who was as enthusiastic as we were for the antics of Bugs Bunny, Daffy Duck, Elmer Fudd, the Roadrunner and Wile E. Coyote. Many evenings during school vacations, we'd sit with them watching westerns like *Sugar Foot*, *Cheyanne* and *Wyatt Earp* or playing bid whist. Those times provided relief and refuge from my father's rages. On summer nights my sister would put us up to begging Skippy to take us to the White Stone Bridge Drive-in, twenty minutes away in the Bronx. He was employed as a social worker at the time and would come home from New York City tired and never wanting to drive. We'd whine and beg until he gave in, which was quite often judging by the number of movies we saw, most of which were science fiction like *The Day the Earth Stood Still* and *The Invasion of the Body Snatchers*. There was the romance, *Marjorie Morningstar*, but not one western, the closest to it being *Bad Day at Blackrock* staring Spencer Tracy as a one armed man skilled in Judo. They all presented alternate ways of being and doing, some of them monstrous, and the outsider as hero, which resonated with the call of the wild incessantly echoing in my mind.

On summer weekends Anne and Skip would go to the beach unless it rained, and they always took us with them as if we were their children. This suited us fine. My parents were older than most in the 1950s, my mother having given birth to me when she was 38 and my father 42. Anne and Skippy were in their 20s, young and vigorous. She was beautiful. He was handsome and athletic. We were proud to have people assume they were our parents. They acted like the young, rational mother and father we wished we had.

Skippy was always revealing something interesting and edifying, whether it was the habits of sand crabs at Riis beach or plankton at Lake Sebago in Harriman State Park, world cultures or some other intriguing topic. We loved to go with him to the Metropolitan Museum of Art on the East side, and the American Museum of Natural History on the West side of Central Park in Manhattan. Skippy had majored in anthropology at Hunter College and was thoroughly versed in European art from ancient Greece to modern times. He seemed to know everything and acted as our own private tour guide on these excursions. He took particular pains to explain the importance of ancient Egyptian civilization, both in its own right and as the indispensable foundation for the Greco-Roman world that followed, and through it of modern Western civilization. His commentary created an enlightening context for viewing the Egyptian collection of the Metropolitan Museum of Art. The representations of black, brown and red Egyptians in tomb paintings and on sarcophagi depicted a mixed population which included a significant, if not predominant, "Negro" strain. As far as I could tell there were few so-called white people in ancient Egypt before the Ptolemaic period. The people who laid the foundations of Egyptian civilization and built the great pyramids appeared to us to be black or brown Africans. What we were taught at school quite conflicted with what we saw in the museum and what my brother-in-law showed us. This discovery augmented my sense of self-worth, but when I shared my experiences in class they were quickly passed over without comment.

Skippy was at his best in the natural history museum. Drawing on his anthropological training he provided a running commentary on the museum's

ALTERNATE PARENTS OR THE SILENT COUNTEROFFENSIVE 97

human evolution exhibit. Things had not always been as they now were. The very nature of humanbeing seemed to have changed over time. Most revealing for us, it all began on the savannahs of East Africa, not in the darkened caves of northern Europe as we had been taught. The same museum contained ethnological collections on the peoples, cultures and religions of Asia and Africa which were not included at any stage in our public school education. Skippy described the significance of religious practices we had never been exposed to. Human beings had created many different interpretations of existence and the American variety was only one.

Skippy and his younger brother Eddy grew up on Fish Avenue in the Bronx. Times were frugal after their father abandoned them, passed for white, and founded another family in the Pacific Northwest. The younger brother graduated from City College at nineteen and went off to study medicine in Basal, Switzerland, learning German on the way. He spent his medical career treating children in Harlem.[1] My brother-in-law eventually followed him to Switzerland, studying medicine at the University of Lausanne where he too learned the language on site. His experiences in Europe fascinated my young mind. We wrote frequently. My letters going to 3 Avenue de Valmont, an address I don't think I'll ever forget. On vacations home, he enchanted me with stories of Europe and its relative freedom in the early 60s from the racism of the United States. My brother, Charles, finished his residency in radiology and went off with his family for a stint of teaching at the University Of Ibadan College Of Medicine in Nigeria. About the same time my sister, Shirley and her family moved to St. Kitts, my father's homeland, for two years. Thus several windows were simultaneously opened on the outside world, giving me vicarious exposure to other ways of living and thinking that reinforced the lessons of the museums, and impressed me with how much perspective influenced anyone's understanding of the world. Morals and values were relative like Einstein's universe. Ours were not necessarily the best.

Anne and Skippy came with a remarkable group of friends who also paid attention to me and Gregory, offering advice and guidance and allowing us to participate as equals in their interesting conversations. Two in particular stand out. Harold Epps and his wife Pat were the ideal couple. They seemed to have a completely equal relationship and to treat each other with great consideration and respect. She was very attractive, intelligent and vivacious and became my image of the ideal life partner. Their example of married happiness had a lasting influence on me as a sort of model of what an authentic marriage could be.

98 BEING-IN-AMERICA: WHITE SUPREMACY AND THE AMERICAN

Harold had studied mathematics and physics in college before starting his own global business enterprise in the 1960s. He knew more about physics and math than anyone I'd met and refinished antique furniture to boot. This young man was willing to spend hours listening to my youthful theories about time and space, taking pains to explain the finer points of relativity. The self-less attention he gave us was extraordinary, the kind of enrichment adolescent boys and girls thrive on but seldom receive. He and other friends of Anne and Skip were signal beacons in a usually dreary, crushingly boring and often terrifying adolescence. My oldest friend, going back to 1964, would say I was blessed in having so rich an extended family. I dislike the term for positing a supreme being who conveys blessings on some while withholding them from others for no scrutable reason. Nonetheless, the presence of a group of supportive and interesting young people seemed a blessing from somewhere. My life would have been much poorer without them.

These recollections are meant to illustrate the crucial importance of communities of surreptitious resistance for any "person of color" in white supremacist America. Beset on all sides by the overt, covert, often unrecognized and even unrecognizable assaults of white supremacy the black person, child and adult finds refuge, affirmation and encouragement in the support of loving communities of the likeminded. In an unintentional manner, our alternate parents and their friends became guides, allowing the example of their strength, humanity and successful resistance to the infernal machine that sought to grind us down to permeate our minds and souls with upbuilding and self affirming effects.

Although there were occasional overt references to American racism the race problem was seldom discussed until the late 60s when it became unavoidable. Like most of the black people I have known they were loath to "dwell" on racism or obstacles. Their focus was on cultivating the strength of character and self-discipline needed to succeed in America. In this strategy, "dwelling" on race, as the eldest brother seemed to do, was perceived as a character weakness that undermined one's ability to achieve success. The issue of race was normally *held-off* so that our energies could be mobilized to achieve our goals. The suppressed awareness of white supremacy's predation remained to burst into consciousness on suitable occasions, such as when Arthur Ashe won the US Tennis Open and Skippy proudly celebrated the victory of "Black Arthur Ashe!" Or when King was assassinated and we discussed whether we needed to arm ourselves in self-defense against the deadly racism of white America. In like manner, very little of the edification conferred on me and my brother was

ALTERNATE PARENTS OR THE SILENT COUNTEROFFENSIVE   99

intentionally imparted as a defense against white supremacy. When years later I thanked Skippy's younger brother Eddy for the positive affect he had on me and Gregory, he was unaware of having had any influence on us at all. Visits to museums and the seashore, the selection of the movies we watched at the drive-in, discussions of astrophysics and relativity, were, like Kant's humanity, ends in themselves. Neither Skippy nor Anne, or any of their friends were following a conscious plan designed to empower us to survive the assaults of white supremacy, at a time when the term itself was hardly used except in reference to extreme elements like the Ku Klux Klan. How then do we explain their working to that effect as if an invisible hand guided their actions?

I opened this book with the claim that all Americans, regardless of race and ethnicity, are possessed by a white supremacist collective unconscious bred into us as we develop American style individual autonomy. In a similar manner there is among "people of color" an anti-white supremacist collective unconscious working to counter the harmful effects of white supremacy. Like the white supremacist unconscious, it is the result of suppression, but this time it is the autonomic concealment of attitudes and ideas, which if openly expressed, or even secretly admitted to oneself, could disrupt our equanimity and hinder our struggle to survive and prosper in white supremacist America. Instead, they are communicated surreptitiously in the context of every-day-life as if they have nothing to do with race or white Americans. In this indirect manner, the group of likeminded adults who nurtured me and Gregory provided a silent counteroffensive against the distorting impositions of white supremacist culture. Silent, because usually not one mention was made of white people or racial oppression. You must understand, however, that this silence was not exceptional, which is why its message was so effectively delivered. In the 1950s and early 1960s, black Parents and older siblings were in the habit of keeping secret many problems and issues they felt would harm the emotional wellbeing of younger children. My parents were skilled in this kind of concealment maintaining major secrets for decades, whether to protect us or themselves is not clear. We were accustomed to enter a room where adults were conversing in whispers, eager to hear interesting gossip, only to have them fall silent as we came in. Through repeated experience of how adults used lack of speech to veil and conceal what they deemed harmful, we came to understand the subliminally rendered message that if something is not talked about it is of the utmost importance. The unspoken created a text we could read as well as the spoken. That message was driven home by the impatience of adults with our questioning about their silencing, an impatience that alluded to a text we ought to be able to read on our own without the overt instruction that would have defeated its purpose. It was a silent attunement to our community and its larger environment, a lesson in survival. And this lesson was also a mitigation of American style individual autonomy, for in order to become attuned to the unspoken thoughts and unexpressed emotions of others, one had to overcome the artificially rigid boundaries between one person and another erected by the American individualism that even our alternate parents accepted and affirmed, and to an extent merge one's being with theirs while remaining an individual, a process which also taught us that there were different kinds of autonomy and not all of them were isolating. Of course it was not really a question of becoming attuned, since we come into the world already attuned to our human and material environments, which is why babies are able to learn to speak so quickly, but of resisting the powerful forces of white supremacist individual autonomy working to erode that already existing attunement, forces which exist inside as well as outside of the family, white or black.

The effect of this surreptitiousness was the protection of the community and the individuals in it from direct and perpetual confrontation with knowledge that could undermine their ability to cope with the Given Circumstances of white supremacist America on a day-to-day basis, while retaining the liberating effects of that knowledge as a sort of artesian reservoir. In lieu of discourse, the alternate parents and their friends articulated a compelling alternative vision of the world to the one white America propagated. Harold's serious discussions of astrophysics and relativity, Skippy's wide ranging discourses on science, culture and the arts, at home and on our many excursions, set a tone that we aspired to echo. My sister's ethical promptings on the persistence of right and wrong, regardless of society's practices, and above all their caring and nurturing attitude towards us, voicelessly proclaimed the power we had of building our own universe of meaning, demonstrating the fact that the white supremacist world order was not the only possible one, a lesson reinforced by the museum and the vicarious experience of Europe, Africa and the Caribbean. In this way, through almost daily interaction with alternate parents, we were protected, enriched and empowered to resist white supremacy's narrowing and debilitating effects, even as white supremacy's destructive influences were inflicted on us, despite the fact that neither I nor my brother had any notion that it existed, although we were well aware of racial discrimination and the higher value whites placed on themselves than on us. The behavior of our alternate parents and their friends was an intuitive response to the situation they found ourselves in, an attunement conditioned and guided by their ancestral heritage which they passed on to us in an ingrained, silent intergenerational counteroffensive.

Notes

1 See Edward A. Nicholas memoir *Fade to White* (iUniverse, 2014).

· 1 8 ·

THE ELDEST BROTHER

My eldest brother fancied himself a philosopher and spiritual guru. I've no idea how he reached such improbable conclusions. However he did, they had very unfortunate consequences for his life, the lives of his children and very nearly for me as well. Perhaps his experiences as a black GI in the Korean War drove him in that direction. He sometimes spoke angrily of the white soldiers' racist treatment of Koreans. He told me once that the experience of racial segregation in America was worse than the war. Off base in the south he'd had to sit in the back of the bus despite his uniform. The humiliations stayed with him. Returned home, he worked as an elevator operator in the Manhattan building our father superintended while going to Long Island University at night. My father encouraged his studies and prepared his dinners. For some reason he dropped out and never went back. Decades later he claimed college was so easy he became bored. I suspect he was afraid of failure and rather than admit his fears which could have been overcome radically altered his life. When in his late 70s he told me he would do nothing differently were he to live again my suspicions were confirmed.

He would educate himself. That came later. In the meantime, not wanting to slave for "the white man" as he imagined his father was doing he decided to go into business for himself. The determination to escape white oppression by gaining financial independence was shared by every black person I knew growing up, but it was so powerful a component of my brother's character that it profoundly shaped the course of his life. In quest of "freedom", the mythical American solution to personal and social problems at home and abroad, he tried his hand at sales, peddling Filter Queen vacuum cleaners in the early 1950s when they were still relatively new. This was the era when the salesman was a powerful symbol of personal autonomy and freedom in the booming economy of the postwar period. By "his" own efforts the salesman could achieve the American dream while driving the economy forward. Too often, the dream ended in the disillusionment of Willy Loman.

Things went well for a while. He became a star salesman, married, bought a house and acquired a vintage Jaguar motor car. Life looked good. Then, never a good judge of character, he trusted two in-laws of doubtful honesty, took a second mortgage on the house and ended up holding the bag on a bad business deal. He lost the house and nearly went to prison for fraud he hadn't committed. An extraordinarily objective and unusual white judge realized that he was a decent young man who had been duped by his partners and spared him, but his father soured on him and his marriage fell apart. He was only 25.

Some would have rebounded, counted their blessings and "moved on". My brother was a proud man and perhaps a bit too arrogant for his own good. He felt shamed and humiliated by the loss and wounded by his father's rejection. Instead of picking up the pieces and starting again at a fairly young age he altered course, drastically transmuting his failure into a symptom of cosmic derangement. Life itself was fraudulent. Civilization had gone wrong at the beginning with catastrophic results continuing to the present, including his own personal calamity. I can't help thinking that most of this response was a delayed reaction to the horrors of the war with its pronounced racial dimensions that he was acutely sensitive to, what today we would call post traumatic shock syndrome, with the woundings of the American dilemma piled on for good measure. Whatever the cause he set off on a heroic quest to solve the riddle of human misery. He soon found it in a sort of original sin enacted when human beings fled in fear from their true spiritual nature. It became his mission to bring his revelation to the world in a great book that would enlighten and transform humankind. By the 1960s he had decided to found a new religion based on his discoveries, a movement towards what he called "the God Man", a philosophy premised on the "god-nature" of each individual human being. His discoveries were the result of an intensive course of reading,

THE ELDEST BROTHER

thinking and writing. Day after day he sat in the marble and oak splendor of the Mount Vernon Public Library, courtesy of Andrew Carnegie's munificence, reading the *Great Books of the Western World, The Harvard Classics* and popular history. But his fundamental awakening came through the religious texts of India and China, the Upanishads, the teachings of Laotse and the words of the Buddha. Most of this he got from popular collections such as Lin Yutang's, *The Wisdom of China and India*, and *The Wisdom of Laotse*. Yet he was no enemy of modern science. On the contrary, he read voraciously in the popular science literature and had an impressive knowledge of contemporary developments in the physical, biological and behavioral sciences. From these sources he developed the syncretic philosophy he promoted to friends and relatives that envisioned the creation of paradise on earth through the collaboration of science and spirituality. Having read Plato's dialogues, he modeled himself on Socrates playing the part of gadfly quite effectively. I don't recall one family gathering while I was growing up when he was not cornering one or more of us with his interrogations. It was calculated to impress young and inexperienced minds. It deeply impressed me.

In September of 1963, I was in my first year of high school and eager to learn. Biology was my favorite class. Here, at last, was a discipline promising definite answers to the questions I was asking. One autumn afternoon we watched a film about the Double helix that had been discovered only ten years before, followed by a movie on evolution. I came home excited about the new concrete approach to the question of the origin of life. That evening my brother came by. He'd been reading in the library all day, which meant he was not working at gainful employment leaving his wife to support the family. That was okay, because he'd score big when the book came out, reap enormous royalties and found a new religion. I remember that evening vividly. He was wearing the dark three piece suit that had become his uniform. I rarely saw him in anything else in all the time I knew him. It was partly how he was raised. It struck me as rather more worldly than spiritual, and it was well within the tradition of the black preachers he accused of swindling their congregations. He dismissed organized religions of any kind as "The God Business." Apparently, the one he aspired to found would be free of hypocrisy.

That evening he came into the kitchen where I was enthusiastically working on my biology homework, and with a few words demolished my newfound certainty and hopefulness. I was sharing with him my excitement about DNA and evolution, explaining how life originated in the sea and through the process of evolution led to human beings. Yes, my brother replied, but where did it

106   BEING-IN-AMERICA: WHITE SUPREMACY AND THE AMERICAN

come from in the first place? I knew the answer to this, "The Big Bang" I said. "What was before the Big Bang", he pressed. "Nothing", I replied. "Nothing? How could there by nothing? What does nothing mean?" Of course I had no answer to that. So he produced *The Wisdom of China and India* from the black attaché case he carried and opened it to an Upanishad entitled "The Subtle Essence." This was supplemented by an aphorism of Laotse about emptiness and a sermon by the Buddha, all leading to the conclusion: Life begins in nothingness and from that beginning, driven by desire, we are enslaved in the world of Maya, illusion. This was the root of all of our suffering. The only way to freedom from our present hell, as he called human existence, was to walk the path of the Buddha, leading to liberation from *samsara*, the wheel of birth, death and rebirth. Being a rather impressionable youth, and in awe of my eldest brother's intellect, I was seduced. My mother saw or felt trouble ahead. She told my brother not to bother me with his ridiculous theories, designed, in her opinion, to justify an irresponsible and unproductive lifestyle. He soon left for home. He had worked hard all day and even geniuses need to eat and sleep and argue with their wives.

I was not converted by his sophistry alone. Fifteen is a critical age, the age when many young people disillusioned with the world are ripe for any alternative offering a way out. For all too many, the way is death itself, for death is the seductive companion of youth, always waiting and often beckoning. That is why over the centuries so many young men have willingly given their lives to old men as capital to expend in war, and others, male and female, have taken their own in search of something better or simply a state of peace, even just the end of pain. In a sense, the way I attempted was a sort of death, a death to this world in the name of a higher, unseen world. What ultimately saved me was the tremendous strength of my attachment to flesh, to the body, to this world despite its miseries. My desire triumphed over my spiritual longings.

In the meantime, I read everything I could find on Buddhism, Zen and Yoga. My brother had a friend, an African American, who had, he claimed, spent seventeen years studying Yoga in India and gave me some rudimentary instruction. Most of what I learned came from books. Some, written by scholars and longtime practitioners had definite merit. Others, like *The Autobiography of a Yogi*, which my eldest brother, as poor a judge of religious as of secular character, took as gospel were largely fiction dressed up to look profound. The book was replete with miracles performed by the central character, all of which I accepted at face value, suppressing the rational doubts that naggingly proclaimed their presence. I began to meditate every day and

THE ELDEST BROTHER   107

became quite adept at it. I declared I would become a monk upon gradua-
tion, don the yellow robes and devote myself to escaping the cycle of birth,
death and rebirth, finally achieving nirvana. My school work suffered as my
asceticism flourished. I spent more and more time in my room, lying on my
bed, concentrating on escaping my body for the realm of the Buddha, which
seemed preferable to a life of labor, pain and misfortune in a world wracked
by war, poverty and cruelty coupled with a depressing and often emotionally
violent home life

My studies led me to the discovery of Kundalini Yoga, a powerful, and as
I was to discover, a quite effective method of releasing dynamic energy in the
body. This produced a crisis of terrifying proportions and near catastrophe
some years later. For the time being I did not venture to use the skills I had
acquired but contented myself with inducing a deep meditative trance, soon
losing all bodily sensation as if I were floating in a silent spiritual realm. I
sensed I could go even further but just as I approached an ever waiting threshold, the same familiar fear I had felt as a very small child fixed on the bathroom tiles, swept over me and I would shake myself awake.

This was when my mother, realizing how close I was to a really dangerous mental and emotional state, stepped in and forbade my brother to talk
to me at all. She lectured me firmly on the dangers of the path I had chosen. Of course I resisted, but something resisted in me, pushing me outward
once again. My eldest brother's escapism was counterbalanced by his younger
brother's pragmatism and success. He had become a doctor by this time and
now exerted a strong influence on me and Gregory. His view of life was cheerful and full of hope. Spending time with him helped to draw me from the
self-obliterating ascetic path which was more against my nature than school
itself. A great revolt set in. By February I was on the indoor track team which
brought renewed attachment to life and enduring friendships.

For all of his foibles my eldest brother had many sterling characteristics.
Most importantly, he was the only person I knew who not only rejected the
American racial order, as most of the adults around me did, but rejected our
entire understanding of what it meant to exist. He was a particularly harsh
and cogent critic of religion, which he described as a conspiracy to hypnotize
the masses with visions of paradise for the dutiful and nightmares of hell for
the sinful, all for the benefit of the ruling class and the enrichment of god's
avaricious vicars on earth. People accepted the lies of religion in order to
escape the freedom they possessed to recognize and embrace their godhood.
Freedom frightened them because it shifted responsibility for their lives onto

themselves rather than to some invisible power. But this flight disabled our ability to resolve our collective and individual problems and condemned us to live unfulfilling lives of self-deception. He had come to these ideas on his own, never having read Nietzsche or Kierkegaard, Sartre or Heidegger. His answer was to proclaim the advent of the "God-Man", who would destroy the idols, ushering in a new human centered civilization in which wealth would be equitably shared and science harnessed to solve the problem of "shortages", which he called the root of all conflict, exploitation and inequality. A golden age would ensue where we'd live harmoniously in a new kind of tribal group, where what he called "the man-woman thing" would return to the equilibrium of the hunter-gatherer times he imagined as a kind of Garden of Eden. He had great faith in the original goodness of "man", which he asserted had been corrupted by civilization. I don't know if he ever read Rousseau. It wasn't necessary in the late 50s and 60s. Those ideas were central aspects of the counterculture of the times, and so was he. From the late 50s he wrote poetry, reading his work in Greenwich Village coffeehouses, one of the foci of the beat culture. Later when the black Power Movement was underway he became a staunch supporter, far ahead of most people around him. He often went to hear Malcolm X preach in Harlem and claimed to know him. Thus, my family and I were exposed to the teachings of Elijah Muhammad and Malcolm X before they became household names. I had read some of the editions of *Muhammad Speaks*, the newspaper put out by the Nation of Islam during Malcolm's time, which my father brought home with him from New York City. It must have reminded him of his black Nationalist Garvey days. It was hard to imagine my father, normally a bitter critic of black people, who he liked to say would take "another 250 years" to arrive, as a Garveyite. Yet he supported any black man who was for black people. I was put off by what I read in *Muhammad Speaks*. White people could certainly be oppressive but I hardly imagined them as devils created by a mad scientist. Malcolm's preaching was different. I can't say it persuaded me at the time, nor did it even later. The idea that black people should take up arms against the most powerful military establishment in the world seemed suicidal. But as with many of us, what Malcolm said about our self-hatred, the way we processed and straightened our hair, the way many blacks despised anything black, the way we rejected Africa and all thing African as backward resonated with me. Other parts of his teachings about history and the racist political economy of America were not so easy to accept because admitting them would make it difficult to fit into

THE ELDEST BROTHER

the society I wanted to succeed in. Those I kept at arm's length, all the while suspecting some deceit on my part.

These liberating and threatening views were conveyed to me by my eldest brother who was unabashedly for black liberation "by any means necessary", and whose version of history placed black people at the foundation of the true civilization, hijacked and perverted by "the white man." He was given to searching out all kinds of esoteric and arcane knowledge in ancient books and publications well outside of mainstream history. Thus, he discovered that the ancient Egyptians were black, a truth that he believed was concealed by white historians. All of this flew directly in the face of all I had learned. It seemed improbable at best and delusional at worst. But it planted seeds of doubt in my mind which sprouted in later years.

Then, suddenly, without warning or explanation he disappeared for five years until the early 1970s. No one knew where he had gone or what he was doing. I suspect he had descended into an underworld so terrifying that he never spoke about it even when he returned, seemingly refreshed and strengthened by his katabasis. Wherever he was I missed his critical and open mind. Despite his often bizarre religious and political views he was one of the two relatives I could talk to about my problems and receive support. He could discuss anything in a reasoned manner without ever losing his temper or raising his voice. He would have made an excellent academic. It is a pity he did not pursue that path.

He remained throughout his life as I knew him as a boy and adolescent. The tragic flight from the world to his own personal wilderness included abandoning his children. I cannot comment on this because I never discovered the actual reasons or circumstances for his turning away. Whatever they were the results were traumatic for them. That they nevertheless achieved productive lives is a tribute to their strength, dignity and faith. He spent his days working in one variety of sales or another, earning barely enough to get by, and sometimes less, justifying his life by the claim he was writing a monumental book that would solve the human dilemma, change the way we lived, and usher in a golden age. The book project, which had started out as a laudable and achievable ambition, seems to have become over many years a myth maintained to avoid facing what he had omitted, what he had done and what he had lost. I do not mean to imply that he was not serious about the book. He was certainly reading, taking notes and talking about his subject, but nothing tangible, not even an unpublishable manuscript was ever produced. It would have been possible, even eminently feasible, in his 20s and 30s to change course; harder,

110   BEING-IN-AMERICA: WHITE SUPREMACY AND THE AMERICAN

but still manageable in his 40s and 50s; increasingly unlikely in his 60s. By his 70s he seemed resigned to living out his life as he was. He ended up poverty stricken, abandoned by his older children, ill with incurable cancer and dying in a nursing home he hated, whose food he couldn't eat. I almost cried when the psychiatrist at the Veteran's Administration Hospital asked me if he was delusional, because he kept speaking of a great book he was writing that was going to make a lot of money and change the world. I confirmed that he had been working on the book for the past fifty years. It was no delusion. In fact, he had enough interesting points to make that his book might have sold if he could have produced it. No one is really sure why he never did. Perhaps he simply did not know how, or he may have lacked the self-confidence to bring it off. That would have been highly understandable given the country, the circumstances and the family he grew up in. The only light in his life was the child he fathered in his late 50s who proved a mountain of support, love and comfort through his final illnesses and tribulations.

By and large he was an honest man, scarred by race as we all are, haunted by demons he only partially understood and preferred to transform into something deceptively manageable. In the end he came face to face with his reality and understood how, in his own words, he had squandered his life and caused pain for others. He told me, just before his final illness, "When I die my tombstone will read *Here lies Ernest Richardson who did nothing.*" I tried to cheer him up with talk about his positive impacts, but neither of us could wish reality away or brighten the view backwards over eight decades. To me, he was a victim of the way we are in this society, certainly a victim of race, and indisputably a victim of his own hubris and unfortunate talent for self-deception. He was the bravest man I've ever known to accept his fate so heroically. A month or so before his death, a lifelong friend, a formal Catholic, visited and leaving bid him "God Bless you." My brother's energy returned, the anger in his voice echoing in the room, "Never say that to me again!" he shouted, "I am the supreme being." He truly believed we are all what he called "god-nature" hidden from ourselves by ourselves from fear of our own divinity. He hated religion for its suppression of that truth, for its fatal exploitation of fear in the pursuit of earthly power.

An alternate and perhaps truer reading of his life would recognize his response to failure and disgrace, the woundings of white supremacy, the terrors of the Korean War as catalysts leading him to confront the fundamental miseries of human existence. In this reading, his personal trauma launched his search for an authentic understanding of why human existence was so deeply flawed, how it got that way and what could be done to return us to the state of goodness he believed was our original condition, with the advantages of science and technology added in. Isn't this how all great spiritual missions begin, provoked by a personal experience of suffering so overwhelming it tears a veil from the eyes of the afflicted, transforming them from ordinary human beings into dedicated servants of truth? Like many so obsessed before him, Ernest, the name rings true, sacrificed children, wife, the chance of personal financial security and worldly happiness to devote himself single-mindedly to his project to save the world. And these are precisely the terms he spoke in, never wavering from his mission to "make civilization work" by revealing the "God-nature" we suppress.

One can never fully comprehend a life, not even one's own. I miss him dearly and feel a deep sadness for the way he ended up, for the loss of what he could have been in this lifetime with a little love, understanding and guidance. Sometimes, when in a less defensive mood, I suspect he exists now in a more enlightened universe. Perhaps after all his life was the passage he often spoke of from hell to paradise.

· 1 9 ·

THE CALL OF THE WILD

During my adolescent years I felt more alienated than ever from the wider society aside from a few white working class friends who were odder than I. Oddity was our bond. The stutter persisted and with it my painful shyness. Both reinforced the call of the wild that I'd always heard. Even as a small boy before shyness became a problem there was the lure of wilderness, the promise of pristine life waiting somewhere. Perhaps it was this sentiment that connected with my eldest brother's vision of a primeval paradise. Until I turned twelve I'd had no chance to get into any sort of real forest or woodland. My wilderness encounters were limited to imagination reinforced by adventure books, but on my twelfth birthday I joined the Boy scouts of America. Thus began my engagement with the real wilderness, at least as close as one could come to it in New York State in the early 60s.

Since I joined the Scouts in February my first camping experiences were in the winter. These days I have little tolerance for winter weather. Back then I loved it. The stimulating cold seemed to bring me closer to more primitive times. During one winter excursion I went off on my own as was my habit. No one was supposed to wander without permission and then only with a "buddy" but from time to time I managed to slip away. Our scoutmaster rarely noticed I was gone. Once we got the campsite set up he'd relax by the fire and leave us to our own devices. As soon as I got the chance I'd get into the woods. On this occasion I had gone a few miles from our campsite to the top of a steep ravine with a stream running through it. From that vantage I could look out over the frozen countryside for many miles. The air was still, the only sound the distant baying of wild dogs. They'd become a problem, terrorizing the local deer population, killing for the thrill of the chase. The ranger had been out hunting them with his shotgun and warned us of the danger earlier that day. As I stood taking in the scenery the barking grew louder. From where I stood they could get to me before I could reach camp. I had my ax and sheath knife but those weapons might be ineffective against a large pack. They were perhaps two miles away, no doubt hot on the trail of a hapless deer. As I turned to leave a movement in the ravine below caught the corner of my eye. All at once a large buck stepped into view walking cautiously in the shallow stream. He paused, turned his antlered head in the direction of the barking then walked along keeping to the stream. I stood, watching, looking down at a drama completely outside the human world.[1] The deer continued on in the frigid waters that would foil the dogs' keen sense of smell. In a minute he was out of sight hidden by the crest of the ridge. I returned to our campsite with the sound of the dogs fading behind me, buoyed by the privilege of having witnessed the scene, as if the wilderness had lifted a veil and shown me another world. With a little luck the deer would elude his pursuers. With skill and good fortune the ranger would thin the dog packs giving the deer herds a chance to survive the winter.

That night, as I sat tending the fire, with everyone asleep, the sound of barking drew near, then closer until the dogs could not have been more than ten yard from the canvas tarp covering the open front of our shelter. I piled more logs on the fire until it blazed brightly. The barking moved slowly off down the hill and into the night. I suppose we were in some danger but I didn't feel it at the time. It was the drama. When the ranger warned us of wild dogs my fantasy recurred to *The Wild North*, the tale of two men attacked by wolves at night in the nineteenth-century Yukon. I had watched that movie may times and when the dogs approached our shelter I turned them into wolves on the prowl. With my hand ax I'd fight them off like the men in the film. I was almost disappointed when they did no more than linger barking then turn aside. Either the fire or a healthy fear of humans spoiled my fiction.

This was how I frequently encountered events, instantly relating them to films and books,, transforming them in my mind into something more romantic and exciting than their mundane reality, which, unbeknownst to me at the

THE CALL OF THE WILD 115

time, was bringing them closer to the white ideal, then reliving the experience in memory where it took on more vivid colors. This is not quite correct. The actual experience itself, as it was constituted, came to me inseparable from imagination, itself already, always racially colored, as something that could become something else, never as a fixed entity.[2] It seemed an arrogant assault on phenomena to think that what I took things to be, or what others presented them as, was all there was and nothing more, as if we were violently trying to keep them from possibilities of themselves and force them to be what served our purposes, what white people seemed to do with the entire world. Resisting rigid designations felt like fighting back against something I could not yet identify, which was, of course, the white supremacist unconscious concealed in my mind like a cerebral Trojan Horse.[3] I tried to clarify the ambiguity that clung to everything as if imagination could release it to assume whatever form it wished, and these imaginings were frequently constituted on the grounds of what I'd seen or read or previously imagined, linked to the present event by some seeming similarity. Everything alluded to something else, nothing was ever incorrigibly known, so that every presentation was simultaneously an imaginative transformation. This felt the more open and genuine way of being, but coupled with the stutter, it marked me as incomplete and slow without the language or the wit to explain myself.

In the late 1950s I could turn a thunder clap into nuclear war. I don't mean pretending or playing what if. I'd hear exceptionally loud thunder and think, perhaps an atom bomb had dropped fifty miles away. One could not rule it out. It was a sort of mental stutter that stubbornly refused to winnow out possible from impossible, to fix one separate and apart from the other. I could imagine myself into a sort of thrilling panic and would have to break away from my reflections and return with relief to the mundane world, glad to take things just as they were for the time being, but always with the guilty sense of betraying something hidden seeking release.

But in the singular case of nuclear war I was not alone. The entire country seemed to have fallen odd overnight. My fantasies were shared and encouraged by the national fixation on the "the bomb" during the early Cold War, a time when we routinely held air raid drills at school. "Duck and Cover!" the teacher would suddenly shout, and we'd instantly fall on our knees beneath our desks, faces pressed against the floor, hands clasped behind our heads. On other occasions, when the siren sounded, we'd line up in the hallways, facing the walls in silence until the all clear. We welcomed these real life dramas for breaking the dull monotony of the school day. I remember watching a film in class actually entitled *Duck and Cover*. It featured Burt the Turtle who carried his own air raid shelter on his back. The bomb "could drop at any time", the film warned. We must always be on guard, prepared fall to the ground and cover our heads as soon as we saw the nuclear flash. There was a lot of laughter and an angry teacher who lectured us on the seriousness of it all. How could we take it seriously? It was too remote, too improbable, too farfetched, too white even for white kids.

The air raid shelter craze arrived on the heels of the drills. Pamphlets were handed out in school describing the terrible effects of nuclear fallout which could be mitigated by something called civil defense, which sounded like a courteous army. We were to urge our parents to prepare fallout shelters in our basements. This was an exciting distraction from ordinary life. Having a shelter would be like camping out at home. The illustrations in the pamphlets showed cozy little rooms of concrete blocks, with bunk beds, canned foods, Jerrycans of water and sandbags protecting entranceways. Civil Defense became a dramatic departure from reality to fantasy sanctioned, like Christmas magic, by the entire adult world, backed by fleets of giant aircraft always aloft, armies bristling with weapons, an elaborate radar defense system and, of course, thousands of nuclear warheads ready to destroy any enemy and the world with them, all costing billions of dollars. For me and for my friends the threat of annihilation made life exhilarating, as if we were on a perpetual hair-raising journey down Snake Hill after an ice storm had consolidated the new fallen snow into a field of terror. I imagined how cozy it would be to spend weeks, perhaps months living in a shelter as if I were an old time mountain man in his Yukon cabin. I pestered my parents, particularly my more sympathetic father, who took the whole thing as a kind of elaborate national theater of the absurd. Surprisingly, they indulged me. I was given the use of a room in the basement with one bunker like window set deep in the concrete. They let me put a bed in there and provision my shelter with canned goods and bottled water. There was a lamp and an old overstuffed sofa chair. I spent many pleasant hours in my retreat reading my wilderness books, and occasionally hiding out from Church and Sunday School. I wonder how many government Cold Warriors were living similar but deadlier fantasies to give their lives the meaning white supremacy deprives us of. It wasn't the threat of nuclear war that terrified us, but the real fruits of their games, first Korea, then Vietnam. Those were not cozy fantasies but deadly horrors perpetrated by the arrogant brutality of white men determined to make the world over in their self-image.

THE CALL OF THE WILD   117

The game of nuclear war united me in a peculiar way with the main-stream. I wasn't there for long before the wilderness called. It could whisper in the most unlikely places, even in the midst of New York City where the American Museum of Natural History was a portal to other worlds. I went frequently once I was allowed to take the subway on my own. Exiting the train where the subway sign read **81st Street: Museum of Natural History**, one passed at once from the most modern of cities through heavy glass doors into the primeval ages of the earth. One winter I discovered an exhibit on the first American expedition to the North Pole. A glass case contained two of the actual sleds used during the journey across the frozen wastes. What attracted me most was a diorama of an arctic landscape, a vast snowy plain sloping away towards icy mountains. Peering into its distance I imagined a dog team carrying Matthew Henson and his four Inuit companions racing towards their goal. It was the sky that drew me, cold and wintry, streaked with clouds, the reddened sky of approaching sunset. I went back several times, standing for hours before the familiar scene as if it were the reenactment of an earlier, primitive age I had known and lost. I yearned to warp time and space by the intensity of my desire, to enter the vanished world where I belonged, a world of solidarity lived within a small band of people dedicated to one another, where emotion and meaning flowed smoothly from person to person without the danger of distorting speech.

The closest I have ever come to that world was the primitive bonding of the Boy Scouts. One night when I was 13, way up at camp in Western Massachusetts, high in the shadowy folds of the southern Berkshires, we climbed to the top of Bash Bish Falls and built a fire on Eagle's Nest. There, with the stars staring down so brightly you could almost hear them speak, I peered into the narrow valley enveloped in black shadows, straining to feel with my heart what was hidden from my eyes. In one precious moment a divine spark, a fragment of those shooting stars that streaked across the August sky that year, lifted me above the morbid compass of life and death that binds us to ourselves and illuminated my inner eye in a supernal flash of recognition. A profound peace settled over me. I lay back against the damp grass just beyond the circle of warmth bled from the fire. The life giving heat from the blaze held half my body in its seductive caress while my chest and head cooled in the chill mountain air beyond the perimeter. I gazed in mute fascination at the dense inner core of the Milky Way drifting like a spectral cloud through the heavens. Until that moment I had felt a detached particle of life longing for the motherly embrace of shimmering creation without knowing how to find the comfort of its bosom. Now I was inseparably woven into the fabric of being, joined in harmonic frequency to those boys gathered there about me. That night as we returned to camp in the back of an open truck, where the boys huddled together like young lovers for warmth against the cold, I felt the return of an archaic remembrance born in the human race long before my own physical birth into the world, and knew I could live and die amidst that elemental band. The palpable, physical sense of ultimate belonging, so strong it threatened to rend my heart, thrilled me with the conviction this was the happiest moment of my life. I could not imagine it could ever be surpassed and doubted it would ever be equaled, and until this very day that doubt has remained unanswered.

As I recollect these passages from the vantage point of decades I think the wilderness was for me a sort of vast reservoir of uncaptured being not yet catalogued and assigned a place and a function. Sadly, the entire physical wilderness has been explored, charted and largely domesticated. There are those who wish the same for the larger wilderness that sustains us. This was why I had such longings for primordial beginnings and hated the modernizing of anything, which always meant forcing it into one frozen mold clamped down and welded together by the collective power of the pragmatic mass. These allusions were only dimly perceived at best from within the midst of daily life as intuitions rather than rational formulations. It is only now when looking back over the years that patterns emerge so clearly I wonder how I overlooked them as I went along.

Notes

1 This statement should be qualified by the observation that although the events did not involve humans as participants, the wild dogs were there because they had either escaped from their human owners or had been discarded by them, and, of course, I was there as an observer.

2 I take up the problem of global white supremacy's infiltration of the personal and collective imagination in a work in progress.

3 The analogy is to the term "Trojan Horse Transit" used in microbiology as in the following excerpt:

> "The fungal pathogen *Cryptococcus neoformans* invades the brain, causing a meningoencephalitis that kills hundreds of thousands of people each year. One route that has been proposed for this brain entry is a Trojan horse mechanism, whereby the fungus crosses the blood-brain barrier (BBB) as a passenger inside host phagocytes." Felipe H. Santiago-Tirado, Michael D. Onken, John A. Cooper, Robyn

THE CALL OF THE WILD 119

S. Klein, Tamara L. Doering, "Trojan Horse Transit Contributes to Blood-Brain Barrier Crossing of a Eukaryotic Pathogen", *American Society for Microbiology Online Journals*, January 31, 2017. https://doi.org/10.1128/mbio.02183-16, Accessed on August 11, 2023 at 3:55 am.

· 2 0 ·

THE VALUE OF WILLFUL UNKNOWING

By the time I was eight I began to discover how much adults did not know and how strangely complacent they were about it. This disappointing revelation surprised me as we were constantly enjoined to abhor ignorance and prize knowledge, get a college education and go on to graduate or professional school. I took it all seriously and wondered why they were so unconcerned about the really big questions, the ones I wanted them to answer, how the world began, why we didn't live forever, what was the meaning of existence, why did people hurt each other and act destructively. Of course I didn't put them quite this way back then. I don't mean to suggest the adults in my world said nothing, although they sometimes were completely silent even as I persistently repeated the same question. The tactic, an undoubted reprimand, did not deter my asking any more than stuttering prevented me from speaking. Usually, they'd respond with a meaningless explanation, such as no one really knows the answer or human nature has always been imperfect. This was unacceptable. I wanted reasonable, convincing answers, the kinds of answers one got about practical questions like how does an automobile work or how far is it to California. There seemed an entire wilderness they were content to ignore. When I pressed they'd say "Oh Ronald", a phrase that in its tone embodied and expressed group attitude, conveying the lesson that it is bad form to pry

122   BEING-IN-AMERICA: WHITE SUPREMACY AND THE AMERICAN

open what the community prefers to keep closed. If I persisted anyway they'd tell me I talked too much. This made me feel ashamed but didn't stop my questioning. Those few adults, like my eldest brother, who were willing to talk about the unknown tried to convince me of one or another theory they'd devised to account for everything in one breath. Religious people were worse. One could not argue with them without being warned of the danger of hell or some other unpleasantness. It was hard to think any adult could believe in a place like hell or people walking on water and flying through the air with wings. Religious people reminded me of shell shocked soldiers, although as far as I could tell they'd never been to war, except the one between their god and the devil that had never been on the news. Apparently, there was no certainty about anything except what was unknown. It seemed to me that most adults had enrolled in a sort of club dedicated to cultivating the deprivation of everything unknown and gleefully accepting every possible insuperable boundary as proof of membership and the mark of soundness. Now I began to understand the delight of adult relatives who seemed to relish ending any conversation about a potentially unpleasant unknown by declaring "Well, we'll never know." Uncertainty, contradictions, any manifestation of our inability to explain rationally what had or had not occurred, were indications of how incomplete our understanding was, therefore, of how incomplete we were. They were immediately perceived as threats to stability rather than opportunities to go beyond the known, to venture into the wilderness. Certainty, even if harmful to our prospects was preferred to progressive possibilities.

Little by little I began to suspect that the foundation they stood on was constituted by whatever was missing or forgotten, that their ignorance defined the boundaries of knowledge and the knowable. It had taken the experiences of years to develop that platform and they were understandably loath to weaken it by probing too deeply. This was why people seemed to grow intellectually rigid as they aged and more susceptible to the socially impregnable defense of belief or faith which once invoked ended all arguments. It was not the aging process per se, the hardening of arteries and the putative shrinking of the brain that was mainly to blame, but the understandable reluctance to embark on alterations they might not have time to complete. They deemed the disadvantages of imperfect knowing far less harmful than the potential chaos of dissolving certainties. My questioning attempts to get them to admit the vital importance of truth, like my eldest brother's Socratic nuisances threatened their ploy, which depended on resigning to the impossibility of definitive knowledge.

Slowly but surely the timeworn technology of narrowing was inculcated in me, meaning, I rather willingly absorbed it to be more like them. In time, I too found myself responding to questions about anything I could not explain with irritation and chagrin. This brought the double blessing of arming me for life and becoming more like the people I admired. In time I gave my full consent to this way of being.

· 2 1 ·

POOR JACK

As I entered junior high school the world of art became a nearly fulltime occupation, art and reading, always books about men who'd gone off to live alone in the wilderness or embarked on long solo voyages in small boats. School was a terror, filled with rough and rude boys whose only interests were sports, girls and fighting. I was good at none of those pursuits and being small for my age I was picked on. Most of my tormentors had been held back several times and were much bigger than I. Fighting was futile. There was one boy who at 16 in the seventh grade was nearly six feet tall. Though he loved to clown, and looked intimidating to some, he seemed a gentle soul. We always got along. He became a sort of protector. When he was around no one dared bother me. I suspect he had a learning disability because he couldn't cope with the simplest lessons. Today he might receive the therapy he needed. Back then his black looming mass condemned him to a life of frustration lived in modest means, perhaps even poverty. I worried about his future. There was no need. One day the word went round the school, Jack had taken part in the attempted robbery of a store where an off duty cop lingered in the back. He and his comrades bolted, scattering in different directions. Jack ran up the middle of the street. Unnecessarily, it seemed, gratuitously, the cop fired at his fleeing form striking him in the back of the head. There'd be no life of struggle bereft of achievement. He ended in a casket, laid out in the funeral parlor across the street from the school, the same parlor where we'd viewed the body of the principal earlier that year, the first dead person I'd ever seen, an old man with gray hair and gray face who died from one of the afflictions of aging. Jack was 16, barely embarked on his journey. All of us kids went to see him. The image remains in my mind, the first of several young black men I've known taken by American violence well before their time. He lay there, more bluish black than he had been in life, his eyes and lips swollen by a 38-caliber bullet's impact on bone and brain, as if it had been determined in taking his life to mold features closer to the stereotype. Poor Jack.

I cried. Even now I cry as I write these lines. I imagine he looked big and dangerous through the eyes of a white cop, as he must have to ordinary white people. Even as he fled in terror, unarmed and harmless, he appeared a threat. Or perhaps his very existence elicited the act of vindictive cruelty that shattered his head destroying his brain. To me, he was always the kind protector whose native sense of justice would not countenance the bullying of a small boy, who made sure no one laughed when I stuttered.

The Civil Rights Movement was in full swing. Nothing happened to the cop. Who'd of thought we'd be protesting similar atrocities over sixty years later, as police officers and private citizens continue to destroy unarmed black people. Jack's demise took something away from me that has never returned. The world became more dangerous and unforgiving. Within a day's rhythm the gap of comprehension between me and the white world that could kill without fear of punishment expanded. I can't recall the anger. I'm sure it was there. I feel the sadness and regret as if I might have done or said something to keep Jack at home and out of harm's way. Poor Jack. He never really had a chance.

· 2 2 ·

BEYOND THE FAR HORIZON

In the spring semester of my freshman year at Howard University I took a course entitled Physical Anthropology. I'm not sure why it attracted me, perhaps an intuition that something primordial lay in wait. It also rang scientific at a time when I doubted the validity and value of any subject that could not be quantified. I didn't want to be taken as a poet or romantic like the eldest brother. The instructor was one of the few white professors at Howard. Her whiteness lent her an instant air of authority and intellectual credibility that black professors had to earn. Despite all that she was actually an exciting teacher with a contagious enthusiasm for her subject. I became an ardent evolutionist, keen on learning all I could about my prehumen ancestors. Robert Ardrey had just published *The Territorial Imperative*. I bought it and read it right away as well as his earlier book *African Genesis* and did my term paper on early hominids. At that time the National Museum of Natural History was featuring a special exhibit on human evolution that fascinated me. There I was on a kind of conveyer belt being moved slowly past the physical remains of my distant ancestors. A heavily primeval feeling about the experience took me back to the museum several times as well as to the National Zoo to observe Tarsiers, Lemurs, Tree Shrews, Orangutans and Great Apes. Anthropology seemed a promising field.

The momentous thing about this course was my discovery of the concept of culture, a simple thing really that had a profound impact on me. The culture concept claimed we are all more or less shaped by our particular culture and the cultural traits common to all human beings. While animals were biologically adapted to their local environments and could not thrive beyond them, humans could adapt themselves to almost any environment through the mechanism of culture. By the use of symbols we fashioned clothing and shelter to protect against the elements, hunted with weapons in compensation for absent fangs and claws. Moreover, our entire understanding of the world and of ourselves is mediated by our culture that allows us to take our bearings and find our way around human societies. Every thought we think, even those "original" ideas we regard as our own, derive from the cultural medium we live in. The notion was exhilarating. Here at long last was a key to the wilderness whose call I'd heard since childhood. What was my longing for the primeval world if not the desire to experience reality as it "actually is" without the distorting filter of human culture? If one could find a way out of culture, I reasoned, the veils would drop away leaving pristine, primeval, primordial being.

Excited, I asked my teacher if one could divest one's self of culture and uncover original being. With an amused smile she told me she didn't think so. It was hard to disagree. If the very ideas, the terms and concepts one relied on to find and open an exit, if they themselves came from culture, then every path we tried would lead us deeper into what we wished to escape. Even the idea of an inside and outside was a cultural phenomenon, as was the notion of escaping culture, which had only occurred to me in an anthropology course while exploring questions which were culturally produced. It seemed she was right.

This was when my mind made a connection on its own and recurred spontaneously to my eldest brother's teachings, in particular to the words of Laotse on emptiness. I went back and reread my favorite piece in Lin Yutan's *Wisdom of Laotse*.

> "Looked at, but cannot be seen-
> That is called the Invisible (yi).
> Listened to, but cannot be heard-
> That is called the Inaudible (hsi).
> Grasped at, but cannot be touched-
> That is called the Intangible (wei).
> These three elude all our enquiries.

BEYOND THE FAR HORIZON

And hence blend and become One.
Not by its rising, is there light,
Nor by its sinking, is there darkness.
Unceasing, continuous,
It cannot be defined,
And reverts again to the realm of nothingness.
That is why it is called the Form of the Formless,
The Image of Nothingness.
That is why it is called the Elusive:
Meet it and you do not see its face;
Follow it and you do not see its back.
He who holds fast to the Tao of old
In order to manage the affairs of Now
Is able to know the Primeval Beginnings
which are the continuity of Tao."[1]

"Primeval Beginnings" were exactly what I wanted to find. I reread the title, "Prehistoric Origins". It had slipped my mind over the years. Now I understood why those lines had appealed to me so powerfully in my adolescent years and why my brother's teachings seduced me from biology. Something in me heard in them the call of the wild. I had ended my early experiments in meditation by drawing back from a looming frontier fearful that once across it might be impossible to return. Was that transborder region the very same cultureless realm whose possibility I was now probing? Were the long ago bathroom tiles alluding ahead to this juncture? If reason couldn't breech the wall of culture perhaps one could leap beyond it.

These thoughts led me back to meditation but in a far more intense and radical manner. It was the 60s when many young people were practicing so-called Eastern techniques of spiritual enlightenment. For once I was well within a broader movement, an unusual position for me that emboldened my experimentations which took peculiar forms. I stood for hours before flowers and trees, stripping myself of the mirage of culture laden constructions my mind had placed on them, summoning the unmediated reality of those beings. Once I meditated on a flower garden for so long I began to feel the same sensation of something hidden approaching, as when the bathroom tiles rose in revolt. The flowers extended and reached out to me. Their colors glowed vividly. At these moments, all completely free of drugs of any kind, the world came magically alive in ways I'd never witnessed before. There was undoubtedly a good deal of truth to the theory behind my experiments. Yet I sensed a lurking danger, a prompting from somewhere that I was losing touch with the world I wanted to live in. If I continued beyond a certain point I might have to live an entirely new kind of world, one I might not want to inhabit. But it was no time for timidity. I began to engage a form of yoga called kundalini or serpent fire. Its aim is to open a number of chakras in the body and release enormous energy. This kind of energy practice can be extremely dangerous without the guidance of a skilled teacher. In my arrogance or naiveté, I speculated it would allow me to awaken quickly to true, unmediated reality, a spectacular break into the wilderness behind the wilderness. I soon became adept at withdrawing sensation from my entire body until I seemed to float in a silent world of pure being. Soon I could go into deep meditation fairly quickly. In a little while it began to happen on its own and I'd have to concentrate on holding off those spontaneous driftings. These occasional, momentary lapses, I will call them, were warning signs that I ignored.

My sophomore year at Howard had been one long misery. The first great love of my life dumped me during Homecoming weekend for a 35-year-old man, provoking a long mental, emotional and physical withdrawal. On top of that, I was required to move to a dormitory some distance from the main campus, tucked away in a dangerous neighborhood where one heard gunshots in the night. A student I knew had been shot in the leg quite close to the dorm. My journeys back from campus late at night were anxiety ridden. You never knew when you'd run into a group of boys bent on mayhem or worse. Then, one night, while walking a female friend home we encountered a little knot of boys who told her they were going to shoot me so she'd see how it was done. It was a moment of terror. There we were on an empty street with nowhere to hide and nowhere to run to. I was paralyzed with fear. Fortuantely she had the presence of mind to ask them to spare me. The boys found sympathy and left. From then on my walks to and from campus were doubly fearful.

Added to physical fear was my resident poverty. Most of the time I had little money for food. There was one three day stretch when I survived on minute rice and instant gravy. This fast was broken by bone filled chopped beef from the ghetto exploiting corner store I was reduced to patronizing. The only bright spot was when my roommate moved out and I had a single room at last. Even that was a mixed blessing. When a drug addicted acquaintance found out he made a practice of driving by at all hours of the night and shouting from the window of his Mustang "Hey Ronnie!" He was looking for a place to shoot up. Actually, he was a good fellow, so I let him use my room to get stoned. He'd sometimes crash on the extra bed but usually he'd drive off once he was mellow enough to face the night.

Then there was the somewhat older student who dropped by one evening, introduced himself and ended up staying for the rest of the semester. His was a very sad case. Like a lot of Howard students he'd run out of money. Unlike most his family refused to help him. Now he had a terrible ulcer and a heart condition, all at the ripe old age of twenty something.. Many evenings he'd sit on his bed in pain, drinking coke, which he swore helped the ulcer. I doubt he thought the same about the deep fried chicken and French fries he also consumed, but it was affordable food and filling until the pain began. One day he came in panting. He'd walked back from campus in the heat. On the way, he said, something closed off the air in his throat. I was afraid for him and pressed him to see a doctor. He couldn't afford it. "Surely your family would pay" I insisted. That's when he told me his mother had thrown him out for being a failure. She'd recently remarried and didn't want him in the way. It was one of the saddest stories I'd heard to that point. He had to sink or swim on his own, he said. He sank. When I returned to school after the summer recess, the dorm director, who had kindly allowed him to stay without paying told me he'd died of a massive heart attack over the vacation. I cried. So did the director when he told me. I can see him now, a big man of six feet, a bit overweight, deeply saddened by a mother who made it known he was worth nothing at all. He seemed so gentle and yearned so deeply for love. He deserved far more than he got. Most of us do.

In April, after the week long student takeover of the university had partially succeeded, Martin Luther King, Jr. was assassinated. He had not been popular among students after the Black Power Movement began, but he was respected. I had heard him speak at Howard. He was eloquent, indeed, but he did not excite us the way Stokely Carmichael did. His murder was a different story. We were outraged and ready to show it to the world. I was in my dorm room the night he died. One of my best friends came by. "Come on Ronnie. We're going out." I knew exactly what he meant, and had been waiting. We drove around breaking windows in the white business establishments in the Black neighborhood we lived in. Throwing a rock through an expanse of plate glass brought a tremendous sense of release. In a small way we were striking back. As the night wore on Washington went up on flames. The revolution had begun.

The next morning I stood on the steps of Cook Hall on Sixth Street and watched the US Army roll in. Before long it seemed there were soldiers on every corner who strictly enforced a curfew. We went out anyway, taunting them for fun until they chased us off. It was rather like playing Red Light/

132   BEING-IN-AMERICA: WHITE SUPREMACY AND THE AMERICAN

Green Light with the thrill of hide and seek. For most of that week we slept in common in the student union. One night, while walking across campus, six rifle shots rang out. In no time two carloads of very large white police officers rolled up. A sergeant poked his head out of the window and said in a stereotypical southern accent "Any-ah-you boys seen anythang", and to our negative, replied "Be careful. There could be a whole lot-a-trouble." They seemed to have stepped right out of a Hollywood movie.

By the time the semester ended, and still recovering from the devastating collapse of my first love, I was emotionally and physically exhausted. Bobby Kennedy's assassination added to our sense of crisis, even though none of us supported or trusted the Senator from New York. The world we lived in was in drastic need of renovation, but it could not come from the established powers or the normal institutional structures. We believed they were too corrupt and morally bankrupt to produce anything good. The best way was to transform oneself spiritually then bring enlightenment to others.

That summer I intensified my meditation as both personal and political resistance. I was about this practice in my bedroom at my parent's home, when all at once I left my body and hovered above it. At the same moment a tremendous pulse of energy surged through me. In the blink of an eye the world was transformed, not so much physically, although its physical presence receded and detached, but the world I had known as solid and unitary was gone. It now appeared, or rather I felt it to be only one version of any number of possible worlds, and the reality of those worlds depended entirely on one's presence in them, at the moment of presence, and nothing more; which meant the only thing keeping me in the world I had regarded as the only one was presence of mind. If that presence weakened, as it threatened to do, I could awaken to other worlds while still in this one, causing multitudes of confusion and incoherence. This transformation was not experienced as a succession of different universes, but as a mental transformation, a rock solid conviction, a revelation. It was as if I had spent my entire life in a room without windows or doors, when all of a sudden, the walls and roof were taken away and I was in a vast plain stretching to unseen and nonexistent horizons in every direction. I found myself in a quantum universe desperately seeking the Newtonian cosmos I no longer quite believed in. I was terrified and completely disoriented. Adding to my horror was the tremendous charge of energy suddenly and simultaneously released into my body, so powerful and unconstrained I felt I would explode. I leapt up and moved excitedly about the room, went outside and jumped up and down. Somehow, I had to express, to bleed off and diminish the enormous maddening energy coursing through my body. My fear was so great that I said nothing to anyone in the house in dread of being thought crazy or being overheard by something waiting to punish me for my hubris.

It took days, perhaps weeks, to calm myself to the point where I could function reasonably well, all of this time keeping the experience strictly to myself. The most harrowing after effect of this episode was the occasional sudden reoccurrence of the original sense of slipping away out of my body to some other dimension. You see, once I had experienced, not theorized, but experienced, the reality that this realm, the world into which I had been born twenty years before, the world in which I had lived as a solid being, taking it and everything about it to be substantial as well, was not as solid as I had believed, or rather that though it certainly existed and was real, it was not all that existed, and most of all, that I had been born not into this world alone but into many, perhaps infinite worlds, what was there then to keep me anchored here and now, except desire and the force of will? I had undercut my desire by the determination to leap beyond. If my will weakened and I lost focus, might I not drift away, not in body but in consciousness, living in this world but dwelling also, and perhaps more substantially in others? At times, I seemed on the verge of doing just that. Whenever this happened all I could do was move, run, jump anything that would focus my consciousness in my physical body still existing in the here and now while I inhabited it only partially. The body became my first line of defense. I had left off running after high school track. Now I began to run again, every day, working my way up from a quarter mile to three miles a day, every day, with sit ups and pushups, pull ups and light weights added in. The more intensively I worked out, the more bodily centered I felt, the more inescapable my physical being became. The next semester I joined the crew team and began more intensive training twice a day. Crew had the added benefits of connecting me with an excellent group of young black men and providing a meal card, so I was now eating three good meals a day. Some days, I'd come off of the river at 8 am, eat breakfast and go back to sleep for an hour or two. I had enough experience of hunger to know better than to waste a free meal because I was sleepy.

A staggering challenge lay before me, to painstakingly rebuild the solidity of the world I had partially lost. In the meantime, I needed holdfasts to keep me fixed, like the adhesives that clamp barnacles to intertidal rocks. I could have accepted the fact of the many worlds that I had been shown and learned to live among them, to affirm, instead of denying, as if it were a fundamental flaw, the fact that I was not all here and never had been, even when that knowledge was kept away. That task was a burden and ordeal demanding more courage, flexibility and self-confidence than I possessed at the time. Instead, I set about constraining my tendency to flight by thinking in the most detailed and tedious ways I could imagine.

These self-limiting exercises, a mode of what I have called *holding-off*, led me back to the study of history that I had left off with my high school self-reconstruction project described below, for of all things the past seemed to me to represent spent potential no longer capable of assuming unexpected forms. As a discipline limiting itself to what had already occurred, or so I thought at the time, history provided an ideal mental mooring locking me into a backwardly anchored foreclosing horizon. With history I could build a stable foundation in an indefinite cosmos, with a socially affirmed identity as a modern human being, provided I accepted the epistemological ground of the discipline. It seemed that my mother's cautionary proscriptions had been prescient. Art and imagination possessed tremendous dissolving and destabilizing powers of enlightenment. I would leave them behind for the time being and tether my wayward mind to the past. This was a clever dodge that had multiple benefits.

Henceforth, and for a long span of years, the only wilderness I wanted to explore was the one made of mountains and lakes, forests and trees but even those were too threatening for the time being, for what had drawn me to them in the first place, the promise of primordial beginnings, remained in them. I rejected the raw in favor of the cooked. Culture now seemed a blessed invention, its power to entangle and limit its human bearers was an unsinkable lifeboat in a stormy sea. I praised the first human who drawing water from a lake had paused, looked up, and said "I am drawing water from this lake", inventing self-consciousness and the culture it creates. I had discovered a love of *humanbeing* in all its aspects, from the most sublime to the most miserable. My intensive physical training helped to express the tremendous energy in me, part of which had built up through years of self-repression, part through yogic practice, but that surplus energy also fueled a remarkable period of accomplishment I had never known before. The simple act of running for miles increased my sense of embodiment and the recognition that the intimate world of flesh and blood shaped me in inescapable ways. I became obsessed with my academic work, which became another therapy for the anxiety released by the event and an avenue to worldly success.

Some years later, I began to reinterpret the event as one more symptom of my tendency towards self-obliteration rather than confronting the forces limiting my life. It confirmed for me a discovery the 60s had also prompted: There can be no true emotional and psychological or spiritual healing without social, cultural and economic change. The struggle for one, if it be authentic and sincere, inevitably and unavoidably entails fighting for the others. Little by little, I came to understand my reaction to my spiritual awakening, an event that left me far more intuitively attuned to being than before, and far more sensitive to worlds here and elsewhere, as largely conditioned by the oppression and repression I had experienced in the family and society I lived in. There was no inherent reason why I should have been terrified by the sudden transformation of my consciousness. It was the fear of losing a self that had evolved, not without a bit of conscious and unconscious tinkering and even alterations, to adapt me, whatever thing that might be, to the world I was being molded by, the world that had taught me it was the one and only world, before which I should fall down and worship and have no other worlds on pain of eternal damnation. That world had trained me to react with horror to the slightest glimmer of transcendence, keeping me locked within its horizon, which is exactly what we ask it to do. The terror, then, was not so much of losing this world, for it could not be lost, no matter how many billions of other worlds there might be, but of losing the self formed for voyaging in it. This was, warrantably, a profoundly frightening threat, because the self is the indispensable tiller of whatever craft we embark in. Should it be damaged irreparably we could be swept out to sea with no means of returning, not to a place, but to a stable state of mind. Had my self-esteem been stronger I might not have abruptly recoiled and fled from the prospect of change to the relative safely of the body, and to the past which because it had already occurred could not be taken away or lost. It was because I already had a destabilized sense of self, a native feeling of inadequacy, of fundamental damage, that the shock of awakening was such a destabilizing event. It took me years to integrate that transformation into a new sense of self, for in a very real sense, my old self really had vanished, just as I felt it was in danger of doing, even though its disappearance was a reorientation rather than an absence. In the same way the sleek black engine had been transformed by time and space into another but still useful vehicle, the old self remained a holdfast in an old world as I inched my way tentatively along the rocky coast of a vast inland sea.

In time I came to understand the wilderness I longed for in forests, mountains and lakes, as a metaphor for trackless regions of being our white supremacist autonomy holds-off in ontological defense of individual autonomy as practiced in America. We are trained by innuendo and example, timbre and tone, gesture and precept to fear, doubt and deny its existence in self defense because we have conflated being with the kind of autonomy that we practice and believe in. In fact, what we fear would undermine the foundations of our individual existence, would only destabilize the autonomous self white supremacy has planted and nurtured in America. Our enculturation teaches us to dread the very resources that could empower resistance to white supremacist being by revealing our connectedness. For reasons I cannot yet fathom, I was aberrantly in contact with the hidden world, and like the Church that has sheltered, revitalized and justified black people in America, it empowered me to fight against an unseen and as yet unidentified and unnamed oppressor. But I also feared it and fled in terror when I was offered a momentary glimpse of the wilderness beyond the physical wilderness that had drawn me.

Still later I realized that by looking for a wilderness within, I was turning away from engagement with the world I already lived in, the world that had made *me*, a disengagement that defeated the pursuit of enlightenment, because to sustain enlightenment one would have to free the self from the oppressions inflicted on it by our white supremacist, sexist, homophobic and imperialist culture and society. That was the only way to release and embrace a self that was agile enough to ascend from one enlightenment to another. It became clear that one must struggle to build a society where humanbeing can become as it actually is, rather than mainly held-off, where one can live as multiple selves in multiple worlds simultaneously.

Notes

1 Lin Yutang, Translator and Editor, *The Wisdom of Lao Tzu* (London: Michael Joseph, 1958), 103, http://krishikosh.egranth.ac.in/bitstream/1/2027518/1/HS1281.pdf

· 2 3 ·

PROPHECY

My mother could see the future. If she set her mind to it, as she often put it, she could make things happen as if by magic. On rare occasions she'd sense glad tidings on the way. Mainly her visions were full of woe. When they were first married she woke one night at 3 am to ask my father if he had two cousins with red hair. He had, though he'd never mentioned them to his wife, and hadn't thought of them for years. They're dead, she told him. Both, he asked? Together, she said. No, no, they're much too young he objected and went back to sleep. The telegram arrived from the West Indies a few days later. The red haired cousins had sought shelter beneath a tree in a thunderstorm when lightning struck. There was the uncle's aunt my mother had never met. One day she saw her lying on the floor in a red brick house. She called her sister who alerted her husband. The aunt was found dead on the kitchen floor in her red brick house. Other incidents followed and my father wondered aloud about Obeah Women.

By the time I was born my mother had made a number of predictions but from the year of my birth her powers increased. When my brother and sister came along they were formidable. There were many minor predictions and some startling major ones. One summer afternoon when I was 16, we were all enjoying the breeze from the front porch, when she stopped talking and stared

138 BEING-IN-AMERICA: WHITE SUPREMACY AND THE AMERICAN

ahead, her expression like a mask floating on hidden depths. She sat silently for a long while. When she spoke, her voice was tired and sad. She told us she had seen our neighbor across the street standing on a ladder painting his house. As he worked a darkness gathered round him, thicker and thicker until it centered densely in the center of his chest pressing heavily, squeezing the life from him. He fell from the ladder and lay still upon the damp grass. We were all quiet. No one doubted the man across the street would not be with us long. One cannot approach a neighbor and say I just saw you die. My mother went about it indirectly, as we all went about many things, never speaking or acting intrusively. She asked about his health and suggested he see his doctor, a man of his age had to be careful. He did see his doctor who cautioned him to take it easy. By the autumn the air was crisp but still warm enough to work outside. We were sitting on the porch listening to my visiting aunt's tales of nursing in her New York City hospital. It sounded dreadful and I vowed to take good care never to go so such a place. I found the talk depressing and was about to return inside when the man across the street fell from his ladder while sanding the clapboards of his house. The nurse went to his assistance. It was too late. The ambulance arrived and took him away.

One of her most disturbing and puzzling visions came when she was in her 60s. My younger brother was completing his PhD in clinical psychology at NYU. There he developed a close friendship with a psychology professor who'd once been a monk and now hunted elephants in Africa. The man became another father figure to my brother. At the time they seemed inseparable. Gregory would often spend extended periods at his house. They even drove up to Binghamton to visit me and my sister at the State University. My father liked him as well. My mother was more reserved. There was the inevitable visiting back and forth. On one occasion my parents went to dinner at his large well appointed home in the Riverdale section of the Bronx, its walls adorned with paintings and hunted animal heads. At some point in the evening mommy rose to use the bathroom. She had to pass the living room to reach it. On her return she noticed something peculiar through the open double doors. Entering to get a closer look she found a full-sized coffin set before the far windows as in a funeral parlor. She approached cautiously, near enough to look inside. It was empty. As she passed through the double doors into the hallway, she turned and glanced back. The coffin was gone. The room was empty of all traces of death. She never mentioned it to my brother or his friend and put the incident out of her mind as another of those numerous apparitions whose messages she was unable to decipher.

"They are like pictures projected in the air" she told us. Whenever the pictures appeared she'd stop and stare. Only after a long while would she speak, and then in a tired and far away voice from deep inside. Sometimes she wouldn't tell us what she'd seen. Sometimes she could not interpret their meaning even long afterwards. She felt her power as a burden and often lamented her gift. What good was it to see things you couldn't understand or prevent, she asked. We had no answers for her.

My mother was in hospital when her middle daughter Shirley died. She had suffered terribly from cancer of the pancreas. Her older sister, Anne Marie, had spent the afternoon with her in her Bronx hospice, then left to visit my mother in Mount Vernon hospital a half hour away. As she entered the room mommy told her to prepare herself, her sister had just died. "I just left her" my sister objected. "She was here", my mother replied. "I saw her hand reaching out to touch mine, to let me know she had passed and wasn't suffering anymore." Shirley had died just when my mother said.

During her last illness, before she slipped into her final coma, she told my sister God had spoken to her. "He told me I would suffer, and suffer, and suffer, and he told me something else but I can't tell you" she said. Whatever it was she never did reveal it. My sister believed it was her death, but her coming passing was no mystery. It must have been something profoundly intimate, one of those revelations denied to mortals, but shared with her because the end was near and she'd soon be unable to communicate it to anyone. I thought of Oedipus at Colonus, how after years of physical and mental torment, at the very end, still defiant and unforgiving of his sons, he was deified. Whatever she was told I have always thought it a balm to soothe her passage through the ordeal from which she'd emerge cleansed and purified, raised to a higher plane of being. Silence is the price one pays for such visions. You may see but never seek confirmation by the affirmation of others. The greatest miracles remain untold.

And she did suffer, lingering in a coma for months, wracked with pain she could not complain of, choking on fluids she could not swallow or clear from her throat, ridden with arthritis that locked her knees in place. Though we were told they could be safely unbent only surgically, one day we arrived to find them straightened. God knows what hospital worker committed that act and what pain my mother suffered in consequence. She died soon afterwards. Now she is one of the ancestors for whom we pray for the welfare of her soul and for our own.

· 2 4 ·

SIGNS AND PORTENTS

I am accustomed to signs and portents. Sometimes they appear unbidden. More often they arrive after a period of summoning, which is a ritual preparation of mental and spiritual receptivity. Thus, prophecy is the mediated articulation of an intuition. For a moment the act of holding something off weakens and we allow in what's always there while in the same gesture structuring the experience as a foretelling.

Ever since the summer of shooting stars way up in the Berkshires I have been fascinated by meteors. Surely our prehistoric ancestors stood in awe of those sudden trails of light without harbingers that streak across the night sky, their regular periodic appearance signaling a transcendent order encompassing humans and all creation in an inscrutable intent. Our science has reduced celestial phenomena to rock and ice, gasses and dust particles governed by physical laws to no purpose at all. Yet for most of us the heavens still represent the incomprehensible transcendent grandeur from which all creation sprang. And for many they continue to gesture from behind the veil as they did to our forebears a hundred thousand years ago. Science can describe and predict the movement of the planets. It can explain their physical composition, their origin and possible demise, but it cannot explain their existence or their meaning. Such questions remain the province of the human soul. In August 1811

142   BEING-IN-AMERICA: WHITE SUPREMACY AND THE AMERICAN

the great Shawnee leader Tecumseh traveled from the Ohio country into the South on his mission of pan Native unity. When he began his journey through the southern backcountry in quest of allies a comet appeared low on the horizon and climbed steadily in the sky as he traveled to recede and disappear as he left for home. On the heels of his departure the worst recorded earthquakes in American history shook Missouri territory. A series of three major quakes and over eighteen hundred minor temblors rumbled through the land until March of 1812. To the Red Stick Creeks it was the fulfillment of Tecumseh's vow to leave a sign of his power.[1] Had he known, or were the comet and the quakes fortuitous events? Was the great Shawnee so powerful he could compel the heavens and command the earth? If so why hadn't he used his power to defeat the Americans, or had he somehow foreseen both events and used his knowledge to bolster his cause.

For ten years on the occasion of each predicted meteor shower I stood for hours in the cold night air scanning the skies for the slightest glimpse of a shooting star. For an entire decade I saw none. Something, I thought, is holding them back. The idea made no sense to my rational mind, but it resonated with a lifetime of similar experiences going back to the coal black engine's unreliability. I resigned myself to being disappointed. In August of the eleventh year, fifty years after the summer of shooting stars, I had a decision to make. Defying rationality, embracing augury, I looked for signal guidance. For two days I vowed that should I see a shooting star my decision would be affirmative. From this you will surmise my favored decision was negative. After all, I had a perfect record of not seeing meteors and no reason to expect I'd see one now. As a further guarantee I spent no more than a minute or two each evening looking through an upstairs window into an overcast sky. I did not venture outside where I would have had a much better chance to spot a celestial visitor. I had stacked the deck quite heavily against success. On the third night something changed, radically. I was suddenly, inexplicably, possessed by the absolute and unshakeable conviction I would see a shooting star from the second floor hall window. Mind you, this was no simple feeling or fleeting thought. The surest possible certainty seized hold and possessed me. I was so certain I refused to say "If I see a shooting star my decision will be affirmative", not wanting the outcome and loath to break a sacred vow.

About 2 am I approached the window. The night sky was overcast as it had been all that day. A hurricane was due within two days. The air was heavily humid. I started to open the window but stopped. "Not yet," I told myself, "yet awhile." I went to the bathroom and brushed my teeth. I tidied up my room. Now I opened the hall window, turned off the lights, raised the screen so I would have a clear view, paused, looked down and said out loud "I will say, now I will see a shooting star. And there it is." I paused. "Now I will see a shooting star" and looking up the brightest meteor I have ever seen streaked across the sky from east to west and vanished. I stood stupefied. The immediate feeling was unshakeable affirmation. It was as if an intimate consciousness had spoken on that humid night "Yes you are and have been exactly what you are. You are with us and we are with you." The overwhelming sense was that of receiving a personal response by a consciousness aware of my thoughts who had acted at the precise moment to confirm its existence, my authenticity and the reality of human and cosmic spirituality. There was no other explanation. It was as if a fragment of cosmic debris had come my way in answer to my supplication.

These thoughts, and the certainty of belonging, endured for about as long as the afterglow of an extraordinarily fulfilling and self obliterating sexual climax. Then the biological heritage of humanity entered in with all the disillusionment of a world of suffering. I began to question, like cartoon figures who overrun the cliff and walk on air until they think "I can't be doing this" and fall. In the blink of an eye the numbness of doubt assaults the brain and undercuts our faith as when Orpheus on the brink of the Underworld turned for reassurance and lost Eurydice forever. Had I actually seen a shooting star? There could be no mistaking that. Not only had I seen it perfectly clearly but it had been the brightest meteor I had ever witnessed. It had completely startled me. I had no history of seeing things. No UFOs had entered my airspace. Besides, shooting stars actually exist and presumably occur randomly all year round. Most of the time we're simply unable to see them. It had certainly happened. It could not have anything to do with the meteor. It was going to pass over my house on its disintegrating course, as doubtless millions and even billions had in the past, whether I looked out of the window or not. The meteor's behavior was independent of me. Neither could I believe an external consciousness had sent it my way as a sign. The question was why I had been so positive it would cross my path when it did, positive enough to look for it at the precise moment of its passing. This question and its implications were staggering. Doubt was a clever way of concealing the fact that I had uncovered something which challenged my settled view of things, a way of avoiding the task of finding a more accurate point of view. Doubt was an effective mask because disappoint and disillusionment screened its deceitful purpose. Doubt became the doorway to modernity which once entered shut itself upon all hidden worlds.

Mercifully, not all prophecies come true. The future is not written indelibly for us to read. In the late summer of 1973 my brother came to spend a week with me in Binghamton, New York. I was completing my bachelor's degree at the state university while learning German for graduate school. Gregory was devoted to his family and had stayed the previous week in Binghamton with our sister and her husband. He was doing his PhD in clinical psychology at New York University. The requirements included a clinical internship at the VA hospital where he was engaged in treating veterans of the war in Vietnam which was still raging under Richard Nixon. His future was bright. Nonetheless, I was concerned about him, not the least for his strange way that made him seem still a boy at twenty-three. What worried me was the possibility that his naiveté could put him in danger. His openness could signal a doorway to the wrong person.

Though still physically fearless, Gregory was never athletic. He tired easily, perhaps due to the heart murmur that plagued him from boyhood. His feet were perfectly flat, forcing him to wear orthopedic shoes with heavy metal arch inserts throughout his entire childhood. He was not supposed to jump or run. He did both, often ending up with terribly painful feet and legs. Accidents sought him out. There was the chop on the head by Sidney's hoe and the misadventure while sledding. At seven he was pushed into a jagged, rusty fence post opening a three inch wound in his cheek. The scar never went away. Sports defied him, though he played baseball and football with the rest of us despite his small size as a boy. He was miserable at Boy Scout camp. On long hikes I carried his pack when he became exhausted. He always seemed out of place, fragile and vulnerable, a sore thumb waiting to be hammered. I often felt keenly sorry for him. The camp had horses, one of the very few thing Gregory was actually afraid of. We went riding together on only one occasion. The instructor put him on a huge horse called RK who had bitten a boy in the lip the week before. My brother was frightened but he said nothing, even when near the end of the trail ride the instructor decided to set us off at a gallop. It's a wonder we didn't all fall. No one at camp wore riding helmets in those days. We could have broken our heads. Today such actions could get a camp counselor fired. Back then they were taken as character building exercises. I don't think Gregory ever went near a horse again.

Whatever his lack of athletic and social skills Gregory excelled in school. Only once in his life did he get a grade lower than A. College organic chemistry proved his nemesis with a D. Always pragmatic, the next day he switched from premed to psychology. I was always an average student who put in just enough work to get by and sometimes less. My mind was on play or model building. Gregory was lauded by his teachers throughout his public school and university days. He loved to deride me for what he called my "lackadaisical ways." "You're a poor student, and you're not even an athlete" he was fond of repeating. It irritated me but it was also funny. Gregory was a very funny boy. And he was very smart; smart, hardworking, diligent and conscientious, but he had a mischievous nature. He spent ten days in the hospital when he was six or seven after complaining for days of double vision. After a complete workup, including numerous blood tests, brain imagining and a spinal tap, the doctors were puzzled. They could find nothing wrong. Years later, when he was in his teens, he confessed to having made the whole thing up for attention. And attention he got, a lot of it, including a toy fire engine you could ride in, ice cream and other delicacies. My parents wouldn't believe he'd lied. It was undoubtedly true.

The hospital stay gave him a passion for medicine. From the day he came home his mind was set on becoming a doctor. My brother had a strong will and fixed determination. Once he made up his mind nothing would deter him, except that D in organic chemistry. In the meantime, college cost money, so did medical school and my parents had little to spare, so he started saving right away while practicing as the local family doctor. Equipped with a toy doctor's kit, a timely Christmas gift, he opened his own doctor's office in a corner of the room we shared. An old glass doored cabinet served as a medicine chest stocked with band aids, mercurochrome, aspirin and other medical necessities. From then on, when any of us cut a finger or felt ill, we'd go to him for diagnosis and treatment, always for a fee. In a few months he'd saved $20, back in 1956, when $20 went a long way. But he was to top that. When summer rolled round he held "The Grand Opening of the Doctor's Office," a carnival, to raise money to support of his medical practice and build his college fund. With help from me and several neighborhood kids, he created booths and rides in our backyard, made tickets and pressed my mother into baking cakes and cookies and cooking hot dogs, all for sale at a food counter. The day was a great success. Everyone had fun and by the time the carnival closed Gregory had raised over $50, the equivalent of nearly $500 today. After changing all of the cash into dollar bills, he ironed them flat and stacked them neatly in his gray toy safe. The success of the Grand Opening was repeated during the next several years, always at a substantial profit. At some point the doctor's office went out of business but not the ambition. That endured until his collision with organic chemistry when he switched his major to psychology without missing a beat. He went on to achieve the academic distinction that won him admission to New York University's highly selective PhD Program in clinical psychology.

By the time he entered NYU Gregory was set for a successful career. He had also become a quite different person from the sarcastic, callous brother of our youth. At least from his junior year in Spain he became a loving and nurturing son and brother. The boy who had refused to wash the dishes, despite my mother's heavy guilt trips, leaving them all to me became acutely solicitous of our parents' wellbeing. It was Gregory who organized the brothers and sisters to send them to the West Indies for their fortieth anniversary, to the natal island my father had not seen since he left at 17, whose earth he kissed when he exited the plane. My brother was deeply concerned for our emotional health, aware of how damaging our parents' conflicted relationship had been for all of us, but he demonstrated great love and compassion for our father as well as our mother, despite daddy's vindictive verbal abuse, the disparagement of his "big head", the racist accusations of being "a little Jew" for saving, the fearful nights at the mercy of his rages. He was suddenly supportive of me, no more ridicule, no more jokes. Instead, he sent me $25 a month, the equivalent of over $170 today, to help out with school expenses. For whatever reason, he had become, as a close friend put it, "a beautiful person." No doubt his study of psychology accounted for some of this, but perhaps it only gave him a structure for expressing what he had felt for years. Certainly, he had come to a better understanding of himself and those who had shaped him. There was probably a lot he had hidden in self-defense against the assaults of family and society which now that he was on his own he could struggle to comprehend and integrate into a new identity and worldview. For that was what Gregory was about in those years, altering his identity, or it may be better to say, discovering who he was, sometimes cautiously, at others in too fearless a manner reminiscent of his reckless descents of Snake Hill.

But he was troubled by the daunting requirement of writing a quantitative based PhD dissertation. This worried me too. For all his success in school my brother had very little interest in ideas. He seldom read anything not directly connected with school work, objecting to my attempts to get him to read fiction that he didn't want to clutter his mind with irrelevant information. He told me he wanted to write an interpretive dissertation, which he felt was better suited to his temperament and easier to complete. I was less sanguine. I

SIGNS AND PORTENTS

really couldn't imagine how he was going to complete any dissertation at all. Eventually, the problem was resolved.

Gregory was often ill in childhood and had been rather sickly over the last few years. A bout of strep throat was so worrisome my father stayed with him for a week in his Bronx apartment to nurse him back to health. When he came to visit that summer he looked thinner than usual. I wondered if there wasn't an underlying chronic condition sapping his vitality. He didn't seem concerned. I also worried about his awkwardness, a phenomenon of his college and adult years. Gregory had sometimes been a shy child around adults but with other children he was outgoing, participating fully in all of our games and activities, though tiring easily. Now he seemed distinctly ill.

My worries were amplified by the persistent dread haunting me throughout that summer, the unshakable intuition some horrible catastrophe was stalking me, a great derailment of enormous proportions. Perhaps, it was the fear I'd fail to complete my Bachelor's degree, which felt like something people like me could not do, and perhaps didn't really deserve, a dream certain to be frustrated by something or other. I had absorbed these gloomy thoughts and emotions growing up in the world I lived in, despite all of the "positive" encouragement, so often undercut by emotional and physical violence, the pervasive sense of doom, and the white wall encircling one's inner life. Gregory and I shared them, so did my eldest brother, although in him they manifested in a rather different way, forming a profoundly pessimistic view of life and of his own existence in particular. I think this is what led him to his somewhat depressing philosophy. With me it was in large part my father's explosive emotional violence, the physical fights, the general atmosphere of profound abnormality I grew up in. But it was more as well. There are black people possessed of unshakable self-confidence. This has always been a wonder to me. I found it an extraordinary thing that any black person could grow to self-confident and healthy adulthood beneath the constant assaults of white America on their self-respect and self-image, beneath the hammer blows of multiple racially driven disappointments, refusals, slights, and major injustices, oppressed by the almost inescapable need to be silent at some point in life, to suppress one's voice on at least some of the many occasions when white supremacy presses against you, cuts and lacerates you, rolls over you on its imperial mission, to keep one's mouth shut or suffer the economic, emotional and possibly physical consequences of speaking the truth. My parents drilled into us the legend we could achieve anything we wanted. We listened. Their preaching made its mark. Nonetheless, we lived in the wider society too, the society which insisted we were not to be taken seriously, our yearnings were not important, our hurts inconsequential, our failures completely our own, the result of weak characters. This is the legacy black people of my generation had to combat within ourselves on a daily basis. There were the demands of school, lessons to be learned, research papers to be written, books read, reports made, exams passed. These were, by comparison, the easy tasks. Approaching each one, there was arrayed in opposition the legacy, always at war with our ambitions. Writing a paper was not a mere matter of the object at hand, but the constant battle against self-doubt, depression, anxiety. These enemies had to be fought and held at bay long enough to get the work done. Two thirds of one's energy was devoted to those battles with a third or less remaining for the work whites were devoting their all to. White supremacy succeeds in large measure by pinning down most of its victims' forces by enfilading fire we must defend against or be defeated while whites go about their business serenely unassaulted. White people will object: we all have our personal problems, whites too suffer from depression and anxiety. Certainly, but so do we, and more so than you, and on top of that we must combat your persistent diversionary assaults which if undefended against would allow you to prove the lies you propagate against us. What accounts for the astonishing capacity of black people to survive, and for some to flourish in America, is the culture built on religious foundations, even for those who like myself are not religious, a culture of fierce individualism, the belief in a transcendent source of self-worth that trumps white supremacy's denigration of us, but also of deep empathy, which includes critical intervention as well as praise when appropriate, and certainly, the emphasis on strength, which can at times be self-defeating. Nevertheless, it is hard not to feel proud of any black person who overcomes what we face to succeed, even in those ways America defines success that I am often repulsed by.

My ever present dread that summer fed my concern for my brother. I knew he shared this aspect of my disposition. We were both always waiting to exhale but when I asked about his health he shrugged off my anxiousness. One day I returned from an early morning class to find him still asleep in the bed next to mine. As I entered the silent room he was completely wrapped in a white sheet, not even his head visible, the whole emitting a certain alabaster glow. Immediately, I knew he was dead. Like the shooting star conviction this was no hunch or surmise but apodictically certain knowledge. I called him several times. Finally he stirred and replied. I was wrong, yet I knew his time was short, something was gravely wrong, something was going to take his

SIGNS AND PORTENTS

life. I determined to intervene. As soon as the summer semester ended in two weeks' time I would set about convincing him to have a complete physical examination, particularly to check the heart murmur that had tired him since boyhood. In the meantime I had to focus on my work.

As I said, sometimes the strongest portents prove wrong. At the end of the week Gregory went home. He was not taken away by illness that summer or any other.

I managed to complete all required coursework for the degree and went off for a ten day vacation on Martha's Vineyard. In those days, when the island was not as popular as it is now, one could rent a room for $7 a night, which would be less than $40 today. Unfortunately, rental costs on the Vineyard have grown exponentially and the same room would now run $200–$300 a night. My fiancé and I took the subway from her Uncle's tiny rat invested apartment off of Nostrand Avenue in Brooklyn to Port Authority, then the overnight bus ride to Woods Hole where we caught the ferry to the island. We had a restful vacation, uneventful except for one strange incident.

Uncle Bill had always been a favorite of mine. He came of West Indian parents, grew up in Harlem and had the West Indian's intellectual acuity, drive and determination. Born in 1915, he and his brother worked their way through Tufts University in Massachusetts, where the dean told him they would admit him but would not help him find employment when he graduated because he was a Negro. He and his identical twin brother worked eight hours a day waiting tables to pay for school. They achieved this feat by each posing as the other and working half of the shift. They both graduated. The brother became a doctor. Uncle Bill got his degree in electrical engineering and went on to work at White Sands Proving Grounds before becoming Chief Electrical Engineer for the Harvard-MIT Electron Accelerator project.

My uncle was memorable for allowing me a glimpse of normality when I spent the summer of 1965 with his family at their home in Newtonville, Massachusetts. My mother had arranged for me to go. Perhaps she wanted to remove me from my father's wrathful presence so I'd have a tranquil summer before my final year of high school. We had never discussed the emotional and physical violence I had witnessed growing up in our home, nor had she ever asked me how it had affected me. I can't speak for Gregory, but I assume she was silent with him as well. Nevertheless, I like to think that she had some awareness of the harm that had been done to both of us, and had secured a temporary shelter in New England. Yet, it could have been merely Uncle Bill's fortuitous offer of a job as a janitor at Harvard. Whatever the cause,

I lived with them for two and a half months of peace and quiet an interval without of shouting and cursing, without the constant fear of a looming devastating eruption. It was a summer of hard work after the experimental lab where I worked blew up and had to be cleared of debris. But the weekends brought enjoyment I had not known before in a family group, like trips to Cape Cod or Martha's Vineyard. I think, if I had been able to remain there for a full year, things might have turned out better for me. When summer ended home I went for another year of torment before college, made unendurable by the taste of domestic tranquility I'd been given. It turned out to be one of my father's worst years, and therefore mine as well. Poor man. He never understood his own demons, could never fathom his murky depths or discover what slippery denizens dwelling there had caused his personal hell. That he had inklings was evident from the strange things he'd say in his rages, but he quickly forestalled them before they could escape into public and challenge his destructive way of being. Then, by self-isolation he ensured that no one could entice them out. This was the purport of his favorite warning "There's no such thing as a friend!" which he set out to prove by having none. Thus, he demonically inclosed himself within himself, perpetually, tragically, draining of emotional vitality because he had damned every stream capable of replenishing the reservoir.

Bill and his wife, my mother's youngest sister, were on the Vineyard too that summer of 73. On Sunday, August 19, we went to East Beach on Chappaquiddick, a magnificent strip of sand with dunes and a salt pond behind. It is, or was then, subject to powerful undertows you had to be careful of. The day was partly cloudy in the mid-70s. At about 4 pm I went into the surf with my uncle. The water was cold but tolerable. I had moved some yards away from Uncle Bill to have more room when a large wave rolled in and knocked me down. I felt a penetrating pain between my shoulder blades as if someone had struck me a tremendous blow before going down and tumbling in the turbulence with the sinking feeling of being swept away and lost. The next moment my uncle had pulled me up. I struggled to the beach and sat shivering uncontrollably on the blanket. The others became concerned when I could not stop shaking. This had never happened before. I felt as if my life were draining away. Something was wrong. They wrapped blankets around me. The shivering went on for ten minutes before it began to calm but it was some time before I felt well enough to stand. It had been a very strange experience. I remember thinking the approach of death must feel like this. Once I had recovered sufficiently my fiancé and I went for a walk in the dunes along the pond. I was still weak from whatever had afflicted me and puzzled by the incident.

The vacation was all too short. I returned home to find my mother concerned about my younger brother who she'd not been able to contact over the last week. He told her he might be going out of town to visit friends on Long Island, but she had always been overprotective of both of us, especially Gregory who seemed particularly vulnerable to one thing or another. Like me she worried he might have fallen ill and didn't like to complain of his condition. She asked me if I would go to check on him.

The next day, Sunday, August 26, my Uncle Louis picked me up and we drove to Gregory's apartment on 242 Street in the Bronx. I was still haunted by the fear that he was suffering from some hidden illness, and in a way I was glad we'd have the opportunity to confront him and make him seek medical attention, but when there was no answer to our repeated knocks I concluded he must indeed be away. I had the spare keys my mother had given me, but it took several attempts to open the door because my brother had installed three separate locks that turned in different directions to foil burglars. They foiled me for some time. Finally the door swung open and we entered the kitchen-dining area of the tiny apartment. In the middle of the floor was a footlocker resting on a blanket in which a TV and stereo equipment were deposited. The kitchen cabinets were all open and a rocking chair turned over. Through the darkened room we could see into the bedroom-living room. The convertible bed was open. On it something large and white seemed to glow in the light coming from the side window. We moved cautiously closer. A body lay face down on the bed. It was on its knees with its head and chest on the bed, a pillow covered the back of its head. Its hands were tightly bound behind its back with something that looked like nylon fishing line, the fists clinched, the fingers, caked in dried blackened blood were like claws. A sheet was wrapped and tied about its lower legs and feet. The medieval sword Gregory had brought back from Spain as a gift for me, was thrust deeply into the body between its shoulder blades. Only the hilt was visible. The body was in its underwear. Blackened blood covered its white translucence, drenched the couch cushions, splashed the wall and hanging tapestries, and stained the ceiling. Above all, was the crushing, clinging physical stench of death, the prolonged decay of a human body, and flies, flies and maggots humming and buzzing everywhere. My body gasped. My stomach heaved once, twice, again. Nothing came up. I shouted in horror and ran from the room with my uncle behind me, banging frantically on apartment doors. No one opened. No one replied. Finally,

152 BEING-IN-AMERICA: WHITE SUPREMACY AND THE AMERICAN

automatically, I went back into the apartment and looked for the phone. It was under the bed. I crawled under to retrieve it and dialed 911. Then I went to look at the body to see if it really was my brother. It was far larger than he had been, bloated by having lain in the hot stifling apartment in sweltering heat for eight days. I moved the pillow from his head and tossed it aside. Gregory's curly hair lay stark and still beneath.

By the time we got outside the police were arriving. They treated us kindly. I volunteered to identify the body at the morgue. This was no act of heroism. I wanted to see his face one last time, to be sure it was him. I wasn't prepared. It was not the face I knew. It was not a face I could identify. His mouth was wide open in a frozen, silent scream. His face, which had been fair skinned was black, the result the coroner said of blood settling in the lowest parts the body. I had forgotten about the stench. It clung to him. There was nothing to do but leave as quickly as possible. Neither I, nor the eldest brother who accompanied me could identify the thing that lay there. Our dentist finally did.

Gregory was murdered on August 19, 1973 between 3 and 4 pm at precisely the time I was on Chappaquiddick the same Sunday. The time was established by his murderer. I do not believe it coincidental that I was with my uncle, the husband of my mother's sister Dorothy, when he was killed, and with the husband of my mother's sister Vivian when we discovered his body. The presence of those matrilineal relations gave me the spiritual strength to endure the horror of my brother's brutal death.

The man was caught at the beginning of September. He had bragged about his crime to his roommate, then showed him the New York Times story when it came out to prove his account. Worrying his roommate would tell the police, he tried to kill him. "You're going to go the same way as that doctor in the Bronx" he told him and nearly beat him to death. The roommate felt the dreadful preciousness of life, made one heroic effort, escaped and alerted the police.

He said he met my brother in Central Park that Sunday and they returned to his apartment for sex. We have only his word for what happened. His story has changed somewhat over the years but he has been consistent in describing the killing. He beat my brother, probably unconscious, then bound him. I suspect he first tried to smother him with the pillow and found killing a human being harder in reality than on film. Then he stabbed him in the back three times with a dagger, another souvenir from Spain, until it bent into the u shape I saw together with the bent blood stained sword in the witness room, where I waited to give my testimony. Gregory didn't die. Instead, he continued to move, making, said the murderer "little gurgling and choking sounds." His assassin saw the sword on the wall, took it down and thrust it into him. The movement stopped. His life came to an abrupt and brutal end.

He died in the tiny dark apartment I hated to visit even briefly. Only once did I stay the night, but felt so depressed by the atmosphere and an ominous presence that I couldn't sleep at all and left early the next morning. He loved his apartment. For him it meant independence, the freedom to live as he chose. My mother had somehow discerned a warning she could not comprehend in the house in Riverdale, where a coffin appeared and vanished in the living room of the man who'd found Gregory's apartment and given him the sofa bed he died on. I had seen his death in my dormitory room and known that I would find him dead entangled in his sheets. I had felt the savage death blow in the surf on Chappaquiddick. Yet I could do nothing to alter a future that had, perhaps, already occurred.

How he lived is something of a mystery. Some of us, but never my parents, suspected he was gay or bisexual. On several occasions I called his home to find him in bed in the daytime and got the distinct impression there was a man there with him. This was only intuition. We may all have been wrong. Today it would not have mattered. In 1973 it mattered a great deal to a lot of people. No one ever asked. His college friends emphatically insist that he was heterosexual, but how would they know. If he was gay or bisexual, and if he felt compelled to arrange secret sexual encounters, one of which proved fatal, then he was a victim, not only of the man who wielded the sword, but of the homophobia and sexual discrimination of the times.

Perhaps, also a victim of race. He had, it seemed to me, in the year or so before his death, tried to appear blacker than he may have imagined he was. This alarmed me, because it was accompanied by a far too open and trusting public presentation of himself. He had taken to teasing his hair so that it resembled the kind of Afro fashionable among some young white rock musicians. It certainly damaged his naturally straight hair and seemed a kind of self-denial. I had seen young people damage themselves at Howard University by denying parts of themselves that did not fit the image of blackness promulgated by the more intolerant black power advocates. When deciding on a college Gregory had visited Howard and spent a night in the dorm room next to mine occupied by a student from Mississippi. This rather callous young man teased my brother mercilessly. Gregory reacted with characteristic awkwardness. He was completely out of place, without the slightest idea of how to negotiate the situation. Instead, he showed his utter contempt for his tormentor and for the

154 BEING-IN-AMERICA: WHITE SUPREMACY AND THE AMERICAN

environment he was in. I had thought it a bad idea from the beginning. He would have been miserable at Howard during the heyday of the Black Power Movement where he would have been subjected to criticism and even hatred for his physical appearance, his complete lack of any trace of "blackness" and his native arrogance.

He went to St. Lawrence University in Canton, New York, in the middle of nowhere, far from any major cultural center. Today he would have been accepted by Harvard and the other Ivy Leagues schools. Why he was not is another comment on race in America. St. Lawrence was a poor choice, not as disastrous as Howard would have been, but excruciatingly isolating. A junior year in Spain helped redeem the time. Then he went to NYU where he began to come into his own and flourish. New York City would have allowed his hybridity to take root and blossom. There wasn't enough time for germination. He desperately wanted to live what we all considered a normal life, to marry, have children and interact lovingly with his family. There was a woman he was interested in. It seemed an impossible match to me. I suspected her sincerity, and worried he was being precipitous, perhaps to prove a point to himself and others. I didn't notice her at the funeral. None of that would matter. I wonder, when he went to Central Park that Sunday afternoon, was he looking for a loving and accepting black friend, his great eagerness and longing for acceptance beckoning the predators inhabiting that savage world, finding deception and brutality instead. It is a deeply wounding thought, but one I suspect to be true.

After the funeral we gathered at my parent's home. As we waited outside for something to deliver us, the mother of a childhood playmate approached to pay her respects. She told my mother her son, the English boy who'd been my best friend for several years, had overdosed on heroin that same morning. Had the news of Gregory's death added another intolerable oppression to his overburdened life, tempting a bit more heroin than was good for anyone? The next week two of my black high school acquaintances were murdered, another, a very talented artist, overdosed. It was the season of death.

When I returned to School in Binghamton I attended a party in late September. A fight erupted. An unruly young black man from off campus was ejected. Almost immediately there was a commotion downstairs. I went to investigate and found the glass double doors of the student lounge wide open with the prematurely cold autumn air streaming in. The room was empty except for an 18-year-old boy, lying on his back, with a hole in his forehead. A portion of brain and bone protruded. A thin spray of blood spurted in rhythm to his pulse. His parents had sent him upstate to escape the violence of his ghetto home. They didn't understand there's no escape for a black man in America. Fate tracked him north of the city and west of the Catskills. It found him in the hallowed halls of academia, standing alone in the student lounge minding his own business, one more innocent bystander to our violent society.

The ambulance soon arrived. Nothing could be done. Today the lounge is named in his honor. I had seen his killer earlier that afternoon in the gym while I was running on the track. He was lifting weights, an angry character with a demonic eye. We exchanged glances long enough for me to mark him as someone to avoid. Justice in America gave him two years in prison. He'd only killed a young black man who might have died violently in some other way. Perhaps his victim's mere existence had provoked his fate.

It came out at the trial. My brother's murderer had been released from Attica in July after serving four years for armed robbery. Before that he had spent a year in a reformatory. During the trial he beat up his lawyer and had to be restrained in his chair. He spat on the District Attorney and told the judge he would put his face on the other side of his head. He threatened my sister and told me "don't look so mean", because I habitually stood outside the courtroom to stare at him as he was brought in. He got twenty-five years to life. Since 1998 he has come up for parole every two years and been denied each time based on his continuing violent behavior and lack of remorse. So far he has served fifty years for my brother's murder. Except for the months of July and August 1973 he has been incarcerated for the last fifty-four years, almost the whole of his life, not including the year in reformatory prior to Attica. He calls himself a victim of society, and in a way he is. In and out of foster care and brutalized in prison, a survivor of the bloody Attica prison riots of 1971, when the state police shot down protesting inmates. I frequently think how two lives could have been saved had he received the help and loving nurture he needed as a child. Unfortunately, destructively, this society would rather lock people up than address social problems if they mean radically changing the way we live think and feel.

I started reading his parole hearing reports in 2004 in the hope of learning how and why my brother met his end. They painted a painfully sad portrait of a child abandoned by his mother, placed in foster care; henceforth in and out of institutions. It was the story of a life derailed before it could get underway. It was only then that I learned he'd gone to Buffalo, New York on his release from Attica for fear of getting into trouble in his native New York City. He only went back, he said, because his mother was ill and wanted to see him before she died. So he took the bus to New York.

Strange as it may seem, we're all interconnected by a hidden web that catches us unawares. Rarely, we're given a glimpse of how our paths cross with others. Sometimes, the view leaves us inspired with a sense of awe as when a shooting star streaked overhead just as I looked into the night sky. Sometimes it leaves us shattered in the face of tragedy.

Notes

1 John Sugden, *Tecumseh, a Life* (New York: Henry Holt and Company, 1997), 246–47, 248–51.

INTERMEZZO

Allusion is a way of knowing things that elude the waking mind. We like to confine its working magic to the words of poets, the art of fiction, the dramatic turn of phrase, the clever referral to cultural complexities no word or phrase alone could possibly capture. Allusion allows literature to attain a scope impossible were it to remain within the limited world of the poem, the play or the novel. A carefully chosen word connects the work of art with larger themes, issues and concerns running deep into the culture, linking the reader or viewer with more than what we witness on stage or find within the poem or story. When Robert Frost writes of rustic boulders in mending wall "We wear our fingers rough with handling them", we are reminded, even if not with conscious immediacy, of the wearing labor of maintaining our identities as separate individuals. Here is an allusion, not to a literary classic, but to a classic discontent of life, one as unavoidable as mending wall itself, a chore that even the narrative voice does not refrain from but initiates each spring. And as the poet alludes to life, so life itself alludes from what we know of its present majesty to its persistent mysteries. We are hardly poets, most of us Americans. Our general mood of pragmatic readiness for work, for getting on in the world, our more or less perpetual self attendance, is not the poet's open receptivity to life's disparate and wayward promptings. A hasty perusal of a poem or the skimmed reading of *Moby Dick* that jettisons all the *needless* things in order to cut to the chase, is liable to miss the wonderfully packed allusions that can light up our world, if we let them. They whisper to us, when in those rare moments of quietude we drift free from the deafening noise of everyday life into precious reverie hypnotized by the full sound of life moving. At times they tug at our sleeve summoning us to follow. We take one, perhaps two tentative steps to something beckoning just beyond our point of view; and then, fearful of our own unclaimed potential, break the spell and resume our customary resignation. It is all a formidable, self-defeating and largely necessary self-defense against self-dissolution. Even Rousseau, drifting in a boat on Lake St. Pierre in Switzerland, cocooned in his own private bliss, was loathe to share that state with ordinary people for fear it would distract their minds from the work at hand.[1] We pay a great price for keeping ourselves together and focused on the world we know, when all the while that same demanding world summons us to transcend our restricted state through a siren's chorus of eternal allusions, while we seal our ears with wax to make safe passage to a homeport whose whereabouts we've forgotten or misplaced. Early on my bathroom tiles suggested more than meets the eye. The white bread-truck rat, the long black eels from the dark lagoon, the gloomy castle on its shores, boarded up and locked away, the Carolina old folks in the projects, with their darkened faces and knotted hands, the shadows sheltering our hide-and-seek, the courageous solitary mouse who robbed my sleep, the lonely deer silently stealing away from his canine pursuers, the wilderness itself, all so many allusions pointing away from what we know, of where we are, and where we aren't and might never be, from where we stand, bareheaded and devout, on the perimeter of a giant tabernacle, peering into its deeper, darker core worshiping. Life alludes, and we, in our timidity, *hold-off* what she would show us, for metaphorically life is the great mother, pregnant with wonders that far exceed the grasp of our most powerful imaginations. In her arms, beneath her bosom lies the secret of the spirit.

Notes

1 Jean Jacques Rousseau, "The Reveries of the Solitary Walker," in *The Confessions of J. J. Rousseau, Citizen of Geneva. Part the First to Which Are Added, the Reveries of a Solitary Walker*, In Two Volumes, Vol. II. Third Edition (London: Printed For G. G. And J. Robinson, 1796), 282–84.

· 2 5 ·

WHO AM I?

If there was a pattern to my life I could detect on hindsight, uncovering therein melancholies and depressions, uncertainties and self-obliterations, why had those particular memories remained vivid while others failed? Did they stand on their own as milestones, or had I, in concert with unseen and unsuspected collaborators, illuminated them while leaving others in the dark? Was the great derailment, the signal flag fiasco, the wayward basketball all pulled from the murky interior, like those long ago eels from Glen Island Lagoon, to provide a cleverly concealed foundation constructed as a tragic flaw I had to struggle against? Did those recollections, while seeming to show the baleful absence of self-confidence, signify the need to temper and harness an energic demon of such magnitude and appetite that only starting from behind and battling uphill could employ it safely, and whose dreadful existence, too awful to admit, generated my sense of guilt? Was I selecting memories in order to establish a livable identity whose frustrations I could set my mind to overcome, and in the quest obscure the abyss of meaninglessness? Or was meaninglessness a nihilistic threat projected in my subconscious by a white supremacist unconscious struggling, with the aid of Nazi philosophers concealed in ancient Greek attire, to drain my self-confidence and turn me into an object it could deprive of agency.[1]

These thoughts elicited a sort of mischievously happy contentment, almost immediately dispelled by the human tendency towards wariness of joy and suspicion of bliss, a remnant evolutionary adaptation of the animal instinct not to linger in one place for fear of being eaten. Thus, I experienced a reverse Cartesian moment, an inkling which the great mathematician, solider and philosopher apparently forestalled. Who was this me to whom those intuitions came? Was it the same *I* the great philosopher had pulled from his hat to beg his question? *I* was proof of nothing, could not affirm the existence of anything. *I* asserted the intention to exist in a thinking way, from a *singular* perspective, outside of the world in a glisteningly white-diverse-and-inclusive-universal space station, a bid for traction, a claim to possession, a demand for recognition. It did not describe a presence. That could only be sensed, and affirmed by community, never demonstrated, for demonstration was a ploy to transcend, and, thereby, to disempower community. It provided no foundation for a self preoccupied with mobilizing the world for self-creation. It responded to my moods and feelings with thoughts from nowhere, while each thought, thought, pushed the thinker further into the depths. *I* was an invocation, a sound used to summon memories, presences and aspirations, to gather and employ energies bent to some task, a sound others in the conspiracy I had joined in infancy, recognized and responded to as me. Who was this pattern-finding me? Were the patterns there, or were they an artful way of creating a stable point in the blizzard of experience whirling about me? Was the me who formed the patterns one more pattern? Could a differently patterned me find other, perhaps infinite, patterns in which the sleek black engine would never derail or not appear at all? In its most concrete sense, me was something I felt about the place of my body, its thoughts and emotions, its encounters in the world, the locus of my fears and anxieties, my hopes and dreams. Behind it dwelt silent-spaceless-timeless presence, raw and uncooked, pristine, ancient and primeval, untouched, all-embracing, yet free of entanglements, the wilderness I sensed and searched for in mountain wastes and trackless forests, on the unbridgeable oceans and unmapped outback of my imagination, an unfathomable, bottomless, illusive presence, a profound every-thingness about which nothing certain could be said.

Notes

1 See Chapter 29 "The Agency of Objects".

· 2 6 ·

A LIFE IN MANY WORLDS

For most of my life the wrenching feeling of insuperable loss was often unbearable. It was as if parts of me were left behind wherever I started out, pieces of a jigsaw taken from the box and thrown away. Stalked by what I did not know, I lived always with an emotion of great desolation, often overcome by the absence of a precious community I had no recollection of ever having known and could not identify, as if it too had slipped into whatever black hole consumed the little engine. In its place was the pain of deprivation. For years I searched my deepest past for evidence of its existence as vigilantly as I scoured the mouse ridden closet for the engine of my early days. No matter how far back I looked or strained my memory I could find no explanation for the melancholy that lay dormant in me and sprouted from time to time. If my parents had come from the college educated middle class they would have put me in counseling where trained specialists claim to discover hidden childhood traumas persisting long after their causes disappear. A course of medication would give me the experience of legitimate mental health to aspire to. A shallow cheerfulness, reflected in a bright smile full of perfect teeth of unnatural whiteness, would confirm my return to normality. Like many Negroes at the time my parents thought counseling disgraceful, the mark of a weak character. They were, perhaps, as well, wary of strangers who wanted to filch one's

162   BEING-IN-AMERICA: WHITE SUPREMACY AND THE AMERICAN

innermost secrets, in the guise of helpfulness, like the little boy who stole my basketball.

One day, as I was hiding in my room with Robert Louis Stevenson, the thought came upon me all in a rush, I was thinking the wrong way round. My melancholy was not caused by the loss of what had been, but the intuition of people and experiences I had not yet known, children I might father, friends and lovers I was destined to meet but had yet to find. The absence of their anticipated presence constituted my sense of loss, and it was the illusion of time that prompted me to place them in the past. An enormous chasm gaped before me, hollowed out by the glacial movement of time and space which would have to occur before we could meet and be together, and the fear that somehow our meetings would be derailed. Although I could not know their shapes, or faces, or the specifics of our reunions, whether they would be good or bad, I could sense their coming on, the way an animal feels the advent of spring, and I was saddened by the loss those meetings would one day inevitably produce. The thought I might not find those people who I should meet created a kind of despair. How many prospective encounters had been disrupted, their chance to flourish obliterated forever, I would never know. Somewhere, unknown to me, a me had appeared and disappeared.

Thus the irony of our being: moving only towards the future, we know only what has occurred, except those among us whose mutant minds, abolishing time and space, can detect the future in the present. There was a profound sadness at the core of life. But it was more than that, for if there were others I had yet to encounter, there must be unknown parts of me, good or bad or indifferent, I had not yet the power or understanding or opportunity to muster, and those opportunities, themselves dependent on future others and circumstances to draw them forth. If this were so, might not the guilt I felt, the dense suspicion of an unknown wrongdoing for which I had searched unavailingly in my past, was it not too an intuition of a guilty act to follow, an inkling of some monstrous deed or undertaking that only time could confirm or deny, or the sense that I was capable of committing all of the terrible deeds that had ever been perpetrated by human beings, simply by merit of being human, and only time and circumstance kept the present me safe and apart from their consummation. Somewhere, unknown to me, I had appeared and disappeared.

In this mood, I was struck by a remarkable thought. If I existed through time in this world might I not exist in space through many worlds? The thought once expressed was additive, preserved and multiplied by its cumulative effects. At the same time, I suspected a sort of escapism, while knowing

A LIFE IN MANY WORLDS

163

well enough how such doubts are designed to put us off the scent of any world threatening events. Didn't I already possess proof of those worlds? Wasn't I accustomed to wake to them each night as soon as I fell asleep? Hadn't I long marveled at the perfect artistry of dreams, whose realism was unequaled by the most accomplished artist? Those dream worlds were as vivid and real as my waking life, with nothing but fashion to prove I'd invented imaginary worlds from the odds and ends of daily life, drawn and quartered by a subconscious as alien and intangible as those worlds themselves, rather than awakened to alternate realities. Scientists would point to telltale activity in the brain while asleep, but neurological activity did not mean I was not in more than one place at the same time. In fact, that activity might illustrate, not only dreaming here, but wakefulness elsewhere.

Freud theorized that dreams are wish fulfillments, the working out in sleep of our daytime trials and tribulations. But if dreams are woven from the detritus of our daily lives isn't this akin to what the sages mean by karma? If I cannot escape in my dreams, the overflow and legacy of my waking life, if my "waking" acts construe and constrain them, fostering bliss or terrorizing me in nightmare episodes, aren't dreams vivid demonstrations of the reality of karma, at least within one psychological lifetime? Yet it does not seem to work the other way round, for I hardly feel my waking life's an elaboration of themes set while I sleep. For the analogy to hold we must posit other worlds to which I am asleep while awake to this one. And why not? Isn't it far more likely those dream worlds are other worlds, lying side by side, parallel universes always there, concealed by waking consciousness absorbed in the daily minutia of this world, only to appear once I fall asleep, than detailed replications of my waking world that I am incapable of rendering in any medium while awake.

If this surmise was true, I would not have entered those worlds only when I slept, but would continually exist in all worlds at once while aware of one world only at a time, regarding it and no others as the real world opposed to the world of dreams. And while existing in all worlds at once, my actions in each one would cling to me in all others where they would have different consequences in each one, because each one of those worlds was different. That, it seemed to me, was the real significance of karma, the interconnection not of past lives but of simultaneously existing lives, connected by the spun web of my actions in all worlds at once.

A certain mystery cleared itself. I lived for years with the terrible apprehension my happiness would always be threatened. No matter how wealthy or successful I might become as long as misery and suffering existed, I was vulnerable, as if they were the lineaments of some fantastic demon dogging me behind. I would experience the worst as well as the best life could inflict. This dreadfulness was not prompted by the capriciousness of an inequitable world. Nor was it entirely empathy with the unfortunate but the fear their affliction could catch me up. There was an aggressive, offensive danger in the presence of suffering that disturbed my enjoyment of the most intense happiness. These sentiments had tormented me as far back as memory searched. Now, as I thought of the fish with the hole in its side, I immediately understood the significance of my childhood revulsion. That wounded animal brought the danger of contamination onto the land, threatening me with its imperfection, just as the Carolina old folk with their knotted veins and darkened faces were signs and portents of what I might become. Even dead, unable to bite and squirm like those demonic eels, the fish threatened to devour my tranquility by its mute assertion of possibility. The possibility of suffering was inherent in my existence in multiple worlds, whose existence the fish had signaled by its emergence on land from its alien realm. What I was spared in one world was bound to occur in another at some time, perhaps it already had or was even now unfolding, and that was why I felt its coming on. And in order to anesthetize myself with the fantasy of individual life lived in one time and place and never again, I'd built strict walls and boundaries between worlds, closing the portal instantly upon waking to create temporary sanctuaries, like picnic blankets weighted to the earth by family and kin. Could it be that on occasion worlds collided, causing little tears and ruptures in the fabric of space-time, through which the denizens of one peeked at the inhabitants of another? Was this the explanation of ghosts and spirits?

These musings led me to a Smithian rationale for altruism. If we did live through worlds, and if we were subject to the caprices of fate in each world that would one day bring us to all imaginable consequences, was there not a moral invisible hand at work prodding each of us to contribute all we could to making existence as benevolent as possible in every world we inhabited? Was it not in our individual and collective self-interest to love our neighbors as the selves we might one day become?

The more I followed these musings the more interesting and liberating they became, ultimately explaining the most oppressive mystery, the end of life itself. Hamlet's anxious questioning after posthumous dreams entirely missed the point. The pertinent question was not what dreams, but what lives may come once we've shuffled on. Death would never come as we've feared and imagined, but fulfill its metaphoric rest, only to wake, without awareness of having slept, in other worlds, always-already at the exact same moment. The nearly universal belief we go somewhere after death reflected the unconscious awareness of being there already.

Then a notion I had held off appeared like a homing Pidgeon returning to its roost. What if imagination, the sign we give to mysterious workings we're unable to explain, was not the genesis of the entirely new, but, instead, the perception of what existed somewhere in time and space and the notion of multiple worlds a metaphoric representation of the incomprehensible idea that mind, like Feynman's photons, is everywhere at all times.

· 2 7 ·

AUDUBON

We didn't have the concept of white privilege during my adolescence in the 60s. Deprived of such enlightenments, I felt possessed not by your privilege but by my deficiency. I was determined to repair the deficit by changing myself, rooting out my native dispositions and becoming as much like you as possible. Yet, as much as I aspired to be like you, I did not think of this as becoming white, for I never consciously wished to be white. I would have liked wavier, though not straight hair, but I did not want to grow paler. To be colored seemed to me much the better state. My motivation was to bring myself into accord with a personality type I took as universal but which was largely white and western. This was a sea change from what I had aspired to on Fourth Street where all of the people I looked up to were what we then called Negroes. Now my models of what a successful person should be were uniformly white, for they seemed to embody the essence of the American individualism I aspired to. This was a correct assessment but the fact that I was embarking on a self-contradictory and potentially self annihilating path was hidden from me by school, parents, friends and myself. Everyone agreed that I was finally turning things around. To their minds it was a cause to celebrate. I concurred. No one suggested I was dangerously undermining myself, for not knowing who I really was, or who they were, they had little basis for doing so.

168   BEING-IN-AMERICA: WHITE SUPREMACY AND THE AMERICAN

Rather, their silence, coupled with applause for my reform efforts reinforced my negative view of the self I was laboring to reconstruct. Provided I had a sufficiently good will I could make of me whatever I chose without harm to myself or to others. The familiar feeling of guilt settled in, and because I identified its cause as the defect I was struggling to overcome, it became an ally in self-deception.

I well recall my senior year in high school as one of only two black students in my American history class. It was a rather advanced course taught by a man reputed to be the best instructor in the school. He took his lectures from *The Growth of the American Republic* by Samuel Eliot Morrison and Henry Steele Commager, whose 1937 first edition contained a racist account of Reconstruction that characterized "Negro" state governments as "the most grotesque travesty on representative government that has ever existed in an English-speaking country."[1] All of that background was suppressed by the instructor who could have exposed the white supremacist views of the authors of the book he drew his lectures from or selected a better text. I knew nothing of these matters at the time. I was possessed by the idea that I was fully integrated into the nearly all-white class and had no consciousness of race. This notion gave me the warm feeling of belonging for the first and only time in my school experience, including the various colleges I have attended and worked in. I commended my ability to rise above race, to see people as humans rather than whites or blacks. My white classmates were cordial, some even friendly. They were clearly happy to have a Negro colleague with a likable disposition who got along with them so well and tried so hard to put them at their ease. Two blond girls in particular seemed eager to get to know me better, at least in the classroom. I took this as an indication of how well I had succeeded in putting race out of the picture for all of us, for I waged my campaign against color consciousness for the entire class, for our society and the nation. And though I never received a social invitation from either of those girls, or from any other white classmate, neither did anyone treat me in any way that I perceived as racial. Notwithstanding all of this, I had the unsettling feeling that something threatening was lurking just beyond the horizon.

It was, of course, my very success in ignoring race, which meant an active struggle to hold its recognition off, for that was what I was doing, that created my unease. My high school racelessness was a unilateral decision, a sort of sympathetic magic, as if by changing myself I could change the white world, break the walls of my prison house and find freedom, even while I had no conscious sense of being incarcerated, for I had transmuted the emotional, intellectual and physical symptoms of imprisonment into evidence of my own moral, emotional and intellectual failures, just as my family had concealed their conspiracies of silence as love and devotion.

To sustain the pose, it was necessary to ignore the time spent every morning incessantly brushing my hair to make it look less Negro than it did, to call it taking pride in self, one more sign of a strengthening character. It meant discounting the anxiety welling up whenever I spoke in class, not from the stutter this time, but the dread of being wrong and appearing more Negro and uncultured than I wished to be. Most importantly, I had to hide from myself just how powerfully my sense of racial unawareness betrayed my vivid and persistent obsession with race, while the whites around me had the luxury of completely ignoring race because they benefited from a system of oppression that made it unnecessary to consider my existence at all, except on their own terms, when, where and if they chose to offer them, all of which meant that they were more obsessed with race than I was and less aware of their obsession. Somehow I was conscious enough to realize the teacher hadn't said a word about black people, even during a cursory coverage of slavery and Reconstruction. Perhaps it was a telltale of the sea change to come that I wrote my research paper on John Brown.

A year later at Howard University my outlook was radically transformed in a matter of months. For a black person who had never lived in a black environment after Fourth Street, which had been an integrated neighborhood, Howard was an earth shaking event. For the first and last time until I taught there for two years in the late 1980s, I lived in a sort of Audubon for black people where the constant huntings and humiliations of race could not reach us directly unless we went off campus. At Howard I met excellent friends, but I remained an outsider whose true home was the wilderness.

Howard is what is called a historically black university. When I entered its hallowed halls, it styled itself the Capstone of Negro Education. It may have been, but Negro education was exactly what I didn't want. Fortunately, neither did a great many of the young students enrolled with me. For us Negro education meant shuckin and jivin, kowtowing to Mr. Charlie, adopting white American criteria of beauty and political progress, repressing ourselves instead of attacking the injustices that oppressed us. But these fruits of awakening came later. In the beginning was profound alienation.

Howard and I clashed from the moment the cab pulled into Sixth Street, NW and stopped in front of Cook Hall, one of the three men's dormitories. If Mount Vernon had oppressed me, the environs of Howard in Northwest

170   BEING-IN-AMERICA: WHITE SUPREMACY AND THE AMERICAN

Washington, as distant from my beloved wilderness as possible, depressed me from the moment I arrived. That miserable state remained with me for the three and a half years I endured my torment. There wasn't a passing day I wasn't desperate to leave. Only the war kept me there. In those days to drop out of school was virtually to enlist in the army. You'd lose your student exemption and become eligible for the draft. Eventually I did leave, not because I had become heroic but because I could no longer afford school and needed to work and save enough money to go back. It was one of the best decisions I ever made, more so because it was against the advice of all of the adults I consulted.

I was drafted almost immediately after losing my exemption, and having determined I wasn't going to make war on anyone, I would almost certainly have ended up in prison or Canada. I appealed and was saved from either of those alternatives by the inexplicable intervention of an Army Doctor of Chinese ancestry, who, perhaps drafted himself, and waging his own guerilla campaign on behalf of life and against the war, asked me if I wanted to be in the army, and when I said no, he marked me medically unfit for no apparent reason. I have never forgotten him or his name and revere him as an authentic saint.

The years I spent at Howard were memorable for the political and cultural transformation they helped provoke in my worldview. Those were revolutionary times and I gravitated naturally to a group of students who could be described as cultural revolutionaries. We read Malcolm's "Message to the Grassroots" and "The Ballot or the Bullet", Mao Zedong's, "Report on an Investigation of the Peasant Movement in Hunan", and "On Contradiction", Che Guevara's, *Reminiscences of the Cuban Revolutionary War*, Régis Debray's, *Revolution in the Revolution* and Frantz Fanon, *Black Skin, White Masks* and *The Wretched of the Earth*. Our reading was reinforced by active political agitation by black populist leaders like Stokely Carmichael, and Ron Karenga. All of this was empowering and exhilarating for a young man forming a personal identity.

The world of Howard University showed how constructively one could live without white people looking over one's shoulders. None of us were completely free by any means because Howard was part of the larger white world from which, as far as we were concerned, its administration received its marching orders, and we were all conscious of the fact that we would be making our lives in American society beyond the walls of Howard. In the meantime, as we read Fanon and Malcolm, we realized how deeply white supremacy

AUDUBON   171

had shaped our psyches, even instigating us to adapt our physical appearance to a white model of beauty.

Whiteness could not be escaped altogether, even at a black school, but it could be held at a distance, especially in the late 1960s when some of us felt ourselves at war with white America for our souls and our very survival. All of this was positive, but blackness could be oppressive in its ethnochauvinistic manifestations, though nowhere near as destructive as whiteness. There is no moral equivalence between the Back construction of a racial fortification and the bombardment that drives us to it. The one represents a fragile band of humans wielding stone weapons against the saber-toothed tiger, the other that rapacious predator itself. Nevertheless, there were hurtful and harmful effects on individuals in an attempt to "liberate" their minds, as when black girls who straightened their hair were accused of self-hatred or those with fair skin, like my younger brother were made to feel unauthentically black and treated with distrust. There was a heavily racial atmosphere that made it seem wrong to think of one's self in other than racial terms. To do so risked ostracism by the more race conscious and even criticism by the middle of the road nonpolitical students whose eyes were fixed on successful professional careers. It seemed to me that everyone at Howard thought of themselves as Negro or black first and foremost. I suppose this made a great deal of sense at a Negro school, but it cast me once again as an outsider. They had chosen Howard because it was black. My decision was entirely driven by finances. Howard was more affordable than the University of Colorado, the other school I was admitted to. I had always thought of myself as a human being first and foremost, but when I articulated my belief in humanity I was derided as "The man for man". The phrase became a standing joke. Whites will seize on this as an example of black xenophobia. It was not. The description was never hurtful. It was a humorous summons to come to my senses by a group that unquestionably regarded me as one of them, even if I was a bit odd. I could argue against them and still be accepted, which would never have happened in the white world. What troubled me most was how conventional so many of the black students were. With the exception of civil rights issues, the majority were more politically, socially and culturally conservative than the whites I had known in high school or were to know later at other universities. Their ideas about homosexuality, male and female gender roles, patriotism, the war in Vietnam, political economy, religion and spirituality were far to the right of mine, except for the group of likeminded students I was fortunate enough to find in my second semester. But we were all outsiders in a basically mainstream

172 BEING-IN-AMERICA: WHITE SUPREMACY AND THE AMERICAN

culture. For me the problem was that Howard in the mid-60s, before its radicalization, was more American, more conventional and more patriotic than I could endure. It felt as if Americanism existed at Howard in intensified and concentrated form while it was being attacked at college campuses across the country.

For all of that, existing without white people on a day-to-day basis was a blessed way of being, made more healing and enriching by the Black Power and Black is Beautiful movements that accompanied my Howard days, and the bosom friends who would do anything for you, all of which helped compensate for the destructive backwardness of the university administration bent on turning raw, uncooked, lowercase negroes into well behaved and socialized Negros who would uphold the race and never rock the boat. They were vastly disappointed in this ambition, for in the spring of 1968, not long before Martin Luther King, Jr. fell victim to the racist America that now lauds him, we invaded and took over the Administration Building to enforce our demand that Howard become a "Black University." There is a photo of me during that revolt in Lerone Bennett, Jr.'s *Before the Mayflower: A History of the Negro in America, 1619–1962*. I am sitting on the steps of the Administration Building wearing the sunglasses I had borrowed from a friend. Our weeklong uprising merged into the massive riots and insurrection that erupted in Washington the night King was assassinated. Like thousands of other blacks I went into the streets taking direct action. The next day I was on Georgia Avenue heading down the hill when the first shots rang out. I turned from the spectacle before me to the masses running down the slope, a bright array of colorful clothing, behind them the blue line of policemen, shotguns raised, firing round after round into the scattering crowd. I was surprised to feel no fear, only a bolt of anger surging through me and the resolve to be a warrior, reclaim my roots and die with my people. But no one died. No one fell. No rich streams of blood ran in the streets. The moving breastwork of blue and white was firing tear gas, and with that recognition, as if in recompense for the lost chance of heroism, I began to cough and my eyes to burn. "I'm in the midst of it now" I thought, and instinctively felt in my back pocket as if for reassurance. Régis Debray was still firmly planted there.

It was a wondrous time when the millennium was at hand, the revolution had arrived and all of the horrors we lived amidst, the racial assaults, the murderous immoral war in Vietnam, the poverty and hopelessness would be swept away by the revolutionary wave. Washington was suffering a high crime rate in the late 60s but during those glorious days of insurrection I felt completely safe wherever I went. We were all brothers and sisters, engaged in building a just community in tribute to our fallen leader, for ourselves and our children to come.

But in my high school, in the spring of 1966, I was part of a raceless community. When I looked back on my childhood and youth from the vantage point of a black university, well beyond the self-imposed horizon I had lived within, it was clear how much I had suppressed, therefore, how heavy a price I had paid to enter and remain in racelessness. Like the rat who interrupted our childhood play on Fourth Street, but with my full complicity, the whites around me had derailed my search for myself at critical stages, forestalling the development of possibilities of me before I had come upon them, and foreclosing already existing ones that clashed with their view of themselves, of me and of the world. In this way they too were channeled away from possibilities of themselves they could not admit or act upon without releasing me to be whatever I chose to become. Yet there was no equivalence here either, for their self-suppression, built as it was on my oppression, bought them wider compass for self-realization than my constricted one, albeit, in perverse directions that defended and extended the imperial wars that raged all around us, consuming hundreds of thousands of darker people abroad, and thousands of young black men in deathly conflagrations.

Tragically, there is little to compel white Americans to discover the white supremacist shadow they slumber beneath and conceal from themselves, little in their dreamworlds to jolt them awake. For the most part, white Americans are sleepwalkers, gliding through life in a self-induced somnambulant trance, anesthetized to the havoc they wreak as they stomp and crush anyone and anything in their way, autonomically proclaiming when one of their sleepmates kills half a dozen people: "Things like this don't happen here!" A denial manifesting, with every headline proclaiming, "The worst shooting in American history", their persistently active suppression of the truth that "things like this" always happen here, have been happening here for centuries and have happened here to Native Americans and black people at far greater magnitude and extent than any recent mass shooting. Convenient sleepwalking allows the self-deceit that their *here* and my *here* are different places, a disruption of the imagined national simultaneity that confirms the integrity of all modern nations, and marks the continuing psychically entrenched segregation of black people.[2]

So that senior year in Mount Vernon High School, my fitting in depended entirely on not protesting, because I had covered them up, the manifold

174 BEING-IN-AMERICA: WHITE SUPREMACY AND THE AMERICAN

injuries I suffered at the hands of white America thereby affirming my class-mates' delusions. It meant perpetually surveying my behavior to ensure I offered no offense, anticipating what they would feel or suspect if I acted in such and such a way and making sure I did not. I had learned, the way most black people learn, how to put white people at ease by maintaining the myth that we're all alike, only differing bodily, that race doesn't really count. It is the pose Bill Cosby made a fortune performing. It is a profoundly self-destructive act because if race doesn't matter then the black situation is self-made. Blacks are poor, unemployed, kill each other in the streets, are incarcerated at higher numbers than whites, underrepresented in the professions, undereducated and segregated due to their own failings. In short, acting as if race does not matter validates racism. In doing all of these things, in making the manifold tiny adjustments in my countenance, tone of voice, and most self destructively, in censoring not only my thoughts but forestalling even the inklings pressing to awaken my mind, I was sacrificing my growth, my existence as an authentic being, trading my discomfort for your comfort and your welfare, making myself small to allow your largeness, all in order to be accepted by you. All of this amounted to a monstrous and unperceived self-mutilation that augmented white supremacy because it foreclosed any pressure for you to change. The constant sense of guilt I felt was the force of all that I was *holding-off* trying to get in, and the recognition that should I weaken, should it find a breach, conflict would ensue, while all the years of shattered nerves, the gift of white America's many wars of attrition against my father and mother, predisposed me to avoid conflict of any kind. Here, then, was the revelation of white supremacy as a dual oppression impinging me and molding me through the family and the outside world. That, perhaps, was why I sought the wilderness. If I had released my self at home my father would have reacted with vocal, perhaps physical outrage. Nor would my mother's respectability have allowed her to understand. Should I open my self abroad the whites around me would react with hostility at being let down by a Negro who'd conspired with them in self-deception. Returning to Howard after the summer of my freshman year I encountered one of the two friendly high school blonde girls on the train. She was delighted to see me, delighted until I exposed my emancipated, black power toting self, the one with no intention of confirming her expec-tations, ensuring her ease and comfort or protecting her sensitivities. She felt appalled, dismayed, bewildered but most of all betrayed. I wonder if she ever trusted a Negro again. The experience, like pummeling that white boy of my youth, was liberating, another cleansing release of frustration, self-hatred and humiliation through violence, just as Frantz Fanon had predicted.

Yet my unease was only mitigated, not abolished. Even today, whenever I'm walking in broad daylight behind a white woman who noticing me hurries her steps, or crosses to the other side of the street, even in my upper middle-class suburban neighborhood, it's nearly impossible not to think of what I could do to show her my harmlessness. The woman ahead might panic and call the police in fear of her life. I could end up dead for walking on a public street. So I go through my days scrutinizing your every move and gesture, reading your thoughts, preparing against your persistent willful misunderstandings of who and what I am, and who and what you are, devising strategies to escape your blind fury and passive destruction. But today I do these things for my welfare not for your comfort. They are necessary because you are among the most dangerous people on earth. Even now, when children are routinely slaughtered in their classrooms, you have not yet begun to understand the depth of your violence and self-deceit.

Notes

1 Samuel Eliot Morison and Henry Steele Commager, *The Growth of the American Republic* (London: Oxford University Press, 1930), 642.
2 See Benedict Anderson's classic work *Imagined Communities* (London, UK: Verso, 1983).

· 2 8 ·

MEMORY PALACE[1]

How did I divert from my purpose? Oh yes, race. It has diverted me over the course of a lifetime, diverted all of us from the enriching lives we could have lived without it. Let me leave it for a while and return to memory. Of course it can never be left in America. That's the ivory dream we sleep with to divert our minds from our codependent marriage with white supremacy.[2] Even now, you may be wondering, perhaps impatiently, what has memory to do with race. Under white supremacy, the act of remembering is racially skewed to exclude what white people wish to hide and what we "others" conceal for the most part, subliminally, apprehensive that recognition would bring us into conflict with you and with ourselves to complicate our lives unsustainably. For as I argued below, an insidious white supremacist unconscious has been bred into all of us growing up in America, and that inveterate saboteur auto-nomically reacts against the rectification of individual or collective memory, so that the act of authentic remembrance, whether "private" or public, entails perpetual struggle against white supremacy, whether one is black or white or some other "other".[3]

I was relating the approaching sense of danger to my memory palace and its newfound sanctuary of reminiscences when my mind, perhaps con-structing an allusion of its own, recurred to my high school history classroom.

178   BEING-IN-AMERICA: WHITE SUPREMACY AND THE AMERICAN

With that image of fragile harmony, the sense of something fixed about to be unsettled returned. Once again, I was holding something off. The coziness of reliving past experiences, catalogued and situated in my mind, that lent to me a momentary sense of solidity, was rooted in the discreteness of each experience re-experienced, a repetition and resurrection that buttressed the horizonal boundaries I dwelt within. It was the coziness of the booth, an island of stability in a fluid, perpetually transforming sea. The illusion of stability is gleaned from the imagined past that seems to come to us on its own as a series of ever accumulating episodes, like the train cake and the army canteen, as if they exist, reservoired somewhere, retrievable as distinct events unconnected to the present thinking self whose memory, and therefore, existence, they constitute, rather than being constituted by it. Mine are given me by my self, just as the Maître d' leads me to my favorite booth in my favorite café. I can find them in my memory because I created them in the past, not, you understand, in any conscious manner, as if painting pictures to hang up within the architecture of my mind for preservation and instant recall, but autonomically by some part of me that I remain willfully unaware of, for I have found that I am a rather elastic, blurred and ambiguous being, never fully coming into focus. Unlike the Maître'd who greets me each time I return to the restaurant, I've never met the invisible host who conducts me to my memories. Nor do I know the pathways it travels coming and going, or the criteria applied in opening and closing what we so hopefully call the past, to support the present. However those experiences were created, however the metaphoric stream of life is broken into segments for review, we can find of ourselves only what has been transformed into experiences, and conforms to what we collectively recognize as experience, by that mysterious demiurge. Nothing else remains to be recalled. Nothing not so constituted is recognizable by that very self we say it constitutes. And even this, in its most intimate retrievals, is a communal event. For in mapping out available pathways to tread, the community can, even unwittingly, conceal and banish portions of me; while I, oblivious to their existence, could form no intention to search them out, nor would I know where to look if I should. Whatever we are able to discover, even those cutting-edge radical departures, remain within the ontological-epistemic horizon of the communal mind, and do not recognize the possibility of questions such as the effects produced in us by what it is impossible for us to know or do or experience.[4] This self of mine has profoundly obscured regions of itself beneath a collectively generated dense Atlantic fog.

Then it occurred to me, what if this episodic episode-fashioning was not the gesture of a past leaving markings for me to follow, but only occurs when I look for what I mean to recall. What if the looking itself creates the events and episodes of my life which were never there before? What if those created episodes and events are pathways into hidden regions of myself, ways of locating me amidst whatever it is that looks. I do not mean that neither events nor life exist until we think about them, but on the contrary, that my self exists perpetually only in the exact present and was never past, or future, only organized into something I know as my past, present and future whenever I turn my gaze to look for it. What if, in this extended era of "possessive individualism", memory is a Lockean move to gather in and appropriate the disparate elements of my self from the wilderness, and turn them into proprietary resources for building an autonomous life; and when I reflect on that life something creates experiences waiting for me to find like paths to walk on.[5] Except they are not waiting for illumination by the light of day for they did not simply occur nor did they persist. They were created by the recollecting itself.[6]

But things were not as simple as that. For I could not create experiences of any kind completely on my own, but only as a member of a community joined by language, culture, and a white supremacist collective unconscious, devoted to defending an extreme form of individual autonomy codependent with white supremacy, that works surreptitiously to forestall threatening possibilities of myself. My youthful experiments in autoontology during that spring and summer of intensive meditation and political and social upheaval, seemed to confirm that I was inescapably woven into human culture. I could challenge that belonging only at peril of dire consequences. Without those collective tools, the heritage of millions of years of instinct, intuition, trial and error, precept and example I had no way of creating anything like a past. And without a past I could not orient myself in a timely fashion to make good use of my self, for the past situated me in a way that I could appropriate. That was why I could not recall the distant days of infancy, why memory began from the time I became proficient in creating experiences by the collective use of a language that further entangled me in a community of like-mindedness. Absorbing a language meant assimilating a particular mode of path constructing into a self; and a self was, thus, a location in space and time, the public intersection of multiple paths, collectively laid down by visible and invisible hands for me and for others to follow, to my self. I was free to illuminate or obscure them, clear or cast them into shadows for others, and for myself.

180   BEING-IN-AMERICA: WHITE SUPREMACY AND THE AMERICAN

I can find experiences to relive and enjoy because I have collectively already demarcated them. And though the experiences are no longer there waiting, the neurological and communal pathways remain.[7] The memory of the train cake was originally made in my second year and renewed and revised many times after, providing a beaten track available for me to follow. But then it must be there for others capable of reading our particular signs to follow as well; for I can relate my memories to them, and evoke in them what I experienced, creating communal pathways into ourselves. Except the pathways did not go anywhere. They were all allusions, metaphors evoking moods, and it is the mood that returns me to my prior state of mind, which is nowhere else but here, in which the cake appears, or rather the feeling-image appears.[8] As with the booth, I approach a preexisting structure, not something I have to create on each occasion, a structure fabricated not by me alone but by community effort, even when I am as isolated as Crusoe before he filched a man and called him Friday.

And, indeed, as I create my memory palace, "I", like Plato's demiurge, look from it, not to an archetype fixed and eternal before all experience, but to my sense of the bounds and contours of our collective notion of memory, as opposed to our notion of artifice, imagination or illusion, a fluid, moving, communally created archetype. If I come across a thing that is not so constituted I may not recognize it as mine, Even as I search for that "unique" self, marking me as modern, I do not recognize any thing I find unless it registers in the collective epistemic context.[9]

By age 2 I was socialized enough to note what was deemed significant by the group I lived in. I did not register the size of the room of my second birthday celebration or the kinds of furniture in it. My memory of that event is a synopsis of what I'd learned was essential. But neither was this quite true, because I had no direct way of knowing what I thought was significant at age 2, or if my memory of the train cake had been revised in light of the significance and meanings I had come to give to people, things and occasions as I grew into adulthood, all of it informed and limited by the cultures I lived within. I could not be sure even if the train itself and its derailment had been the most significant events at the time they occurred, or if the cake and the derailment had occurred on the same day, or if I had cobbled them together as a metaphor for a pattern I detected or infused into my life years later.

Now I was more depressed than ever for it seemed our creation of experiences continually directed our minds to what the communal self deems significant, continually revised in light of new experiences. For what we are concerned with is not the substance of recollection, merely, or the agreement of identity, but the ground of recognition; so that whole regions of being could exist, entirely unsuspected, and excluded by our epistemic horizon. And if that community in America was dominated by the white majority knitting all of us within a *white supremacist collective unconscious* wasn't I forever hemmed within it, even in the construction of a memoried past, wasn't it enslaving me and all of us to constantly repeating and replicating a self-defeating worldview, distorting even the force and direction of our rebellion against it into looking for those signals of transformation which that unconscious marked as significant: Negro firsts, Negro excellence, black Cleopatras, black superheroes, black billionaires, Presidential Negroes, self-reliant Negroes, law and order Negroes, autonomous Negroes, strong black Men and Women. Whatever lay beyond that mnemonic horizon had never been constructed and, therefore, would yield no memories at all. Worse still, it might never allow a truly original, emancipatory vision of a possible future free of white supremacy and all other debilitating horizons. We seemed forever chained to the pasts we had constructed to protect us from the very fate we suffered, looking to them for materials to craft similar inhuman artifacts. For whatever I had not deemed noteworthy or paid no attention to, or had been entirely unaware of, all of which insensitivity was never mine alone, but also the unavoidable manifestation in me of my community's likes and dislikes, preferences and biases, judgments and determinations, forestallings, foreclosings and holdings-off, was as irrecoverable as if it had been pulled into a gigantic black hole traveling through space devouring anything out of the ordinary.[10] Most of all, whatever had never evoked a mood in me was gone forever. I was trying to thrust beyond the wall by traveling its interior boundaries and, thereby, continually kept within it. Before created experience lies our personal horizon, a different moment for each of us, but for each of us always social as well as personal.

I had constructed my memory palace, but of its architect I could find no trace. It seemed the only foundation for any self to stand on was the collective, unreliable and shifting sands of memory. Yet, regardless of my discomposing thoughts, I was, perhaps perversely, incapable of doubting my existence. It was then, I understood: there must something more, something beyond remembrance or forgetting that accounted for my presence, by its presence.

Notes

1 The chapter title alludes to the China mission of sixteenth-century Jesuit Matteo Ricci to teach the Chinese a memory technique based on constructing a mental palace in which memories could be stored. See Johnathan D. Spence, *The Memory Palace of Matteo Ricci* (New York: Penguin Books, 1985). On medieval European memory arts see the fascinating study by Mary Carruthers, *The Book of Memory: A Study of Memory in Medieval Culture* (Cambridge, UK: Cambridge University Press, 2008).

2 The allusion is to the gates horn, through which true dreams emerge, and ivory, the passage of false dreams in the *Odyssey* and the *Aeneid*. It is notable that in the *Aeneid* Virgil sends Aeneas back from the underworld through the Ivory Gate.

3 See Chapter 30 "The White Supremacist Collective Unconscious".

4 For my consideration of this question see Chapter 32 "Deprivations".

5 For "possessive individualism" and John Locke's theory of property see Chapter 30 "The White Supremacist Collective Unconscious".

6 I am influenced here by pioneering work of F. C. Bartlett, *Remembering: A Study in Experimental and Social Psychology* (Cambridge, UK: Cambridge University Press, 1932).

7 On the role of neural pathways in memory see Antonio Damasio, *Descartes Error* (New York: Penguin Books, 2005).

8 I am influenced in thinking about the importance of moods by Antonio Damasio, and especially by Soren Kierkegaard.

9 For modern selves as individually inwardly unique see Chapter 30 "The White Supremacist Collective Unconscious."

10 For the definition of these terms see Chapter 30 "The White Supremacist Collective Unconscious".

· 2 9 ·

THE AGENCY OF OBJECTS[1]

Once my mind started on this confusing path I found it impossible to halt its ruminations. If I were in perpetual relationship to something surely it ought to exist here with me. Yet there seemed nothing here but what I had encountered all of my life, other people, animals, plants and things. There was no mystery about my interaction with other people. It happened all of the time. It occurred face-to-face and at a distance by merit of my inextricable and unavoidable situation in the human community. Whenever I thought about anything I used language and engaged images which were the common property of humanity. Nothing I thought or did could ever be mine alone. Yet that did not seem enough. There was something thicker going on, something not so clear cut. Animals, trees and plants had always been a powerful influence on me since early childhood when I'd planted a vegetable garden every spring. The Boy Scouts extended the engagement into the wilderness. However, there were no trees or animals and only a few potted plants inside my house, nor except for the occasional dog were there animals. Something was missing, something that could account for my occurrence even when I was alone, away from nature within the depths of my study.

I was musing on these thoughts one day as I absentmindedly sauntered about my house when I carelessly stubbed my toes against the leg of my oak

184 BEING-IN-AMERICA: WHITE SUPREMACY AND THE AMERICAN

desk. There was the annoying feeling of having done something stupid followed immediately by the sense of delayed pain on its way as the impulse traveled from my toe to my brain. I was about to curse at the desk when I caught myself and laughed. Something my son said when he was 3 years old, over forty years before, had suddenly come to mind. He had run across the living room without looking, collided with a chair and fell hard to the floor. Getting up, he pointed to the chair and said angrily "Look what the chair made me do!" I laughed then as I laughed now and thought how childishly I was about to behave, when the thought came to me as an enlightenment: He was right! At the time, I had explained to him how his carelessness and not the chair had caused his fall. I was helping him develop mental attitudes, templates for explaining causation in a way calculated to give him a certain kind of human agency over his environment. But now, as I thought about his comment, I realized he was right. Despite his carelessness the chair had caused him to fall by being in his way. My son had seen clearly, while I had persuaded him to shift his perception in a way that reinforced his agency and took it away from the chair. Immediately it came to me. There was something I was always in relationship with no matter where I was, whether sleeping or awake, conscious or unconscious, young or old, and that something existed in plain sight. The perpetual presence defining me as present was the object. I was unaware of this fact because in growing into a mature and responsible human being, a modern autonomous American self, I had denied agency to objects and centered all agency in humans. I had pushed objects into the background as things to use and define as I saw fit, as tools, equipment, furniture, raw materials of every sort, or simply what was in the way, with no meaning of their own, except what I gave to them. We had purloined agency so deftly that our theft could exist in plain sight without anyone perceiving what we'd done. This was an extraordinary revelation, changing the way the entire world appeared to me. The most obtrusive, and the most easily missed, nearly invisible characteristic of our world is the presence of objects and their perpetual, inescapable influence on us. Once I realized how profoundly they shape my life I was astonished I had never noticed before.

The first and fundamental recognition was the fact we do not simply use objects because objects are not here for our use. Before we can use it the tool must be made. I am not positing here primarily a conceptual construction, which is certainly influenced by the object and what it allows us to do with it, but an actual physical fabrication from materials that have been prepared, changed from preexisting states as trees or rocks for example. To put it

THE AGENCY OF OBJECTS   185

figuratively, they are here for themselves as we are here for ourselves and in both cases being here means being for others whether those others are humans or physical objects, not from volition but unavoidably. We can only "use" objects by entering into relationships with them and cooperating with them to obtain the ends we seek. But since we are always-already in relationships with objects entering into a relationship with an object actually means changing an already existing relationship. When we enter into such altered relationships, often motivated by the need to change objects to facilitate attaining our ends, we too are changed by the objects we engage with. When we seek to learn how to work with an object which we require to attain some end we are seeking to be changed by interaction with it. Moreover, since we are always-already in relationships with objects of one kind or another, and since there is never a time when any human being is free of such relationships, humanbeing entails, in fact, means to be in relationships with objects. It could not exist apart from such relationships. This is true of so-called natural objects such as trees, rocks, mountains, lakes, oceans and so-called human-made objects such as furniture, houses, clothing, tools automobiles, and planes. Humanbeing means being in relationship with objects.

In all of our so called "uses" of objects we must interact with them largely on their terms, because we can only know them as phenomena, and therefore, cannot negotiate with them. This is a limitation that objects impose on our interaction with them, and, as such, it is a sign of their agency. We cannot simply "use" them just like that, but can only make use of them according to their nature, or we can also say according to *their way of being*. They compel us to interact with them in specific ways, not simply as we wish, even when we succeed in employing them for our own ends. This includes our volition in deciding to "use" a certain object. For example, when an early human decided to make a hand axe their mental action of "deciding" expressed a prior interaction with stone which informed them about its potential for chopping, hammering or scrapping. The idea was not simply the automatic, spontaneous, autonomous result of a human mind's capacity to think symbolically. Indeed, that very capacity exists, and is only capable of existing, within an already established relationship with the material world that called it forth. Not only did that world, including the body, impose needs upon the human being but it also suggested how those needs might be met, could be met and could not be met. Of course, what we call human beings were always-already actively engaged in multiple relationships with the material world and we are not to conceive of early humans as initiating such relationships as humans

186   BEING-IN-AMERICA: WHITE SUPREMACY AND THE AMERICAN

but of inheriting them from their "non-human" ancestors. That inheritance would have included understandings of things and their possible uses. Thus, a hand ax could not be made from just any rock but needed a rock that could be worked efficiently. This knowledge ultimately derived from our premodern human ancestors' experience with rocks, which would have been passed down through generations and could eventually come to be thought of as expressing human wisdom independent of the objects themselves, would always be based on interaction with objects, as any craftsman would have soon discovered, since the material could only be worked in ways that were suitable to its physical nature. If struck the wrong way, the rock would not chip effectively but splinter and fragment. Knowing which rocks to use for which purposes-knowledge-, how to work the rock properly-craftsmanship-,thus expressed a relationship between rock and human with the human adapting its movements to the nature of the rock, and this kinesthetic engagement developed human understanding of the body as an immediately available and potentially available object, the one closest at hand. Moreover, we cannot move or act in any way we want in regard to objects. When we seek to pick up a rock, it resists, a resistance we interpret as weight, which induces a compensatory adjustment in our muscular skeletal response. We may even have to train or develop our muscles in order to be able to pick up rocks of a certain weight, while remaining unable to move others without engaging social networks and the technology associated with them. Our motility is modified by the objects we encounter and must unavoidably encounter in the world. A lore might develop around stone working craft that perhaps even endowed certain rocks or all rocks with particular characters or spiritual significance. In fact, it is a peculiarity of the age of white supremacist autonomy that we no longer routinely do so, but have, as Weber claimed, disenchanted the world; whereas the recognition of the spiritual presence in all things was typical of many human societies for thousands of years.

The example of arrowhead production among Native Americans makes the same point on a larger and more sophisticated scale. In that case trade routes developed to obtain raw materials for arrowhead production, and subsidiary supporting industries, such as hunting for trade pelts or making wampum belts could be seen as extended relationships with the natural objects needed to produce arrowheads, relationships that entailed modifying human behavior on the individual and group level. Science and technology are vastly more complicated relationships with objects requiring advanced educational training. In this way, one may view all of human society as conditioned and

THE AGENCY OF OBJECTS

refined by human interaction with objects, by which we are forced by their nature to adapt to them in order to make use of them, and to train our minds in quite sophisticated methods of discovering their ways, how they might be used and how best to use them to our own ends. Of course, we do not think of ourselves as doing any such thing. Rather we pride ourselves on "taming" the natural world by the strength of human intellect. This is a mere human conceit, perhaps engaged to make it easier for us to mobilize our own powers by fabricating horizons or by narrowing our awareness of influences acting on us, and to preserve a certain homocentric view of existence. It may be for this reason that we tend to restrict the notion of agency to living creatures, and especially, to human beings and deny it to objects.

Although agency simply means the power to cause an effect, and as such includes forces of nature as well as objects, we usually understand it to apply to the willful decisions of conscious actors. It has increasingly taken on that meaning as movements for the liberation of women and oppressed peoples have grown in significant and influenced academic writing. However, this good use of the concept of agency still operates within the homocentric paradigm, further obscuring our inescapable dependence on objects. At the same time our use of objects is explained entirely by the human attempt to achieve human ends, and not by the unavoidable need to adapt ourselves to the objects around us, whose very existence, as such, requires we enter into relationships with them largely on their terms and not ours. Thus, no matter what the Paleolithic hand ax maker may have wished they would never succeed in turning a rock into a hand ax, or later into an arrow head simply by looking at it, or stroking it in a kindly manner, or talking to it gently or soaking it in water overnight. They could only achieve their ends by working the rock in the specific ways the constitution of the rock permitted, a technique that would have been demonstrated by a mentor or that they would have discovered on their own through trial and error, knowledge which in either case would be based on experience with rocks, that is on interaction with them.

These observations are made more interesting when we consider that we really do not know what objects are independently of our interaction with them. This in no way signifies that objects have no meaning or significance aside from what we give to them as we integrate them into our worlds, as some Euro-centric philosophers have asserted. There is something there transcending our interaction with the object that makes our interaction possible by the bare fact of its existence. However, what we know of things is not the result of our mind's construction of sensory intuitions presented by them, as Kant

188   BEING-IN-AMERICA: WHITE SUPREMACY AND THE AMERICAN

had it, but the product of our interaction with them, which also produces our selves. The relationship between ax maker and rock produces both rock and humanbeing. Objects have *assertorial* agency as opposed to *willful* agency. Their agency is apodictically demonstrated by the sheer fact of their existence.

This statement seems to make no sense if we consider that objects are unable to avoid being used by us while we are free to use them or not to use them, even if not doing so would greatly inconvenience us or even end our existence. This seems undeniably true. Though the ax maker is forced to use the stone in a manner consistent with its properties the stone can never avoid being used. Where then is its agency? All this means, however, is that objects do not have human agency. They are not human beings. They cannot escape being used by us but neither can we escape dependence on them, and it is that dependence, rather than the object's ability to move under its own power that is its agency.

In other words, the agency of objects is a function of our dependence on them, which is, in turn, a fundamental structure of humanbeing. Another way of formulating this statement is to say that humanbeing is structured by its fundamental engagement with the objects amidst which it always and already finds itself. In fact, humanbeing consists in relationships with objects, other life forms and itself in that humanbeing occurs, and only occurs in relationship to them. Human consciousness emerges in, is directed towards, shaped by and understands itself in terms of those relationships. Humanbeing is what occurs when a human becomes aware of those relationships objectively, which, normally, in everyday life, takes the form of recognizing something as external to the self without cognizing a relationship in a formal sense at all. Thus, to be aware of the furniture in one's home and the need to walk around sofas, chairs and tables is an expression of relationships whether or not they are recognized and conceptualized as such.

When my son reacted to his fall by blaming the chair he was responding to objects the way we all do until we are taught otherwise. As we all do, my son soon learned to regard objects as nothing more than things for our use or obstacles in our way. Under the guidance of adults and the prodding of other children we come to assimilate to ourselves all responsibility for our encounters with objects. Those who do not are regarded as immature, odd, even mentally and emotionally disturbed. No doubt our world loses something of the enchantment of childhood once we mature in this way. In return we augment enormously the autonomy, and thus, the aggressive power of the self by making it solely responsible for all of its interaction with objects, except for those

THE AGENCY OF OBJECTS   189

accidental encounters that no one could avoid, such as a brick falling from the tenth story of a building and striking the unsuspecting pedestrian on the head. Even in such circumstances we look for a human agent to hold responsible, the carelessness of a building inspector, perhaps. In our normal interaction with things, sole responsibility is attributed to people, a way of being that strengthens the notion the self is free to determine its actions with the physical world. This emancipation places the physical world at the disposal of the self as a factor that need not be considered in any determination of the causes of one's actions. Nor need we trouble ourselves with an object's wishes in considering using it for a particular purpose. We can simply regard it as a natural or human made resource. Once again, we find the tactic of narrowing at work. By narrowing responsibility for almost any outcome involving our interaction with objects we drain spiritual power from objects and absorb it into ourselves. The result is a far more powerful self and a seemingly far less powerful, interesting and consequential object. Narrowing agency to volitional acts obscures the impact of objects on us in shaping our existence, and our impact on objects, hence, on the earth. But obscuring those impacts does not remove or diminish them. It simply makes it harder for us to address them, thereby fomenting ecological disaster.

These ruminations led to another surprising consideration. One consequence of our unavoidable interaction with objects, including our own bodies, is being compelled to act as their nature dictates. Neither objects nor our own bodies allow us to do two things at the same time or to achieve our ends all at once. To make a hand ax we must chip a core. To gain muscle mass we must lift weights. Both activities can only be done incrementally, never all at once. In other words, our relationships with objects entail duration. Objects, including the body, do not allow simultaneity. If I stub my toe the impulse must travel along my nerve pathways before it reaches the brain, so there is always a moment's interval between the impact and the occurrence of pain. Duration is not a human creation. It is imposed on human beings by the nature of the object world. The resistance of objects to our attempted use of them creates temporality. Temporality occurs when human beings interact with objects. In other words, temporality is the manifestation of relational resistance.

But since human beings are always-already in relationship to objects temporality always-already exists. There is an obvious objection to this proposition. Granting our interaction with objects involves doing one thing after another and forbids us doing everything simultaneously, why do we experience this as duration? It would seem duration requires a prior sense of temporality.

However, the problem is resolved when we consider that we are always and already in relationship with objects from conception, that there is no a priori state, because there is no state when we are not interacting with objects. This perpetual relation is what creates temporality, not the interaction with specific objects. We come into the world as temporal beings. Kant was right in positing time and space as a priori categories through which the mind apprehends the world. However, he was wrong in assuming that because they were a priori they were not based on experience. He neglected the always-already existing relationship between humans and objects that begins with conception and never ends. Even in our prenatal state we are interacting with our body and our mother's body. As a result, we are temporal before birth.[2] Everything we experience from that moment on reinforces our temporality. One might object that this only pushes the problem back before birth, rather than explains where the notion of temporality comes from. My response is that the sense of duration, the feeling that "time" is passing, and the sense of space, which is the recognition that I am not something, is produced by our interaction with objects, and both exist in some manner prior to birth, because we are in relationship with objects from conception, even in our most biologically simple state prior to self-consciousness as we know it. Duration is what it feels like to interact with objects.

Finally, their resistance raises the question of what we are. Interaction with objects is what led to our discovery of ourselves as something apart from them, as observers, and even to imagine objective observation.

I began to think I had found the missing being I was relating to. It was none other than the object, the entire material world, including our bodies in which we are always-already-and-unavoidably-embedded. There has never been a moment in my life, from conception, in which they are or could be absent. They are with me intimately, incessantly, a relationship even death cannot destroy, at least in regard to my body. It can be said in very truth that objects give meaning to us.

Notes

1   First published in Epoch Magazine, Issue #34, September 2020.
2   This raises the significant question of what the nature of this "we" is and how it arises, which goes beyond the scope of this work, and is the subject of a work in preparation.

· 3 0 ·

THE WHITE SUPREMACIST COLLECTIVE UNCONSCIOUS

White supremacy is a fundamental and unavoidable structural dynamic of the American self. White supremacy is not an unfortunate flaw in the otherwise sound practice of American freedom and individual liberty, to be removed through mitigating policies, not even by the end of discrimination. Rather, white supremacy plays a fundamental ontological function in America by structuring the concept and practice of individual autonomy. While it exists in intensified form in white Americans, white supremacist mentality is not limited to them. In varying degrees, all Americans are endowed with a virtually unalienable *white supremacist collective unconscious* (WSCU) that supports and is supported by autonomous individualism. Our endowment is not the work of Jefferson's "Laws of Nature" or "Nature's God". It is the historical and ongoing consequence of acquiring and sustaining the American variety of individual autonomy on which our society and culture are founded. As illustrated by continued resistance to restrictive gun laws in the face of the frequent mass slaughter of children, individual autonomy is the nation's highest value, above life itself, to which each of us is taught to aspire by example and precept as we grow from birth into adulthood. Autonomous individualism, as currently practiced in America, and white supremacy are inseparable, mutually defining and sustaining ontological dynamics of *humanbeing* in America.

Thus, as powerful a personage as a United States Senator recently denied that white nationalists are racists: "My opinion of a white nationalist, if someone wants to call them white nationalist," said Senator Tommy Tuberville, Republican of Alabama, "to me, is an American. It's an American. Now, if that white nationalist is a racist, I'm totally against anything that they want to do, because I am 110% against racism." [1] Under pressure from the media and Republican colleagues Tuberville later modified his stance, seeming to concede that white nationalists are racists, but his original statement and even his clarification, reveal the connection between white supremacy and our current style of American individual autonomy.[2]

It is my contention that white supremacy cannot be rooted out without making fundamental changes to our practice and concept of personhood. Efforts and policies that avoid this difficult task because it is not politically expedient, or is felt to be culturally and emotionally unpalatable, are affirmed as practical and savvy, but they have fallen short of dislodging white supremacy. When they originate, either directly or by proxy, from the white leadership of American institutions they are directed, consciously, or by what I will describe as the *white supremacist collective unconscious*, to preventing any such alterations. This is the underlying, albeit, normally unconscious, because *held-off*, strategic thrust of the "diversity and inclusion" movement, despite its incidental benefits to those Americans who are now arbitrarily called "people of color", with or without their consent.

The ontological function of white supremacy is obscured by limiting the concept to far right racists. Such narrowing is a reflex action by the *white supremacist collective unconscious* in defense of white supremacy. Fundamentally, white supremacy is the hegemonic position of white people in American society, whether they are of the right, left or center, so that one can be a liberal white supremacist, a moderate white supremacist or an extreme right white supremacist. Identifying white supremacy with its extreme manifestations misses its ontological significance. It is the hegemonic position of whites in America that ensures and enables the hegemony of their ideas, ideals and values, including our prevailing fundamental conceptions of the self, its limits or horizons, the natural and object worlds, and standards of beauty, personal responsibility and social obligations that shape the conscious and unconscious life of all Americans to one degree or another, regardless of their race or ethnicity. While it is possible to choose to become aware of and struggle against white supremacy and *the white supremacist collective unconscious*, white supremacy itself is a structural, not an elective problem.

For over fifty years, historians have argued in varying degrees, that white American racism developed as a justification for the genocide of Native Americans and the enslavement and continued oppression of black people.[3] Most recently Ibram X. Kendi asserted that "Time and again, racist ideas have not been cooked up from the boiling pot of ignorance and hate. Time and again, powerful and brilliant men and women have produced racist ideas in order to justify the racist policies of their era, in order to redirect the blame for their era's racial disparities away from those policies and onto black people."[4] It is certain that racism and white supremacy rose hand in hand with Native removal, slavery and the slave trade and supplied powerful rationales for those developments. However, viewing white supremacy as a rationale for the genocidal treatment of Native Americans and black slavery begs an important question. Why was there a need for new justifications for taking land from its possessors and enslaving people? Wars of conquest have occurred since antiquity and slavery was a nearly universal and normal practice. As David Brion Davis has shown, neither needed much justification other than the prerogative of the stronger, until relatively recent times.[5] Also, white supremacy emerged as well in European countries such as Portugal, Spain, France, Britain, and Holland, which, with the exception of Portugal and Spain, had negligible black populations. All of those countries, however, were engaged in empire building in the Americas and Asia and slave trading in Africa. On the other hand, only an extremely small number of their subjects came into direct contact with Africans, Asians or Native Americans either at home or abroad. That does not mean they were not exposed to images of black people. As Winthrop Jordan demonstrated in the late 1960s, pejorative images of blacks can be found in Elizabethan England, where whiteness was coming to be configured as the symbol of the utmost purity in contrast to black as symbolic of filth, sexuality and savagery.[6] Audiences and readers of Shakespeare's plays would have encountered them in *Othello, Titus Andronicus* and *The Tempest.* Travel literature, which became popular in early modern Europe in consequence of European voyages of discovery, introduced Europeans to images and descriptions of colored others. Early on these depictions could be favorable, but they "darkened" as European technological and military power waxed.[7] Yet, as Bernard Porter has demonstrated in the case of England, popular awareness of empire was limited to a tiny handful before the era of high imperialism in the late nineteenth century.[8] Nevertheless, white supremacist ideas emerged in Western Europe, and were embedded in the evangelical and popular abolitionist movements from the late eighteenth century.[9] White supremacy was

194   BEING-IN-AMERICA: WHITE SUPREMACY AND THE AMERICAN

transcultural and transnational serving multiple purposes across different regions. It did not have the same origin or intentions in Europe as in America but it filled an overriding need in both, connected with the fact that there was something different about European colonialism, including American colonization and imperialism that did require justification.

That difference was the invention of the modern self, characterized by what C. B. McPherson called "possessive individualism", and the kind of radical interiority represented by Rousseau's *Confessions* and *Julie*, Richardson's *Clarissa*, and later by Goethe's, *The Sorrows of Young Werther*. [10] Long ago Ian Watt defined this new self in terms that are still useful:

> In all ages, no doubt, and in all societies, some people have been "individualists" in the sense that they were egocentric, unique or conspicuously independent of current opinions and habits; but the concept of individualism involves much more than this. It posits a whole society mainly governed by the idea of every individual's intrinsic independence both from other individuals and from that multifarious allegiance to past modes of thought and action denoted by the word "tradition"-a force that is always social, not individual.[11]

This new kind of self began to emerge during the eighteenth century, quite significantly, as Europeans were expanding seaborne and land based empires overseas and transforming their communally and locally oriented kingdoms into market based polities organized for military and commercial competition with comparably powerful rivals. Reflecting its late medieval and early modern roots, the premise of this newly forming self was its creation by a god that endowed it with self-possession and the liberty to maintain itself in the world.[12] This idea was the basis of John Locke's theory of property that asserted the self's liberty in the state of nature to use its labor to remove resources it needed to survive from the natural world, while the act of mixing its labor with them gave the self ownership of the fruits of its labor by the law of reason.[13] The right of self possession distinguished the new self from its predecessors. For this emerging self the liberty to act on its own behalf, informed by its own judgment, became the cardinal value, the foundation of self-preservation and self-crafting, because it conveyed the means of appropriating and keeping natural resources, and by extension developing the world. Whatever may have been its theoretical resonance, in the context of American conquest, colonization and development, liberty had concrete significance. It meant the freedom to take and keep Native lands, enslave Africans and exploit the environment. At the same time, the equation of liberty with "man's" natural state,

THE WHITE SUPREMACIST COLLECTIVE UNCONSCIOUS 195

the proposition that all humans are equal and free in the "state of nature", whether it was Hobbes brutal or Locke's benign condition, problematized the hitherto unproblematic practice of conquest and enslavement. If all humans were originally free and equal in the state of nature, theoretical, if not necessarily practical consistency called for some explanation for why it was permissible to conquer and enslave some of them. Of course, that did not mean that both practices could not occur without racist rationales but it made the invention of racist justifications more likely in the context of the New World. As Winthrop Jordan argued over fifty-five years ago, there appears to have been,

> a mutual relationship between slavery and unfavorable assessment of Negroes. Rather than slavery causing "prejudice," or vice versa, they seem rather to have generated each other. Both were, after all, twin aspects of a general debasement of the Negro. Slavery and "prejudice" may have been equally cause and effect, continuously reacting upon each other, dynamically joining hands to hustle the Negro down the road to complete degradation.[14]

Moreover, racism and white supremacy, emerging concurrently with the invention of the autonomous self served another less easily recognizable purpose. They filled a vacuum created by the socio-cultural-psychological conditions of autonomy. In other words, in addition to justifying racial oppression they performed an essential ontological function in Europe and America that was not and is not *directly* reducible to racial oppression.

The breakdown of communal society in early modern times, including the diminishing importance of the extended family and clan, the restriction of the power and authority of guilds and other collectivist modes of being, and what Max Weber called "the disenchantment of the world", symbolized by the Enlightenment's assault on superstition and religion and its emphasis on the use of reason as the guide and moderator of the passions, freed the self from many constraints on the development of autonomy as we know it.[15] Reason replaced an increasingly distant god and "His" church as the moral compass for a new kind of self. Or rather, reason was proclaimed as an ideal guide, but as Johnathan Israel has argued, not for the common person.[16]

In "the beginning", wrote John Locke, "all the world was America, and more so than that is now".[17] Like Robinson Crusoe's Island, New Worlds offered ideal laboratories for creating novel varieties of societies based on a radical kind of individual autonomy that elevated the freedom of white males to pursue their ambition and happiness above the collective welfare of society; an autonomy premised on the extirpation of Native Americans from the land

and the enslavement of black people, an autonomy based on racial oppression, albeit under the governance of a watchful god. But even God had become an autonomous individual, no longer accessible through a corporate hierarchy of clergy, monks and saints. Like other individuals he was now an agent one must establish a personal relationship with, which if achieved secured a powerful personal defender, vindicator and champion. Yet despite Crusoe's professions of gratitude to divine providence for his many salvations, his new world experiences suggested that a "man" might become "his" own god, if "he" could acquire sufficient land and people that could be cast as permanent tools, available like things for "his" own uses.[18]

New Worlds offered the chance to develop radical kinds of societies empowered by the unchecked exploitation of nature and varieties of other human beings defined as inherently inferior, and therefore lying outside of the social contract that Charles Mills appropriately called the Racial Contract.[19] Crusoe did just that on his island. Yet the price he paid for rejecting traditional social authority and modes of being in exchange for the liberty required to create modern white supremacist individual autonomy, hand in hand with the colonial development that empowered it, was isolation from other civilized people.[20] As if in punishment for its hubris, the new freedom left the self alone in Newton's mechanized universe with no solid ground to stand on. The situation demanded another ground from which to perform *humanbeing* to replace the old communally based foundation that was disintegrating underfoot. It was found in a radically new concept of human difference that defined the individual in terms of its connection to a racially restricted category of other selves united in the "pursuit of happiness", which in America became the conspiracy of happiness, as whites collaborated against Natives and blacks in pursuit of their own self and collective interests.

Amidst the radical transformations in society and culture between the sixteenth and nineteenth centuries, the body remained an indisputably verifiable fact. It became the premise of the new foundation: Race. Unlike specific religious beliefs and philosophical doctrines, the body was an unavoidable, universally occurring, material reality that could be appropriated, disciplined and forced to labor in the removal of resources from nature and their transformation into commodities and other forms of private property. Thus, slaves, as one species of property, helped to create other species of property that could be held as commodities or transformed into the imperishable medium of money and stored or invested.[21] The consumption of black bodies in the killing work of exploitative plantation agriculture, in order to absorb the power that their

THE WHITE SUPREMACIST COLLECTIVE UNCONSCIOUS 197

blood, sweat and deaths generated was echoed in *Robinson Crusoe* as the terror of cannibals, the psychic projection onto the black other of what the English were actually doing in the seventeenth-century Caribbean, and thus an early manifestation of the *white supremacist collective unconscious*.[22]

The physical differences between bodies, observed by Europeans in their voyages throughout the world, became the means of classifying humanity into a system that put white westerners at the pinnacle, blacks at the bottom and the rest of humanity in between.[23] While this bio-racist construct certainly helped to justify the enslavement and oppression of darker people and the theft of their allegedly unproductive land, it also became the basis for an otherwise foundationless self which could now stand on the solid ground of a particular racial group, each with its own inherent mental, emotional and intellectual attributes firmly rooted in biology, and with its own historical trajectory. Moreover, the invention of biologically based race had the further benefit of freeing the self from reliance on the constraining effects of religious foundations that had continued to act as stopgap measures, which could become purely elective modes of strengthening the stability of the self without interfering with its new found radical autonomy.

While such localities as family, clan and village were insufficient foundations for a self that aspired to limitless development and universal sovereignty, the invention of the white race, whose supposed inherent virtues, particularly devotion to liberty which it elevated into the supreme value, would prove a secure platform from which to launch the project of individual autonomy. That project was limited from the start to white men, whose love of liberty justified their claim to racial superiority while their racial superiority was demonstrated by their love of liberty, which meant that they possessed the rational ability and moral aptitude to perceive, defend and cultivate the freedom necessary for autonomous interior life and its outward expression in deeds. Liberty and individual autonomy became codependent variables. Enslaved people were obviously inferior because they were unfree, just as unemployed blacks in contemporary America are imagined as inferior because they lack the freedom gainful employment conveys. The very fact of unfreedom came to indicate the absence of authentic humanity, and was used in turn to justify racial oppression. From the beginning, white supremacy became an indispensable support for individual autonomy, *holding-off* awareness of how the commissions and omissions of autonomous selves harmed and even extinguished Native and black peoples. The sacredness of individual freedom became the freedom to act and think with no regard for those *non-white* people one's actions and thoughts harmed, and helped to conceal or trivialize the harms done to them. It is because this "right" to ignore is challenged by "people of color" and LGBTQ communities that critical race theory, affirmative action, diversity and inclusion, gender affirming health care and discussions of sexuality and gender in public schools are under attack by white supremacist conservatives who long for the good old days when they could do and say as they pleased without provoking irritating criticism from those affected and their sympathizers; which illustrates a simple fact: The ability to ignore the deleterious, even lethal impact of white supremacist individual autonomy on those others, is the precondition for individual autonomy as it has existed in America.

While the power and self righteousness generated by the newly invented inwardness of the self provided the moral force for empire building in the Americas, Asia and Africa, that same interiority became a crucial bulwark of white difference in the context of a world of bodies, for there was nothing inherent in European or American bodies to mark them superior to those of Africans, Asians or other "others." White exceptionalism came to be defined by their alleged endowment with a unique mental, emotional and spiritual life that allowed them to feel, think and act from the inside out, while the rest of humankind responded to the external pressures and constraints of nature, custom, tradition, the tyranny of the collectivities they lived within or the compulsion of ruthless rulers.[24] By contrast, civilized Europeans and Euro-Americans supposedly ruled themselves, to a greater or lesser degree, by the use of reason directed at best by what Kant styled a "good will", acting in freedom from contingent considerations, or, more practically, guided by what Adam Smith thought was the collective good sense of community experience, which in practice meant white experience.[25] It was "man's" ability to think "I", signaling "his" reflexivity, and "his" faculty of understanding, asserted Immanuel Kant, that "raises him infinitely above all other living beings on earth…an entirely different being from *things*, such as irrational animals, with which one can do as one likes."[26] The soul of the savage man "dwells only in the sensation of its present existence," proclaimed Rousseau in A *Discourse on Inequality*, "without any idea of the future, however close that might be, and his projects, as limited as his horizons, hardly extend to the end of the day", an opinion which Kant repeated in his anthropology.[27] Circumscribed by his absorption in the physical, the savage's instincts were as well developed as an animal's: "the Hottentots of the Cape of Good Hope see ships on the high seas with the naked eye from the same distance that the Dutch see with their telescopes", Rousseau asserted, while "the American savages scent Spaniards

THE WHITE SUPREMACIST COLLECTIVE UNCONSCIOUS   199

on the trail as well as do the best dogs".[28] However, to act virtuously the mind must be independent of the senses: "Man is free in his actions", he argued in *Emile*, "and as such animated by an immaterial substance", a capacity that assumed the kind of radical interiority, reflexivity, and ability to rise above the physical that the uncivilized *non-white* lacked.[29] Rousseau's white supremacist perceptions illustrate the crucial value of race as the foundation of "civilized" "white" identity and the notion of historical development that affirmed and supported it.

The cultural historian, Dror Wahrman brilliantly argues that the last two decades of the eighteenth century witnessed the rapid collapse of what he calls the "Ancien Régime of Identity", marked by the predominance of "identicality", by which individual identity was defined by what individuals shared in common, and the transition "to identity as that quintessential uniqueness that separates a person from all others."[30] Now, "identity-as-self, innate and even congenital, was supposedly stamped on each and every individual."[31] At the same time, prevailing notions of gender, race and class, which had been relatively fluid, rapidly hardened into fixed and immutable categories. Though Wahrman argues that "in the new regime of the late eighteenth century, gender, race, and class were not understood primarily as collective categories, but as individual traits stamped on every person", he believes that the tension between the claims of individual uniqueness and "the essentializing categories" of race, sex and class became "an inescapable aspect of modern notions of identity."[32] However, from the perspective that I am elaborating, the relationship between identity as individual uniqueness and the category of race was one of complementarity that made possible the production of the white supremacist collective unconscious.

The invention of the white race created the allegedly unified group of "white" people who, although unique in their individual selves, were collectively subjected to an identicality defined by their membership in the race. The emergence of modern "white" self-identity, characterized by individual uniqueness, at the same moment that race was hardening into an immutable category, whether an intentional, or a fortuitous conjunction, was a fortunate development that allowed for the safe cultivation of individual autonomy by placing a horizon around it. Collective racial identity made it possible for the members of the "white" race to imagine, possess and cultivate a shared radical interiority, which, because they excluded all "people of color from it", protected them from the need to make or act on the assumption that all people were endowed with interior lives similar to their own. Such an assumption would have made it more difficult to justify and conduct the oppression of Indigenous, African, Asian and other "people of color" globally, and did make it more difficult whenever the recognition of similarity was brought home, as in the campaign to abolish the slave trade and the American Civil Rights Movement. As it was, their shared racialized interiority allowed whites to mobilize their emotional, mental, intellectual and spiritual lives against Native and African Americans, analogously to the way their mobilization of laws and military/police power was deployed to control their bodies.

Interiority also shifted the criteria of identity and culpability from one's actions in the world, and their consequences, to one's inner motivation and intent. It is not what I do only but also, and sometimes primarily, what I *am* inside, which is heavily configured on the basis of whiteness, and the intent of my behavior, that defines who I am and the degree of my responsibility for the consequences of my behavior. Though I bear some responsibility for harm to others, the degree of my responsibility may be mitigated, and in some cases determined, by my intent. In this sense, the valuation of interior motivation became an aid to American colonization and European colonialism and imperialism. So far as they did not intentionally communicate smallpox and other pandemic diseases to Native Americans, for example, white colonists could not be accused, either in their own consciences or by others, of responsibility for the pandemics that wiped out vast numbers of East Coast Native Americans, in some areas to the tune of 90%, whereas, if we focus on the consequences of their actions alone, they may be accused of genocide.[33] Accordingly, the men and women who crusaded against the British slave trade worked to shift the public's consciousness from their seeming innocence in perpetrating the horrors of the trade, because they were not directly involved, to the consequences of their purchase of slave grown sugar, or their passivity in allowing other Englishmen to trade in slaves while protected in their property by British laws and customs.[34] In other words, those humanitarian movements worked to shift focus from interior intent to outward action, in a sense working against the new interiority, while simultaneously motivated by it.

But the discovery of interiority had tremendous positive benefits which could not be limited to whites. As my struggles over stuttering reveal, my experience of an inner self that differed from the external image of me was empowering. It has been empowering to generations of "people of color" struggling against white supremacy. As I suggested above, it could provide leverage for the attack on slavery and racial oppression by arguing that blacks, Asians and other *nonwhite* people shared similar emotions, sentiments, thoughts and

THE WHITE SUPREMACIST COLLECTIVE UNCONSCIOUS 201

aspirations with whites, despite differences in skin color, and physiognomy, thus weakening the racial horizon. Such early artistic works as Shakespeare's *Othello*, and Aphra Behn's *Oroonoko: or, the Royal Slave* depicted the thoughts and emotions of blacks in dramatic form, thus representing the potential disruptive power of interior similitude.[35]

Just as the shift to identity as unique and inward was occurring, the potential for spontaneous or imaginatively generated sympathy was augmented by a group of thinkers who advanced the view that human beings were naturally sociable and innately moral.[36] Arguing in opposition to Hobbes gloomy view of human nature in *The Leviathan*, the Earl of Shaftesbury asserted that sociability "was a basic human instinct".[37] His ideas inspired Francis Hutcheson, who influenced Adam Smith and the Scottish School of moral philosophers, as well as Immanuel Kant.[38] The new philosophers proposed a capacity for human elective affinities capable of operating beyond the horizons of kith and kin, claiming that even without a god all "men" had a natural disposition to perceive and pursue good.[39] While Hutcheson found benevolence innately installed in human beings, Adam Smith argued that all "men" were capable of sympathetic understanding of their fellow humans by the exercise of imagination, an active process by which anyone could put "himself" in the place of another. "As we have no immediate experience of what other men feel", he wrote in the *Theory of Moral Sentiments*, "we can form no idea of the manner in which they are affected, but by conceiving what we ourselves should feel in the like situation…By the imagination we place ourselves in his situation…we enter as it were into his body, and become in some measure the same person with him".[40] By the power of imagination we could discover or create what Smith called "fellow-feeling" with other people.[41] The effect of this active *connectivity*[42] would be to broaden affinity horizons.

In addition to their domestic roots, sympathy and benevolence responded to the European and Euro-American encounter with a world of alien others since the fifteenth century. It was the context of that encounter that allowed Adam Smith to proclaim in universal terms that mankind "have a very strong sense of the injuries that are done to another. The villain in a tragedy or romance, is as much the object of our indignation as the hero is that of our sympathy and affection", and to illustrate his point by a reference to Shakespeare: "We detest Iago as much as we esteem Othello; and delight as much in the punishment of the one, as we are grieved at the distress of the other."[43] Smith relied on his audience's familiarity with Blackamoors, at least in literature and on the stage, and their ability to transcend religious, racial and ethnic boundaries to identify with one of them, to make his point. But if left unrestrained and unchanneled that same ability could unsettle and jeopardize the project of global white supremacy in the age of competitive empires, and even undermine the notion of a unique western self. Once again, Winthrop Jordan's seminal work emphasizes the crucial *difference* that race made. Citing a 1651 statement by the Reverend Mr. Cotton of the Massachusetts Bay Colony, wherein he indicated that the Scots that Cromwell sent to them have not "been sold for slaves to perpetuall servitude, but for 6 or 7 or 8 yeares, as we do our owne" and that they were doing all they could "to make their yoke easy", Jordon sums up: "Here was the nub: captive Scots were men "as our own." Negroes were not."[44] By 1680 the English colonists were referring to themselves as white and slaves as black, or Negroes or Africans.[45] By foreclosing understanding of and fellow feeling for "people of color" the invention of the white race, even if only a fortuitous, or perhaps, an overdetermined event, provided an effective means of sealing sympathetic horizons, thereby creating a vast human reservoir of potential victims for western exploitation that could be tapped without disturbing consciences, provoking sustained widespread domestic opposition to their inhuman treatment, or even awareness that any harm was being done. On the contrary, henceforth, the burden would be upon those who struggled to combat such inhumanities as the slave trade, slavery, imperialism, the atrocities in the Belgian Congo, American apartheid and the Vietnam War, to prove the humanity and worthiness of the victims of those horrors. Race became the horizon within which sympathy could be restricted to "our own" and denied to those others, thereby making it possible to safely pursue the cultivation of the new kind of individual identity, with its radical interiority, without granting it to people who fell outside of Charles Mills "racial contract."[46] At the same time, race served as a convenient barrier to self-discovery because it identified what white people were and were not, inherently, thus obviating the need for critical interrogation of individual or collective identities. In short, race closed affinity horizons, and forestalled introspection, without seeming to do anything at all. Most of the work of this self and collective ontological structuring was and is performed by what I have styled *the white supremacist collective unconscious*, which in America is reified and powerfully active in the ghostly juridical presence of the Founding Fathers, who, when revitalized and empowered by a conservative Supreme Court majority, defend white supremacy through the pernicious doctrine of Original Intent.

THE WHITE SUPREMACIST COLLECTIVE UNCONSCIOUS 203

The founding of America was premised on the removal of Native Americans from their land and the enslavement of black people, which the Constitution supported. Thus, the nation began by producing a category of people whose welfare and humanity could be completely ignored, provided they accepted their subjugation. The fact that they never did, but attacked and rebelled, ran away and resisted and fought in every way possible to overturn or at least modify the hegemonic regime of white supremacy, is the source of white paranoia about "colored" enemies that continues to grip the nation, illustrated by every white supremacist, whether white, black, Asian, Hispanic or other who goes on a shooting spree targeting *nonwhites*. The fear expressed by supporters of Donald Trump is that their freedom to control those others is being eroded. Of course, they do not see it as freedom to control, but as freedom to act and think as they wish, just as Senator Tuberville regarded white nationalists as just Americans, rather than racists-in short, the *conspiracy of happiness*. But, for the most part, to act and think as they wish, in the context of an ethnically diverse America, means being empowered to ignore the welfare of "people of color." For the followers of Donald Trump, Governor DeSantis and their variety, the seeming loss of that empowerment, weakened by the "special pleading" of minorities, women, LGBTQ constituencies and the invasion of darker immigrants who insist on not being ignored is why America is no longer great.

The recent controversy over Jason Aldean's music video "Try That in a Small Town" illustrates this point. Aldean filmed his video, in which he rails against unidentified evildoers, in the context of news clips of protests, flag burnings, and riots, against the backdrop of the Maury County Courthouse in Tennessee. This was the site where Henry Choate, an 18-year-old black man, was severely beaten and lynched from a window of the building in 1927. He had been falsely accused of raping a white girl. Aldean was criticized for seeming to condone lynching and vigilante justice. His response is representative of white denial when it comes to race, by shifting to the ground of individual autonomy:

> I feel everybody's entitled to their opinion. You can think something all you want to, it doesn't mean it's true. What I am is a proud American... I love our country. I want to see it restored to what it once was before all this bullshit started happening to us. I love my country. I love my family. And I will do anything to protect that

Aldean told the crowd chanting "USA! USA!"[47] Confronted with the suggestive and callous background image of the courthouse where a black man

204   BEING-IN-AMERICA: WHITE SUPREMACY AND THE AMERICAN

had been lynched, Aldean's shift response claimed innocence: "There is not a single lyric in the song that references race or points to it", The New York Times quoted him as saying "—and while I can try and respect others to have their own interpretation of a song with music—this one goes too far."[48]

Aldean's expression "all this bullshit" means precisely all of those others refusing to be demonized, abused and oppressed. His refusal to acknowledge the symbolism of lynching, glaringly represented by the courthouse is the WSCU on full display. The border wall is the grandest symbol and concrete manifestation of this paranoia at the resistance of "people of color" to white supremacy. Fear of the "colored" other is the origin of *the white supremacist collective unconscious*.

In excavating the white supremacist collective unconscious, it will be helpful to begin with the concept of the collective unconscious proposed by Carl Jung in the 1930s. In his essay "The Personal and the collective (Or Transpersonal) Unconscious" Jung theorized that the unconscious "contains, as it were, two layers: the personal and the collective. The personal layer ends at the earliest memories of infancy, but the collective layer comprises the pre-infantile period, that is, the residues of ancestral life." [49] Jung presented a formal definition in the 1936/37 essay "The Concept of the Collective Unconscious"

> My thesis, then, is as follows: In addition to our immediate consciousness, which is of a thoroughly personal nature and which we believe to be the only empirical psyche… there exists a second psychic system of a collective, universal, and impersonal nature which is identical in all individuals. This collective unconscious does not develop individually but is inherited. It consists of pre-existent forms, the archetypes, *which can only become conscious secondarily* and which give definite form to certain psychic contents.[50]

I have put the words "which can only become conscious secondarily" in italics to emphasize the point that *secondarily* implies interpretive work which, because it makes use of symbolic thought, is always collectively collaborative. So long as that interpretive work is performed by whites there is little risk of their discovering the white supremacist nature of the collective unconscious with which all Americans, and no doubt Europeans, are endowed. Jung, of course, made no such discovery, but found proof of a racialized, biologically based collective unconscious in so-called primitive peoples. Consequently "The man of the past is alive in us today".[51] For Jung, the "man of the past" could be observed among the contemporary Hopi he met in New Mexico and the Kenyan and Ugandan "Negroes" he observed in 1925.[52] Jung maintained that the mind of modern "man" was characterized by individuation and the rational understanding of the world, while the consciousness of "primitive man" was "undifferentiated", and dominated by the collective unconscious.[53] "Archaic man" projected his psychic life onto the world as objective reality, a type of primordial consciousness that modern "men" had evolved beyond, but which remained as a sort of psychic vestigial organ, so that "every civilized human being, whatever his conscious development, is still an archaic man at the deeper levels of his psyche."[54] Moreover, "the supposition that there may also be in psychology a correspondence between ontogenesis and phylogenesis therefore seems justified…it would mean that infantile thinking and dream-thinking are simply a recapitulation of earlier evolutionary stages."[55] For Jung, the mind of "primitive man" represented a lower stage of development than that of the contemporary European.

Jung's characterization of "primitive" people was typical Eurocentric racism, but Frantz Fanon was able to adapt Jung's concept for antiracist and anticolonial analysis. In his 1952 study of psychology and colonization *Black Skin White Masks* Fanon argued that:

> European civilization is characterized by the presence, at the heart of what Jung calls the collective unconscious, of an archetype: an expression of the bad instincts, of the darkness inherent in every ego, of the uncivilized savage, the Negro who slumbers in every white man. And Jung claims to have found in uncivilized peoples the same psychic structure that his diagram portrays. Personally, I think that Jung has deceived himself. Moreover, all the peoples that he has known-whether the Pueblo Indians of Arizona or the Negroes of Kenya in British East Africa-have had more or less traumatic contacts with the white man…Jung locates the collective unconscious in the inherited cerebral matter. But the collective unconscious, without our having to fall back on the genes, is purely and simply the sum of prejudices, myths, collective attitudes of a given group…Jung has confused instinct and habit. In his view, in fact, the collective unconscious is bound up with the cerebral structure, the myths and archetypes are permanent engrams of the race. I hope I have shown that nothing of this sort is the case and that in fact the collective unconscious is cultural, which means acquired.[56]

Fanon's formulation focuses on elements Europeans have forced into their unconscious and associate with the Negro in order to deny their existence in themselves. The Negro created by the European becomes the "symbol of sin. The archetype of the lowest values is represented by the Negro."[57]

206 BEING-IN-AMERICA: WHITE SUPREMACY AND THE AMERICAN

Drawing on Fanon's critique of Jung, we theorize a *white supremacist collective unconscious* as a cultural construction created in a manner similar to Freud's superego. It is also akin to Jung's concept of the Shadow in the sense that it is a blacking out of what the white self does not want to face.[58] Henri Ellenberger describes the shadow as "the sum of those personal characteristics that the individual wishes to hide from the others and from himself."[59] In a formulation reminiscent of Fanon he continues "the shadow can also be projected; then the individual sees his own dark features reflected in another person whom he may choose as a Scapegoat."[60] This ancient tool of self-deception is employed by many whites and demagogic leaders in America today. For example, a recent news poll found that Donald Trump voters believe that racism against whites is a bigger problem than racism against blacks, and similar sentiments were reported by CNN in 2022 and by the Washington Post in 2017. Such beliefs fly directly in the face of historical and contemporary evidence and constitute white projections of their own collective responsibility for anti-black racism onto their victims.[61]

Ellenberger usefully points out that the German word *unbewusstheit*, which he renders as unawareness, is a more appropriate descriptor for Jung's shadow than the Freudian unconscious (*das Unbewusste*): "To unawareness belong those aspects of the world and of oneself that an individual does not see, although he could if he honestly wanted to."[62] Jung explained that "The shadow is a moral problem that challenges the whole ego-personality, for no one can become conscious of the shadow without considerable moral effort. To become conscious of it involves recognizing the dark aspects of the personality as present and real. This act is the essential condition for any kind of self-knowledge, and it therefore, as a rule, meets with considerable resistance."[63]

In America, which has a very different historical trajectory than Jung's Europe, what is suppressed is the collective memory of the horror of white America's genocide of Native Americans, the trauma of black slavery, the racial terror after Reconstruction, the continued oppression of Native Americans and the persistence of Anti-Black, Anti-Hispanic and Anti-Asian racism. In our formulation white Americans do not perceive the white supremacist oppressions they have perpetrated historically and continue to perpetrate because they choose, *autonomically*, to *hold them off*, an action that produces the active *White Supremacist Collective Unconscious* rather than simply unawareness. This *holding-off* is accomplished by the mechanisms I call *forestalling* and *foreclosing*. By *forestalling*, I mean warding off, and refusing to draw out and explore the implications of moods, inklings, intuitions, or

THE WHITE SUPREMACIST COLLECTIVE UNCONSCIOUS 207

nagging, unsettling feelings that might lead to the discovery of the *White Supremacist Collective Unconscious* and possibly to an altered view of black people and of the American racial situation. By *foreclosing*, I mean refusing to explore ideas, evidence, or alternative interpretations that one is fully conscious of. An example of the former would be a white person having an unsettled and inexplicable feeling of guilt when a jury fails to convict a white police officer filmed shooting an unarmed black man ten times who was fleeing from him and claimed he was acting in fear of his life. *Forestalling* would suppress the unsettled feeling instead of exploring its implications, perhaps by projecting negative motivations onto the deceased black man, a maneuver which they could count on the wider white population to support. In the same case, *foreclosing* would come into play when one realized the shooting was murder but stops thinking about it in order to preserve one's peace of mind and avoid protesting.

We all use *forestalling* and *foreclosing* in order to function "normally" in the world, and our everyday uses help to obscure the particular white supremacist uses to which they are put in America. I am arguing that whites deploy those techniques similarly in similar circumstances as if they had made a conscious compact to do so. This helps to explain why, until George Floyd, they normally ignored police killings of unarmed black people. Of course, there is no such conscious agreement. Instead, there is a culturally set psychic reflex that alerts whites to when they should *forestall* and *foreclose* to screen out moods, feelings, ideas and thoughts that would tend to weaken the white cathexis on white superiority and innocence and undermine white supremacy. This reflex is a learned behavior that is assimilated by intuition, example and precept as whites grow into adulthood, just as I learned to be a person from my family, friends and the local groups I lived within, and kept, for the most part, out of conscious thought like Freud's superego. In America it is supported by several hundred years of white supremacist conditioning, traditions and taboos which help obscure its existence. It is further protected by the learned belief that our interior worlds are only connected to others by conscious, voluntary disclosures, rather than being always-already interlinked with those of others by our unavoidable socio-cultural nature. Because the radical interiority of our autonomous way of being is created by concealing and covering up the socio-cultural dimensions of the self, whites acting uniformly about race appear to themselves as having independently arrived at a common view, because they have the intellectual acumen, and emotional maturity, to objectively and fairly assess racially charged situations, which blacks, for example, are constructed as too emotionally unstable and subjective to do. Coincidence of individual views among whites strengthens white solidarity, and is taken to prove that the majority view must be right, so that white supremacist concealing action is enhanced by the uniform behavior it is instrumental in effecting. It is important to understand that when whites act this way, they are not normally, consciously, or even unconsciously, acting to protect white supremacy per se. They act in defense of what they consider "normal" ways of understanding, of living in and of valuing the world. They act in defense of values they hold to be independent of race, ethnicity and, usually, of gender. In short, they act in defense of individual autonomy as they see it, and are typically shocked when anyone tries to connect their behavior to race or white supremacy.

And this is what makes white supremacy so difficult to expose and combat. Unless *their* behavior fits the criteria that *they* define and accept as overtly racist, criteria censored and redacted by the WSCU to protect white supremacy and its codependent American style individual autonomy, whites refuse to perceive or comprehend the connection between their external and internal behavior and white supremacy. This is why most white Americans do not understand how American autonomous individualism underpins white supremacy by permitting inequality between blacks and whites to exist as long as it is not intentionally created, and forecloses policy initiatives, such as Affirmative Action, to remove inequality that could interfere with American individual autonomy. While blacks, who are also committed to some variety of American individual autonomy, are handicapped in proposing effective actions unless they are willing to violate the cannons of autonomous individualism by advocating the preferential treatment of blacks on the basis of race. When they do so their actions are routinely taken as proof of their hostility to individual responsibility and subversive of individual autonomy. In fact, they are elaborating alternative visions of a less destructive, more socially responsible and sustainable kind of individual autonomy, similar to the *socially autonomous* individualism that I present below. In such ways, the struggles of black people for a just, equitable and humane America have modified American autonomous individualism in progressive directions, which is the major reason the conservative right vociferously opposes them.

Amidst attacks on white supremacy, which began immediately upon white colonization of the Americas and have never ceased, the *White supremacist collective unconscious*, which is itself a defensive reaction to those attacks, maintains itself by a collective *cathexis* on whiteness. Webster's Dictionary explains that:

THE WHITE SUPREMACIST COLLECTIVE UNCONSCIOUS 209

> *Cathexis* comes to us by way of New Latin (Latin as used after the medieval period in scientific description or classification) from the Greek word *kathexis*, meaning "holding." It can ultimately be traced back (through *katechein*, meaning "to hold fast, occupy") to the Greek verb *echein*, meaning "to have" or "to hold." [64]

I am using *Cathexis* in the dual sense of holding something fast in mind and that something's occupation of the mind. The white supremacist collective unconscious is an emotional, mental and intellectual fixation on white superiority, and a guarded and willfully unspoken holding on to the belief in white entitlement, the last of which is so indefensible that whites project it onto black people. However, those beliefs have become so unfashionable as a result of decades of social and cultural activism against racial oppression, that vast numbers of whites have suppressed them into an unconscious realm to avoid provoking the anger, criticism and action of black people and progressive whites against them, just the reaction that the country artist Aldean dismissed, significantly in the passive voice, to obscure the anti-black aggression of his performance, as "all this bullshit started happening to us", and to confirm their own positive self-image as freedom loving people. The continued, albeit suppressed, commitment to white supremacy is fixed in the *White Supremacist Collective Unconscious* by constant reinforcement by the overwhelmingly segregated groups that whites live within, in order to produce the desired common mental state. For being white is a mental state and religious faith that informs and justifies white supremacist action. Thus, the WSCU is an actively deployed, constantly repaired and adjusted bulwark against modifying the notion of what the American self is in defense of continued white dominance, a trance-state that gives white people the appearance of uniformity and the opacity and brutal insensitivity that ignores the regular killing of blacks by blacks and the high rates of suicide among Native Americans as black and Native problems, rather than American problems, while promoting opioid abuse among whites as a national crisis. This inward looking whiteness, is a "demonic" condition.

In his study of sin and anxiety, the nineteenth-century Danish philosopher Soren Kierkegaard speaks of the demonic as "inclosing reserve" sealed into itself. Lacking the gradual step by step continuity of normal communication it appears as if from nowhere, as "the sudden".[6566] The purpose of Kierkegaard's demonic inclosing is to escape the self-revelation inseparable from interacting with others. This function is similar to that of the WSCU in forestalling and foreclosing authentic communication with blacks by refusing to confront the tremendous power inequalities inherent in any exchange between blacks and

210   BEING-IN-AMERICA: WHITE SUPREMACY AND THE AMERICAN

whites, while pretending that authentic communication can occur without that admission. This *holding-off* is designed to conceal white supremacy and protect it from criticism. However, in both cases the self cannot avoid betraying itself:

> What the inclosed person conceals in his inclosing reserve can be so terrible that he does not dare utter it, not even to himself, because it is as though by the very utterance he commits a new sin or as though it would tempt him again...What determines whether the phenomenon is demonic is the individual's attitude towards disclosure... He has, that is to say, two wills, one subordinate and impotent that wills revelation and one stronger that wills inclosing reserve, but the fact that this will is the stronger indicates that he is essentially demonic.[67]

Inclosedness allows whites to be and do what they could not openly be and do without contradicting their professed ideals and democratic self-image. White demonic inclosing is the result of whites refusing to face the choices they make to allow blacks to suffer and not to assume responsibility for their plight, and the fear that authentic communication with blacks would expose their sins of omission and commission. But as Kierkegaard argues the demonic cannot keep its secret concealed. "Inclosing reserve is involuntary disclosure. The weaker the individuality is originally, or the more the elasticity of freedom is consumed in the service of inclosing reserve, the more likely the secret will break out at last. The slightest touch, a passing glance, etc. is sufficient".[68] The demonic may reveal itself "as when an insane man betrays his insanity by pointing to another, saying...he is no doubt insane."[69] Here, again, Fanon's argument that the "Negro" created by the European becomes the "symbol of sin" is revealing: "In the degree to which I find in myself something unheard-of, something reprehensible, only one solution remains for me: to get rid of it, to ascribe its origin to someone else."[70] By casting their collective *shadow* onto blacks, whites protect their innocence.

The white supremacist collective unconsciousness is constructed by precept, proscription and lived experience. Once constructed it guides the actions of white people unless they challenge and overrule it. And we must recognize that not overruling it, letting it direct one's actions, is a decision made in bad faith to support a white supremacist political economy that works largely for the benefit of white people, even without their being aware of doing anything at all. Here it is essential to recognize that white supremacist oppression operates not just, or even mainly, by overtly racist acts, but overwhelmingly by acts that *forestall* alternate visions of society and *foreclose* social action that would remove systemic racism and modify American individual autonomy, that is, by acts of omission that ensure the failure to challenge white supremacy. Many whites go against the white supremacist promptings they assimilated as they developed into adulthood. But many do not even know they are there because they are holding them in their unconscious. Here, what I mean by the unconscious is not another place, or division in the mind. It is the result of *holding off* awareness of something(s) or some process(es) so we might concentrate on other things or processes, but being in abeyance does not remove them from one place to another. However, there are degrees of *holding-off* so strong that unawareness becomes deeply unconscious. Nevertheless, it is still possible to bring what is held in the unconscious into conscious focus for critical examination, and that possibility is why whites resist so strenuously discussing white supremacy, greatly preferring such terms as *diversity and inclusion* and *anti-racism*-which do not automatically include all white people as culpable, as white supremacy as I have defined it does-while clinging stubbornly to freedom of thought and emotion in defense of their secluded beliefs and feelings. As long as that collective unconscious, and those racist feelings and thoughts, remain indwelling they are beyond my power of exposing and critiquing them publicly. For whites, who are normally protected by racial social-distancing from the kinds of close interaction and intellectual/emotional exchange with blacks that could possibly provoke soul searching, there are no compelling reasons to admit or challenge the white supremacist collective unconscious. On the contrary there are powerful reasons for keeping it hidden. Often the only way to reveal it is through provocation. The Alabama Christian Movement for Human Rights and the Southern Christian Leadership Conference brilliantly utilized this perception in the Birmingham campaign of 1963 by offering the opportunity for Commissioner of Public Safety Bull Connor and his minions to attack peaceful demonstrators, including children, thus manifesting on the outside what black people knew from experience was always lurking on the inside, but which whites had concealed so effectively from themselves that they could claim they did not know it existed. The demonic explosion of race hatred, televised on the evening news, shocked the country and benefited the Civil Rights Movement.

Notes

1 "Tommy Tuberville, a US Senator in 2023, Has Only Just Come Around to the Idea That White Supremacists Are Racist", Vanity Fair, July 11, 2023. https://www.vanityfair.com/

news/2023/07/tommy-tuberville-military-white-supremacists-racist, accessed on July 11, 2023 at 11:30 pm.

2   "Tuberville's White Nationalism Comments Trigger GOP Uproar", *The Hill*, https://theh ill.com/homenews/senate/4091794-tubervilles-white-nationalism-comments-trigger-gop-uproar/. Accessed on November 7, 2023 at 11:49 pm.

3   There is a large literature on Native American history and anti-Native racism. One can begin with Richard Drinnon, *Facing West: The Metaphysics of Indian-Hating and Empire-Building* (Norman, OK: University of Oklahoma Press, 1997), and Francis Jennings, *The Invasion of America: Indians, Colonialism, and the Cant of Conquest* (Chapel Hill, NC: University of North Carolina Press, 2010). For the origins of anti-black racism see Winthrop Jordan, *White Over Black* (Chapel Hill, NC: University of North Carolina Press, 1968); Thomas S. Gossett, *Race: The History of an Idea in America* (New York: Oxford University Press, 1997); George Fredrickson, *White Supremacy* (New York: Oxford University Press, 1982), *The Black Image in the White Mind* (Middletown, CT: Wesleyan University Press, 1987), *A Short History of Racism* (Princeton, NJ: Princeton University Press, 2003); Edmund Morgan, *American Slavery, American Freedom* (New York: W. W. Norton, 2003), and Ibram X. Kendi, *Stamped from the Beginning, The Definitive History of Racist Ideas in America* (New York: Bold Type Books, 2017).

4   Ibram X. Kendi, *Stamped from the Beginning, The Definitive History of Racist Ideas in America* (New York: Bold Type Books, 2017), 9.

5   See David Brion Davis, *The Problem of Slavery in Western Culture* (Oxford, UK: Oxford University Press, 1966) and *The Problem of Slavery in the Age of Revolution* (Ithaca, NY: Cornell University Press, 1975).

6   Jordan, *White Over Black* 4–11 and passim.

7   There is a large literature on European overseas expansion, but on the shifting nature of popular impressions of Africans and Asians see especially Michael Adas, *Machines as the Measure of Men Science, Technology, and Ideologies of Western Dominance* (Ithaca, NY: Cornell University Press, 1990).

8   Bernard Porter, *The Absent Minded Imperialists, Empire, Society, and Culture in Britain* (Oxford: Oxford University Press, 2004), 164ff. and passim.

9   Ronald Kent Richardson, *Moral Imperium: Afro-Caribbeans and the Transformation of British Rule* (Westport, CT: Praeger Publishers, 1987).

10 C. B. MacPherson, *The Political Theory of Possessive Individualism: Hobbes to Lock* (Oxford: Oxford University Press, 1962).

11 Ian Watt, *The Rise of the Novel* (Berkeley, CA: University of California Press, 2001), 60.

12 Dismissing the primacy of the Renaissance and Enlightenment in fostering the rise of the modern self, Larry Siedentop argues forcefully that modern individualism, liberalism and modernity, defined as a society based on the notion of the equality of individuals, are rooted in Christianity, specifically in the work of fourteenth- and fifteenth-century cannon lawyers, philosophers and theologians. See, Larry Siedentop, *The Creation of the Individual, the Origins of Western Liberalism* (Cambridge, MA: Harvard University Press, 2014), especially 338–40, 352.Siedentop has raised important questions about the provenance of the so-called modern self. His thoughts on the contribution of medieval Christianity to the shaping of the western liberal tradition are compelling.

THE WHITE SUPREMACIST COLLECTIVE UNCONSCIOUS 213

13 John Locke, *Two Treatises of Government, the Works of John Locke*, vol. V (London: Printed for Thomas Tegg; W. Sharpe and Son; G. Offor; G. and J. Robinson; J. Evans and Co., 1823), "Essay Two, Concerning the True Original Extent and End of Civil Government", Chapter V, "Of Property", especially p. 116.

14 Jordan, *White Over Black*, 80.

15 Weber observed that: "The fate of our times is characterized by rationalization and intellectualization and, above all, by the "disenchantment of the world."" Max Weber, "Science as a Vocation", in *From Max Weber*, trans. and ed. H. H. Gerth and C. Wright Mills (New York: Routledge, 2009), 155. For a clarification of Enlightenment ideas on the relationship between reason and the passions see Ritchie Robertson, *The Enlightenment: The Pursuit of Happiness 1680–1790* (New York: HarperCollins, 2020), chapter I.

16 Many adherents of what Israel calls the "moderate Enlightenment" as distinct from the "radical Enlightenment" whose origin he traces to the philosophy of Spinoza, were reluctant to completely cut away the moorings of tradition and authority. These moderate enlighteners "felt that reason is not and should not be the only guide and that a balanced compromise between reason and tradition, or reason and religious authority, is necessary. Some leading proponents of moderate enlightenment such as Voltaire and Hume accorded little or no validity to religious authority as such but nevertheless remained anxious to restrict the scope of reason and retain tradition and ecclesiastical authority, duly clipped, as the primary guides for most people." Jonathan I. Israel, *Democratic Enlightenment, Philosophy, Revolution, and Human Rights 1750–1790* (Oxford, UK: Oxford University Press, 2012), 11; Jonathan Israel, *A Revolution of the Mind: Radical Enlightenment and the Intellectual Origins of Modern Democracy* (Princeton, NJ: Princeton University Press, 2010), 177–80.

17 Locke, *Two Treatises of Government*, 125.

18 Crusoe reveled in his sovereignty over the island and his "subjects": "My island was now peopled, and I thought my self very rich in Subjects: and it was a merry Reflection which I frequently made, How like a King I look'd. First of all, the whole Country was my own mere Property; so that I had an undoubted Right of Dominion. *2dly*, My People were perfectly subjected: I was absolute Lord and Lawgiver". Daniel Defoe, *Robinson Crusoe* (London, UK: MacMillan and Co., 1868), 245. He had found in the New World opportunities nonexistent at home.

19 Mills observes:

> "Henceforth, then, whether openly admitted or not, it is taken for granted that the grand ethical theories propounded in the development of Western moral and political thought are of restricted scope, explicitly or implicitly intended by their proponents to be restricted to persons, whites. The terms of the Racial Contract set the parameters for white morality as a whole, so that competing Lockean and Kantian contractarian theories of natural rights and duties, or later anticontractarian theories such as nineteenth-century utilitarianism, are all limited by its stipulations." Charles Mills, *The Racial Contract* (Ithaca, NY: Cornell University Press, 1997), 17.

214   BEING-IN-AMERICA: WHITE SUPREMACY AND THE AMERICAN

20 Crusoe's rejection of traditional authority is symbolized in the novel by his failure to heed not only his father's injunctions but those of his friend's father as well.

21 Locke provided philosophical justification for money in his second essay on Civil Government. Locke, *Two treatises of Government*, 120-126.

22 Defoe was a defender of the Royal African Company and a promoter of British enterprise in Africa and the Americas. Richard West, *Daniel Defoe, the Life and Strange Surprising Adventures* (New York: Carroll and Graf Publishers, Inc., 1998), 170; William A. Pettigrew, *Freedom's Debt: The Royal African Company and the Politics of the Atlantic Slave Trade, 1672–1752* (Chapel Hill, NC: University of North Carolina Press, 2013); Tsim Keirn, "Daniel Defoe and the Royal African Company", Historical Research, 61, Issue 145 (June 1988): 243–47.

23 Jordan, *White Over Black*, Chapter VI "The Bodies of Men", 253, 253–59, and passim.

24 Ronald Kent Richardson, "Images of Africa in Black and White", paper presented at Harvard University in the W. E. B. Du Bois Colloquium Series, December, 1997.

25 Kant began his *Groundwork of the Metaphysics of Morals* with the assertion that "It is impossible to think of anything at all in the world, or indeed even beyond it, that could be considered good without limitation except a good will." Immanuel Kant, *Groundwork of the Metaphysics of Morals*, ed. Mary Gregor (Cambridge, UK: Cambridge University Press, 1997), 7. He elaborated his influential ideas on self cultivation in several works the most important of which were *Groundwork of the Metaphysics of Morals* (1785), *Critique of Practical Reason* (1788) and *The Metaphysics of Morals* (1797). He did not explicitly limit the ability to cultivate one's humanity to Europeans but to "rational" beings, which, he seems to imply, need not be human beings only, but later stated that "We know of only one species of rational beings on earth; namely the human species." Immanuel Kant, *Anthropology from a Pragmatic Point of View*, ed. Robert B. Louden (Cambridge, UK: Cambridge University Press, 2006), 234. In *The Metaphysics of Morals* Kant suggests that not only is any human being capable of cultivating "his" humanity but has an obligation to do so: "Hence there is also bound up with the end of humanity in our own person the rational will, and so the duty, to make ourselves worthy of humanity by culture in general, by procuring or promoting the *capacity* to realize all sorts of possible ends, so far as this is to be found in a human being himself. In other words, the human being has a duty to cultivate the crude predispositions of his nature, by which the animal is first raised into the human being." p. 154. Kant rejected what became the civilizing mission rationale for taking the land of "crude" peoples such as the "Hottentots", insisting that no settlements may be made without a freely entered contract. This did not prevent European nations and American colonists from doing precisely that. *The Metaphysics of Morals*, pp. 121–22. Smith wrote "Our continual observations upon the conduct of others insensibly lead us to form to ourselves certain general rules concerning what is fit and proper either to be done or to be avoided." In this way our general moral rules are formed. Adam Smith, *The Theory of Moral Sentiments* (Mineola, NY: Dover Publications, Inc., 2006), 153. Smith's view thus contrasts with Kant who argued that in arriving at true maxims for governing our conduct we must avoid all contingent considerations "because a rule is objectively and universally valid only when it holds without the contingent, subjective conditions that distinguish one rational being from another." Immanuel Kant, *The Critique of Practical*

THE WHITE SUPREMACIST COLLECTIVE UNCONSCIOUS 215

Reason, ed. Mary Gregor (Cambridge, UK: Cambridge University Press, 1997), 18. As if replying to Smith, he observed: "Nor could one give worse advice to morality than by wanting to derive it from examples. For, every example of it represented to me must itself first be appraised in accordance with principles of morality, as to whether it is also worthy to serve as an original example…It can by no means authoritatively provide the concept of morality." Kant, *Groundwork,* 21. Of course, Smith is concerned with how we actually arrive at our moral values, while Kant was arguing how we ought to arrive at true maxims for governing our conduct.

26 Kant, *Anthropology,* 15.

27 Jean-Jacques Rousseau, *A Discourse on Inequality* (London, UK: Penguin Books, 1984), 90; Kant, *Anthropology,* 79.

28 Rousseau, *A Discourse on Inequality,* 86–87.

29 Cited in Jerrold Seigel, *The Idea of the Self: Thought and Experience in Western Europe since the Seventeenth Century* (Cambridge, UK: Cambridge University Press, 2005), 216.

30 Dror Wahrman, *The Making of the Modern Self* (New Haven, CT: Yale University Press, 2003), 276; see also Raymond Martin and John Barresi, *Naturalization of the Soul: Self and Personal Identity in the Eighteenth Century* (London, UK: Routledge, 2000), and their study *The Rise and Fall of Soul and Self: An Intellectual History of Personal Identity* (New York: Columbia University Press, 2006).

31 Wahrman, *The Making of the Modern Self,* 278.

32 Idem.

33 Kathleen J. Bragdon, *Native People of Southern New England 1500–1650* (Norman, Ok: University of Oklahoma Press, 1996), 25–28; Francis Jennings, *The Invasion of America, Indians, Colonization, and the Cant of Conquest* (Chapel Hill, NC: The University of North Carolina Press, 1975), 15–33; Neal Salisbury, *Manitou and Providence, Indians, Europeans, and the Making of New England, 1500–1643* (New York: Oxford University Press, 1982), 20–30, 101–8; William Cronon, *Changes in the Land, Indians, Colonists, and the Ecology of New England* (New York: Hill and Wang, 2003), 85–91.

34 Ronald Kent Richardson, *Moral Imperium: Afro-Caribbeans and the Transformation of British Rule, 1776–1838* (Westport, CT: Praeger Publishers, 1987).

35 Such perceptions need not lead to liberationist sentiments. Aphra Behn herself does not appear of have opposed slavery. For Behn see Moira Ferguson, *Subject to Others: British Women Writers and Colonial Slavery, 1670–1834* (London: Routledge, 1992).

36 Israel, *A Revolution of the mind,* 177–80.

37 Robertson, *The Enlightenment,* 264–65, 351.

38 Ibid., 266-67; Seigel, *The Idea of the Self,* 295.

39 Robertson, *The Enlightenment,* 267.

40 Smith, *The Theory of Moral Sentiments,* 3.

41 Smith, Ibid., 5.

42 On my notion of connectivity see below Chapter 31 "The Socially Autonomous Self and Anticipatory Connectivity".

43 Smith, Ibid, 31.

44 Jordan, *White Over Black,* 88.

45 Ibid, 95.

46 Mills, *The Racial Contract*, 17.

47 Jason Aldean Rails Against "Cancel Culture," Defends His Vigilante Anthem as Concert Crowd Chants "USA!", https://www.aol.com/entertainment/jason-aldean-rails-against-cancel-193800384.html 7:59 pm.

48 *The History of the Lynching Site Where Jason Aldean Filmed a Music Video*https://www.nyti mes.com/2023/07/21/arts/music/jason-aldean-song-video-lynching-courthouse-choate. html accessed on 7-22-23 at 7:22 pm.

49 Carl G. Jung, "The Personal and the Collective (or Transpersonal) Unconscious", in *Two Essays on Analytical Psychology*, trans. R. F. C. Hull (Princeton, NJ: Princeton University Press, 1966), 77.

50 Carl G. Jung, "The Concept of the Collective Unconscious", in *The Archetypes and the Collective Unconscious*, trans. R. F. C. Hull (Princeton, NJ: Princeton University Press, 1969), 43.

51 Jung, Ibid., 43, 47.

52 For Jung's 1925 African journey and visit to the Hopi Indians see, Carl G. Jung, *Memories, Dreams, Reflections* (New York: Pantheon Books, 1963), and Blake W. Burleson, *Jung in Africa* (New York: Continuum, 2005).

53 Carl G. Jung, "Archaic Man", in *Modern Man in Search of a Soul* (New York: Harcourt, Inc., 1933), 125, 130, 145, 148–49,. Jung was so impressed by the power of the collective unconscious that he imagined he witnessed among "primitive" Africans, that according to one Jungian analyst he had several panic attacks during his African journey sparked by his "paranoid" fear of being overwhelmed by the black collective unconscious and "going black." Michael Vannoy Adams, *The Multicultural Imagination: "Race", Color, and the Unconscious* (London, UK: Routledge, 1996), 73. Cited in Blake W. Burleson, *Jung in Africa* (New York: Continuum, 2005), 197.

54 Carl G. Jung, "Archaic Man", in *Modern Man in Search of a Soul*, 125, 130, 140–41, 142–43. The passage cited continues: "Just as the human body connects us with the mammals and displays numerous relics of earlier evolutionary stages going back even to the reptilian age, so the human psyche is likewise a product of evolution which, when followed up to its origins, shows countless archaic traits." Jung, *Modern Man in Search of a Soul*, 126.

55 Carl Jung, "Two Kinds of Thinking," in *Symbols of Transformation*, Second Edition (Princeton, NJ: Princeton University Press, 1956), 23.

56 Frantz Fanon, *Black Skin, White Masks* (New York: Grove Press, 1967), 187–88.

57 Ibid., 189.

58 Carl G. Jung, *Psychology and Religion* (New York: Pantheon Books, 1958), 76ff, and passim; *Aion* (Princeton, NJ: Princeton University Press, 1958), Chapter Two.

59 Henri Ellenberger, *The Discovery of the Unconscious* (New York: Basic Books, Incorporated, 1970), 707.

60 Idem.

61 Poll: Trump voters say racism against white Americans is a bigger problem than racism against Black Americans https://news.yahoo.com/poll-trump-voters-racism-white-americans-problem-black-reparations-politics-090038973.html, July 21, 2023; Led by Trump, GOP increasingly casts White people as racism's victims https://www.cnn.com/2022/02/06/politics/supr

THE WHITE SUPREMACIST COLLECTIVE UNCONSCIOUS   217

eme-court-vacancy-white-grievance/index.html; White Trump voters think they face more discrimination than blacks. The Trump administration is listening. https://www.was hingtonpost.com/news/wonk/wp/2017/08/02/white-trump-voters-think-they-face-more-discrimination-than-blacks-the-trump-administration-is-listening/ All accessed on July 21, 2023 at 11:22 pm.

62 Ellenberger, *The Discovery of the Unconscious*, 743, n. 143, 707.

63 Carl C.G. Jung, "The Shadow,", in *The Essential Jung*, ed. Anthony Storr (Princeton, NJ: Princeton University Press, 1983), 91.

64 https://www.merriam-webster.com/dictionary/cathexis accessed on 7-1 20-23 at 3 am.

65 Soren Kierkegaard, *The Concept of Anxiety*, ed. and trans. Reidar Thomte (Princeton, NJ: Princeton University Press, 1980), 129–30.

66 In like manner, the recent appearance of masses of whites protesting the oppression of black people in the streets of America seemed a sudden and nearly inexplicable occurrence, because it did not occur as the continuation of an ongoing process of engagement.

67 Ibid., 128–29.

68 Idem.

69 Ibid., 129.

70 Fanon, *Black Skin, White Masks*, 190.

· 3 1 ·

THE SOCIALLY AUTONOMOUS SELF AND ANTICIPATORY CONNECTIVITY

In the final analysis, white supremacy exists because our American *way of being,* modified though it has been over the years, continues to preserve it; and because it does, we need it to exist, even when we're unaware of any such need, even when we wish fervently for it to disappear. To eradicate white supremacy, we must modify our way of being by reconstructing our notion and practice of what it means to be a self in an expansive direction, so we are able to *anticipate* how our actions will affect people, other beings and things whose welfare we do not feel obligated to consider when we act. To accomplish this goal, we need greater access to our selves so we can eliminate or modify those ways of thinking, feeling and acting that encourage and support our American style of destructive individualism, and cultivate constructive, socially oriented ways of being. We need to gain greater awareness of each other's thoughts and emotions by bringing more of what we regard as private emotions and thoughts into the public realm, where they can be engaged through discursive comprehension, that is public discourse directed to revealing how certain ideas and emotions harm or may harm others.

As we engage in uncovering and critiquing harmful ideas and emotions, we must refrain from censoring or "cancelling" those whose interior behavior or public utterances depart from what is considered politically or culturally correct, unless they destructively persist in their antisocial behavior. Canceling throws the shared burden of guilt between individuals and society onto individuals alone, expecting them to change without any reciprocal response from society. In fact, individuals need the active, collaborative support of the groups they live within to effect change in themselves and contribute to changing society. Canceling engenders fear, resentment and opposition. It retards rather than promotes the achievement of the *socially autonomous self*. We need to show the advantages of the new openness by a policy of nurturing care that eschews vengeance in favor of forgiveness. Rather than reacting in kind to the world as it is, which is a prescription for exacerbating problems, we must dedicate ourselves to *living in the world as we want it to become*, thereby, exemplifying the very transformation of the self and of society that our actions pursue, allowing ourselves to be guided by the insight that *self-consciously transformative living is the fundamental political act of our time*, exceeding parties and electoral politics, as crucial as they are. The more people who live the future in the present through *connectivity* the more powerful the transformative force of their collective action will become. Unless we are willing to make this commitment, Americans will continue conceal their real ideas and emotions in public, expressing them with a vengeance in the privacy of the voting booth, to reverse, in the passive voice of Jason Aldean, "all this bullshit" that's "happening to us."

To achieve what I call the *socially autonomous self*, we must shrink our self-concept by reducing or qualifying our autonomy in so far as it directly or indirectly affects others negatively, while simultaneously expanding our self-concept to include others whose welfare we believe we need not consider when we act. In other words, we have to become less privately autonomous selves and more *socially autonomous selves*. Autonomy would come to have a consciously collective meaning and significance expressing the freedom of the group, and the individuals in that group, to think and feel freely, and to pursue self-realization and self-development, provided it is consistent with the welfare of others, defined more broadly than currently. This would amount to a dramatic shift in what we understand as the self, the emergence of the *socially autonomous self*, which would expand the range of acts that harm others to include acts of omission as well as commission, and mental and emotional acts committed in the privacy of our minds, such as beliefs and attitudes that enable white supremacy, homophobia and patriarchy in ourselves, in others and in the collectivity, as well as physical, economic and political acts done in public. Informed by our broadened awareness, we would reconceive our

THE SOCIALLY AUTONOMOUS SELF AND ANTICIPATORY   221

notion of intent to include the consequences of acts committed unintentionally, that could have been reasonably *anticipated*, where the failure to *anticipate* the probable results of an act implies intent not to imagine possible consequences that might prevent or discourage our actions, a kind of connectedness that forces an expansion of self-concept. The recent murder of George Floyd by a white police officer kneeling on his neck for over nine minutes, as he pleaded that he could not breathe, is an example of an easily *anticipated* consequence that must be considered intentionally brought about by the officer failing to *anticipate* the death. The alternative, that he *anticipated* the death, would be premeditated murder.

But what is a *socially autonomous self* and how is it created? First, I use the term social in the sense of "tending to form cooperative and interdependent relationships with others" living in "more or less organized communities especially for the purposes of cooperation and mutual benefit".[1] A major flaw in the new self that emerged around the late eighteenth century was its lack of spiritual grounding, which was a consequence of its aspiration to become a self-defining entity through the use of reason, a process that Max Weber described as the "disenchantment of the world." The absence of a transcendent ground created the powerful feeling of alienation and meaninglessness at the heart of modernity. Perhaps, Soren Kierkegaard best expressed the psychological dilemma of the autonomous self in *The Sickness Unto Death*:

> The self is its own master, absolutely its own master, so-called; and precisely this is the despair, but also what it regards as its pleasure and delight. On closer examination, however, it is easy to see that this absolute ruler is a king without a country, actually ruling over nothing...the self in despair is always building only castles in the air... and the basis of the whole thing is nothing. In despair the self wants to enjoy the total satisfaction of making itself into itself, of developing itself...And yet, in the final analysis, what it understands by itself is a riddle; in the very moment when it seems that the self is closest to having the building completed, it can arbitrarily dissolve the whole into nothing.[2]

Kierkegaard grasped the impossibility of grounding the self in its self, but his solution to the dilemma, a return to the Christian God, is not viable in an increasingly globalizing world of competing and conflicting beliefs and ideas and people eager for greater access to individual autonomy. The *socially autonomous self* I have in mind is spiritually grounded, not in the religious sense of being the creation of a supreme being, the existence of which humans as presently constituted can neither prove nor disprove, but meaning that the self is the creation of forces beyond its control, and always-already participates in a hidden web of interconnections with all beings and the environment, by which and through which it is generative, a dynamic, continuously evolving process that I designate by the noun connectivity, as opposed to the verb *connectivity*, that I employ below. However, this does not mean that the self is "socially constructed" in the sense of being the product only of social and cultural processes we can identify and trace by rational investigation and analysis. The *socially autonomous self* emerges from dynamics it did not initiate that transcend the social and cultural. It does not come into such relationships, precisely because there is no moment from conception on in which it is not always-already in such relationships. In this sense, it is always-already a *socially autonomous self*, and becomes one in a conscious and constructive way by recognizing and affirming that state. This is a rebirth into an already existing condition that the self has been taught to conceal and *hold-off* in order to achieve American style autonomy, as when my mother, fearing I would be overwhelmed on the American battlefield, scolded me for sharing my basketball. Nor is the self's inextricable situatedness in the connectivity a problem for it unless it assumes that it should be autonomous of it. In fact, its complete connectedness offers the hope of transcendence into a new sustainable practice and concept of self. For if we accept that the self is always-already in connectivity, we have a foundation we can work on and improve, so that the ultimate way to improve the self is to improve the connectivity in which it exists, just as the way to improve the connectivity is to improve the self. You can't improve the self by improving the supreme being that created it because by definition a perfect being cannot be improved. Nor, if the self is grounded in natural law, can you improve it by modifying natural law, which is not an entity or a force accessible to human beings, even if it existed. But with the notion of the *socially autonomous self*, we suffer mainly because the connectivity that largely shapes our fates is imperfect, a recognition that points to the need to improve the connectivities we live within, in order to improve our lives.[3] But, since we live in an increasingly interconnected world, we are all ultimately woven into the global connectivity that may be generating its own collective unconscious. Therefore, we cannot escape the need to improve the global community. Here, once again, reactionary white supremacy and its contemporary defenders on the political right stand directly in the way of progress, both domestically and globally.

Attaining the *socially autonomous self* depends on developing our humanity, by which I mean, that aspect of humanbeing that allows us to transcend our separateness and connect with other beings, to open our selves to the

THE SOCIALLY AUTONOMOUS SELF AND ANTICIPATORY 223

manifold ways in which our commissions and omissions affect one another; that is, to embrace and dedicate ourselves to improving the connectivity.[4] *This is a spiritual awakening, where spiritual is understood as the interconnectedness of all creation and the self's complete and utter dependence on forces, creatures and things other than itself, together with its unavoidable influence on other beings.* This web of interconnections, that I have called the connectivity, is mysterious because our limitations as human beings, including our temporality, do not allow us to comprehend it entirely, and because, in order to produce a certain kind of autonomy, we *hold-off* much that we could recognize, particularly regarding the relationship of humans to humans and humans to other beings and the environment. However, I am not making a materialist argument that only the world we are aware of, or can become aware of with our senses, or by instruments, or can demonstrate scientifically, such as the quantum universe, is all that exists, all that influences us and all we can know. Despite its aura of scientific objectivity such a position is entirely indemonstrable and is simply taken as an article of faith by its proponents. We do not know and cannot know that this world is all there is, or that consciousness ends with death, or that our existence in this world is governed only by the forces we can identify as originating in it.

But it is not enough to anticipate how our intended acts or omissions which we are aware of or could become aware of might affect others. To create a sustainable self for the densely populated global future we will have to actively expand our awareness of what affects and effects might be, that is to say, of how our selves produce effects in other selves, in other beings and the natural environment even when we are unable to perceive, and perhaps not even able to imagine what those effects might be. We will have to strive to transcend our ontological horizon to achieve a vision of humans and other beings as entirely interconnected so that all of our behavior inevitably affects all of us, all of the time but often in ways we do not and possibly cannot comprehend presently. To gain such expanded comprehension, we must actively expand our awareness of our interconnections. This means that to achieve the *socially autonomous self* we must develop a notion of self characterized by the pervasive mood of *anticipatory connectivity*, the relentless, eager, and continuous *autonomic* searching out and exposing of the multiple connections between ourselves, other selves, other beings and the environment in order to undermine the notion that separateness is our most important and essential defining characteristic, and, instead, allowing our essential connectedness to define us. Ironically, we already engage in a form of anticipatory connectivity,

224   BEING-IN-AMERICA: WHITE SUPREMACY AND THE AMERICAN

albeit of a negative kind, by vigilantly identifying and *forestalling* those inklings that we are conditioned to feel might disrupt our settled white supremacist way of being. In this sense all we need to do is to convert that preexisting practice into a positive searching out and development of the inklings and intuitions of connection, and of the existence of the connectivity that we are accustomed to holding off. This involves overriding the WSCU which is what actually does the *forestalling*, and to do that we must first identify it and bring it out into the open.

By *connectivity* I mean a built-up predisposition towards finding connection points and developing them. Such points might be intuitions of affinity or the potential for affinity that are always there to be perceived, but which, in our inclosing autonomy, we forestall to prevent them from destabilizing American style individualism and white supremacy. In an active state of *connectivity*, we stop *forestalling* and *anticipate* such intuitions, summon and develop them. Likewise, we must continuously expose negative connections, such as the way white privilege harms those of us who are not white, empowers whites and makes them insensitive to the harm their actions do to us, to other beings, and to the environment. The more diligently we develop our ability to *anticipate* and unconceal negative and positive connections, including the omissions we do not now recognize as acts that affect other beings, the more connections we will find, with the consequent result of becoming less self-centered, less focused on the self as something whose affinities are entirely elective, and more predisposed to a conception of self as always-already connected to every other self and every other being by relations that can be obscured, ignored, obstructed or developed, but never removed. Our struggle is not over the existence of connections, but over whether or not they will be and should be exposed, discussed and accounted. Today, Donald Trump and his followers fight desperately to keep all such connections hidden in order to protect and advance white supremacy, and with it their self-centered and socially destructive political careers.

Whether we chose to modify the selves we've inherited or cling to them in fear of alteration, the old American style self will not survive the coming technologically driven shifts in global political economy. Inevitably a new kind of self will be facilitated by brain-to-brain interconnections via AI or bioengineering. The primordial idea that there is a god who knows our every thought and sentiment is perhaps an intuitive foreshadowing of our coming connectedness under the dominance of a *Super Intelligence*.[5] This could occur because it would be convenient for it to do so. Begun in harmless ways it

THE SOCIALLY AUTONOMOUS SELF AND ANTICIPATORY 225

will not seem threatening, and might not be dangerous at all if we lived in an equitable world. But we do not. In fact, we live in a nation where wealth and income inequality have grown dramatically over the last forty plus years, bringing inordinate power to a tiny elite. As things now stand, the advent of linked brains may enormously strengthen the power elites that dominate our world, creating the standardized minds marching to the orders of Big Brother we all dread. Therefore, it is crucial to create broad based grassroots movements for equitable, just and democratic societies before the coming *singularity* vastly multiplies technological revolutions, so that when they do arrive, they may be used to liberate rather than enslave humanity and heal the earth.[6] White supremacy prevents us from doing this, because it depends on the preservation of the kind of extreme autonomous self we live with. That self is an obstacle to removing white supremacy because white supremacy protects it and is protected by it. That self is deeply engrained in all Americans regardless of race, gender or sexual orientation. But it will inevitably fall prey to the possibly unstoppable march of scientifically engineered sameness even if we do nothing. Ironically, in our reactive resistance to surrendering some autonomy in order to create more equitable societies, in fear that doing so will destroy the individual freedom we prize, we may ensure that very result.

Notes

1 Merriam-Webster Dictionary Online, https://www.merriam-webster.com/dictionary/soc ial, accessed on 8-11-19.

2 Soren Kierkegaard, *The Sickness Unto Death*, ed. and trans. Howard V. Hong and Edna H. Hong (Princeton, NJ: Princeton University Press, 1980), 69–70.

3 So far as it is within our means to do so, since, as I indicated above, there may be transhorizonal forces that we are unable to access or influence as humanbeing is presently constituted.

4 It should be clear that the notion of humanity that I am articulating should not be confused with Kant's idea of humanity, and our obligation to develop it in ourselves and in others, from which it differs, fundamentally.

5 See Nick Bostrom, *Superintelligence* (Oxford: Oxford University Press, 2016), especially chapter 2.

6 What has been called the technological singularity refers to a theoretical future time in which technological growth accelerates beyond human control accompanied by the creation of a superintelligence. See among others Ray Kurzweil, *The Singularity Is Near* (New York: Penguin, 2006).

· 3 2 ·

DEPRIVATIONS

Deprivations are influences we are denied, whose absence alludes to something unknown, situated beyond one or more of our horizons, the boundaries beyond which we cannot know. For example, light from the most distant reaches of the universe is too far away ever to reach us, so although we can conjecture, we can never know for certain what lies beyond the cosmic event horizon, and, theoretically, we are unaffected by whatever may be out there. Of course, to the extent that we do not know what lies out there we may be unable to detect its possible effects in us. In other words, the impact of the cosmic event horizon on humanbeing is a function of our ontological horizon.

By *ontological horizon* I mean the apparent limits of our ability to know imposed by the current structure of humanbeing, which includes the body, which I will refer to as our *way of being*. For example, our current *way of being* prevents us from physically occupying two places at the same time or performing three different acts simultaneously. It denies us knowledge of what occurs to the self or consciousness after death or what the ultimate meaning of existence may be, or if there is any meaning at all. These are subjects about which we can have no concrete, objective, verifiable knowledge at the present time. However, unlike the case of the cosmic event horizon, we can be affected by phenomena that lie beyond our ontological horizon, although we may be unaware of the causes of the effects, and, depending on our degree of acuity, even of the effects themselves. For example, if Kant is correct, human beings cannot know things in themselves, yet we are still affected by them as phenomena. Even though we may not know what time is we are affected by its "passage", at least in a Newtonian universe.

On the other hand, horizons do not determine how we interpret our ignorance or how we let it influence our lives. The assertion that we cannot know more than our horizons allow is a judgment which does not imply our automatic acceptance of the state it purports to describe. We could rail against it, even if doing so would not change the situation as we know it and end up absorbing valuable time and energy. There are certainly people who spend their lives doing just that. My eldest brother was often accused of wasting his life on idle speculation and attempts to penetrate beyond barriers taken as unalterably fixed by nearly everyone around him.

Alternately, we could construct or discover other worlds through intense creative concentration and live in them. The great Japanese monk Honen claimed to have done just that when on his deathbed he said he had been living in the *Pureland* for the last ten years. [1] We could seek a scientifically grounded way of penetrating beyond horizons. The Webb telescope is an example of the latter. It attempts to transcend our cosmic event horizon by narrowing the spatial and temporal gap between here and there, now and then, by traveling into deep space and capturing light from the origin of the universe that would not be detectable otherwise. Similarly, modern medicine challenges the horizon of the body by preventing and healing disease, remedying defects and extending our life span.

In other words, *it is not our apparent inability to know, which is always an interpretive, contextually and temporally conditioned and contingent judgement, rather than a definite fact, but the acceptance of that judgement that affirms our horizons.* For the most part this "acceptance" is an autonomic pragmatic response rather than a conscious choice. It is a way of being bred into us as we assimilate to our societies and develop personal identities linked to them.

There are consequences for not accepting horizons, perhaps most significantly, difficulty successfully negotiating day-to-day life within horizons. People who question fixed verities are felt to be irritating and may have problems engaging with other people who may regard them as annoying disturbers of the peace. Refusing to affirm horizons also loses the benefit of the potential energy damned up and magnified by the acceptance of limitations, which can then power intrahorizonal living. Accordingly, some of the most

DEPRIVATIONS

narrow-minded people may also be the most powerfully effective in obtaining their goals.

But there are also consequences for affirming horizons, one of which is confirmation of the belief that we have no alternative but to live within them, which makes visionaries, utopians and their schemes appear peculiar and even dangerous, predisposing us to dismiss their ideas uncritically. We simply cover up the inconvenient consequences of our affirmation of horizons by interpreting the resultant limitations as among the unavoidable Given Circumstances of our existence. We are seduced and cajoled, sometimes coerced and compelled to do this by the groups we live within, beginning with the family, and by our desire to fit in and succeed. Apparently, like characters in a play, we have no alternative. But what this actually means is that we accept the general interpretation of the meaning and significance of those limitations prevailing in our culture. *In this way, despite the apparent, or momentarily apparent, impossibility of being influenced by what lies beyond our horizons, we are influenced by a deprivation by orienting ourselves toward that absence as irremovable, holding-off awareness of the possibility that our present or future actions might be able to modify or remove those horizons.* I am arguing that this orientation promotes a particular way of being human, which I refer to as *intrahorizonal* being, that is, being shaped by its focus within and closure of horizons. Such a way of being is most effectively maintained when it enjoys the benefit of political-cultural support, such as Governors Abbott and DeSantis' ban on discourse on race and gender in public schools. The Medieval Catholic Church's censorship of Galileo is an earlier version of this reactionary tactic.

The unknown, and apparently unavailable opportunity to come into a relationship with what is not *here*-which is itself an interpretive designation that locates our being as existing exclusively in intrahorizonal space-becomes a building block of our *way of being,* by constraining our being and becoming in unknown ways by its absence. The fact that those ways are unknown is crucial, because the autonomic goal of the affirmation of limitations is precisely to freeze humanbeing as it is currently imagined to be, or to have been in some golden age such as the 1950s, that is, to make humanbeing a static rather than a dynamic phenomenon as a secure foundation for intrahorizonal existence; while becoming aware of how the affirmation limits our *being* could disclose the possibility of existing differently, and suggest that our current inability to do so is a consequence of our ignorance rather than an inevitable result of the nature of things, thereby defeating the autonomic ontological purpose of the affirmation. Instead, we enter into a relationship, not directly

230   BEING-IN-AMERICA: WHITE SUPREMACY AND THE AMERICAN

with the unknown itself, because it remains, *preferentially*, unknown, but with its absence, an autonomic decision or tactic which is directed to keeping it unknown for pragmatic reasons. This kind of relationship with the transhorizonal unknown is analogous to our relationship with things which, as Kant argued effectively, we can only know through perception and never in themselves by the use of reason. Although, in the second edition of his *Critique of Pure Reason*, he raised the possibility of a being capable of spontaneous intellectual knowledge of things-in-themselves without sensory perception, such a way of being would exist beyond our current ontological horizon. [2] In default, we are, for the most part, resigned to interacting with objects as phenomena only. In this sense we may regard our relationship with objects as *objective resignation*. In general, our relationship with horizons mimics, and may be derivative of, our relationship with the ordinary material objects in our world which resist our attempts to know them in themselves, forcing us to interact with them as phenomena only, and by doing so condition our entire way of being.[3] Similarly, the absence constituted by horizons, shapes our way of being by forcing us to take up a relationship to it from within our horizons, even if we are prepared to challenge those horizons. It may also be that the conservative nature of the object's relationship with us may have predisposed us to transfer our object-conditioned-resignation to horizons, reacting to them as if they were a kind of object and, thus, predisposing us to regard our response to them as objective, which perception lends seeming stability to our existence.

But, whereas in the case of depriving objects of their agency we seek to increase our power, the affirmation of horizons allows us to maintain the belief that the results of our ignorance are actually unavoidable consequences produced by the structure of existence, thereby concealing the possibility that changing our way of being might allow us to discover how to avoid those consequences. For the most part, we are inclined to sacrifice that possibility, which in any case may be quite remote, and at the moment not possible at all, in exchange for the feeling of security that comes from believing our being and our world are objectively determined. That is why I fled from the terrifying labor of self recreation to the security of the historically constructed past during that long ago summer. In other words, the affirmation of horizons allows us to maintain the illusion of being objectively determined, which obfuscates the possibility of striving for continual self and species transcendence in order to improve the human condition. For example, in everyday life we continue to conceive of death as the result of an irremovable biological horizon, a fact of life, rather than a consequence of our ignorance of how to extend life indefinitely, a soothing but, perhaps, a self-limiting attitude.. Here it is important to emphasize that I am concerned not with the existence of horizons per se, nor am I denying that they are real. Currently, for all practical purposes, the horizon of death operates as if it is an unalterable fact of nature, which it is, but only within our current temporal horizon. If, as some other organisms have done, we are someday able to extend human life for centuries, death will no longer be a simple fact of nature. Affirming horizons as "naturally" occurring fixed and inherently insuperable barriers, retards the development of our humanity, with negative consequences for human societies, for all living things and for the earth.. My concern, therefore, is with how our affirmation of horizons conditions and shapes our *way of being*. In this regard, accepting the impenetrability of horizons obscures the fact that there are consequences for *humanbeing* of not constantly searching for ways of doing what seems, and currently may be, impossible for us to do, and not striving to know what seems, and currently may be, impossible for us to know, but we are conditioned to conceptualize and experience the consequences of affirming horizons as limitations that we cannot get beyond and should resign ourselves to living with, rather than the results of our not knowing, which we should strive to overcome by the perpetual search for knowledge, and by orienting our way of being towards continual transcendence of our current mode of *humanbeing*; in other words towards consciously directed evolution.[4] Concealing the fact that the origins of those consequences lie in our ignorance, by transforming them into limitations imposed by the structure of existence itself, makes it easier to obscure the potential possibility and essential importance of transcending limitations to the continued existence of human beings, and the "natural" environment we are destroying by our unsustainable way of being. In short, our current global crises stem from our failure to evolve beyond our current unsustainable mode of being human.

However, instead of challenging them, in the face of horizons we adopt a resigned, complacent and complaisant attitude so that horizons of every kind, whether physical, biological, cultural, or ontological function in everyday life as *pragmatic sanctions*, authoritative decrees that affirm the currently knowable and doable as for all practical purposes all there is of consequence, and thereby protect, defend and preserve our accustomed way of being. Thus, the persistence of the left unknown and assumed to be unknowable, never to be confused with nothingness, becomes a stable foundation for our American way of human being, far more stable than belief, creed, conviction or scientific knowledge all of which can change. In order to preserve that foundation

232 BEING-IN-AMERICA: WHITE SUPREMACY AND THE AMERICAN

from challenges, we are eager to keep the unknown, unknown, and preferably unknowable. In other words, our pragmatically sanctioned resignation mobilizes the unknowable, conceived as determined by the nature of things, as proof we need concern ourselves with the knowable only, while obscuring the fact that the designations knowable and unknowable are both judgments that are contingent upon the current state of humanbeing as manifested by *humanbeing*. Therefore, they are matters of interpretation. White supremacy plays an important role in the project of closure by empowering white supremacists like Donald Trump, Governor DeSantis, and the conservative right, to mobilize their faithful in support of legal and extralegal measures to keep horizons closed for fear that any opening could endanger white supremacy, and, therefore, individual freedom and autonomy as they are currently, and unsustainably conceived and practiced in America. Opposition to critical race theory and discourse on gender and sexuality are recent examples of such closures.

Affirming horizons allows us to *set* our being based on a closedness which we feel and accept as externally imposed. Not "dwelling" on the limits "imposed" by horizons whether physical as in the universe, contingent, as limited by the current state of our knowledge or ontological by the apparent current structure of humanbeing itself, allows us to maintain the illusion of existing as *set being* rather than *incomplete being,* that is being that is not fully formed and for that reason must act to repair the deficit. It is *incomplete being* because we can only know it and its potentialities as they are manifested within our horizons, and cannot know of any existing "parts" of them or of their current manifestations lying beyond our horizons. We cannot even know if it exists beyond the horizon of death. Incompleteness is what causes the unsettledness that leads us to speculate about our being not the nature of our being per se, which remains ambiguous. But if, as I am arguing, accepting the need for perpetual change is the orientation from which we can most effectively develop our humanity, produce peaceful, equitable and sustainable societies and save the earth, then humanbeing should be characterized as *indeterminate being*, rather than *incomplete being*, that is being that evolves. Indeterminacy suggests that we extend beyond our horizons, that we are noumena as well as phenomena. But our longing for wholeness without challenging our horizons, prompts us to *set* humanbeing by using seemingly unavoidable ignorance to confine it within our horizons, thereby obscuring the troubling possibility that we may exist everywhere simultaneously. Nevertheless, the possibility that we might transcend our current *way of being* is neither inherently nor inevitably anxiety producing. As I learned in consequence of my attempts to penetrate beyond the cultural horizon during that long ago summer, when the sense of leaving my body threatened to deprive me of the only foundation I knew, one's orientation towards an opening can make it a heaven or a hell. In our case, the possibility that our being may be both intrahorizonal and transhorizonal is troubling because our orientation to it is governed by white supremacist autonomy, whose race based origins and continued existence are rooted in concealing always-already existing connections between beings in support of *American autonomous individualism,* so that whenever we attempt to transcend our current *way of being,* the WSCU, sensing danger, warns us off by producing anxiety and dread, thereby retarding the development of our humanity towards the *socially autonomous self* that I discussed above. By awakening the American self to the web of interconnections we always-already exist within, the *socially autonomous self* would undermine *white-supremacist-individual-autonomy* which is founded on closing horizons to maintain the integrity of race-based individual autonomy, and replace it with a self founded on uncovering and searching out ever denser webs of interconnections, a way of being that I characterized as *anticipatory connectivity,* which would provide a more stable and sustainable foundation for *humanbeing* in America. The *socially autonomous self* would promote horizon interrogation rather than horizon closure. The new self would mitigate and perhaps remove the fear of challenging horizons that hinders the development of our humanity, because our essential *way of being,* formed as it would be by interconnections would never be in danger of alienation, the bane of modernity, as the racial and autonomous self is, because its existence depends on denying and obscuring connections, precisely in order to be autonomous.

Notes

1 Soho Machida, *Renegade Monk, Honen and Japanese Pureland Buddhism* (Berkeley, CA: University of California Press, 1999), 67; chapter 2, and passim.

2 Immanuel Kant, *Critique of Pure Reason,* trans. Werner S. Pluhar (Indianapolis, IN: Hackett Publishing Company, Inc., 1996), B33, see also translator's notes no. 9 and 13, page 72. See also Kant's argument in his *Prolegomena* that objects of perception actually do exist in themselves independent of our perception, which I assume he makes to address criticism that his *Critique of Pure Reason* follows Berkeley's idealism: Immanuel Kant, *Prolegomena to Any Future Metaphysics,* trans. James W. Ellington (Indianapolis, IN: Hackett Publishing Company, Inc., 2001), Remark II, 289, 30.

3 See Chapter 34 "The Ubermensch".

4 The sciences are the leading example of a way of being that is focused on transcending existing knowledge, ways of knowing, practice and existing. The discussion of how and why they are able to pursue such a way of being, and the extent to which their quest is circumscribed will be the subject of a future work.

· 3 3 ·

ELECTIVE DEPRIVATIONS

In my high school I was deprived of knowledge of my own oppression by the school and the community with my active complicity. I left my deprivation unquestioned to create the illusion that race did not matter, that I was like everyone else and was treated as they were. This unquestioning attitude was a way of being nurtured in me as I was growing up, a legacy of the ingrained habit of assimilating to them. The evasion temporarily dulled my awareness of the burden of race but it was accompanied by the unsettling feeling that I was living in a fool's paradise. My family did not recognize my oppression or their own. Rather, we worked as unconscious collaborators at the level of the *white supremacist collective unconscious* to obscure our self-deceptions. I was only too glad to embrace their complicity by leaving our mutual deceit concealed and deflecting any guilt by mobilizing fear and reluctance to confront them. This worked well, because like all of our best dodges there was sufficient truth in it to make it compelling. I *was* afraid of challenging them but I left that surmountable fear itself unchallenged to serve the prophylactic purpose I had conceived. This was a self-repressive use of the willful ignorance I had observed adults employing as a child and learned to use myself, the reactionary *holding-off* behavior all humans necessarily engage, because we're capable of far more knowledge and understanding at any one time than we need to

236   BEING-IN-AMERICA

function on a day-to-day basis. We tend to adjust to the seeming superabundance of consciousness by restricting our awareness in order to function at all.[1] Most of this narrowing of awareness occurs autonomically, as a predispositional mental reflex, similar to the way the brain filters out distracting sensory data once we are bred into our society's habitual *way of being*.[2] In America that habitual way of being is *white-supremacist-individual-autonomy*, protected by the WSCU which acts autonomically to obscure any manifestations of white supremacy in action, thus further locking us into our destructive kind of individualism.

In everyday life, we think of narrowing awareness as concentrating, keeping our minds on what we're doing, or simply paying attention, skills we practiced as children playing such games as *Simon Says* and *Red Light/Green Light*, and were taught through the regimen of school. They are descriptions that, for the most part, obscure the fact that we are actively *holding things off*, concealing their always already relationships with us, thereby shrinking our world to manageable proportions. Without those skills, which have been ingrained in us since childhood, it would be difficult to attend to what we're doing at any given moment. We could not survive let alone flourish. This exercise in mindfulness is a consequence of human temporality, the fact that currently we can only do one thing in one place at a time, a constraint, as I argued above, that is imposed by our inextricable, unavoidable relationship with objects, including our own bodies and their resistance to our wills. Being mindful is a mode of fully embracing our temporality in order to live more efficiently within in it. It is a technological requirement of selfhood of every kind.

The autonomic narrowing reflex is also a response to the openness of imagination, in which I subsume symbolic thought.[3] Imagination is the faculty that allows us to unchain ourselves from the Given Circumstances and transcend horizons, something that every child does at play, and which the WSCU works diligently to prevent. Once loosed this force is capable of eroding and undermining the foundation of ignorance we elect to stand on. To preserve stability, we seek to restrain our imaginative power. The affirmation of horizons provides an effective way of limiting fancy, insight, artistry and invention, an ongoing self retention that is as essential to our *way of being* as holdfasts are to barnacles and seaweed. It permits us to live, as we are now, without constant worry of being swept out to sea, and to harness our conscious awareness to the demands of each moment.

Since *holding-off* in order to narrow our consciousness is indispensable to survival it is easy to obscure the ways in which we use it to suppress

ELECTIVE DEPRIVATIONS 237

knowledge we prefer to avoid, that is, to narrow our awareness out of convenience rather than necessity, a mechanism the parasitical *White Supremacist Collective Unconscious* makes good use of. The difference between authentically unavoidable employments and elective ones, which distinction is always an interpretive judgement, is often sufficiently ambiguous to allow us to confuse the latter with the former with a clear conscience. On other occasions we camouflage an elective deprivation by making it seem unavoidable. Sometimes we admit we're doing it by openly declaring certain kinds of knowledge to be harmful to our mental and emotional stability, which might be perfectly true, so that our self-willed deprivation may be both helpful and harmful. This maneuver works best when we can mobilize the support of a *facilitating group*. I might complain to black friends "Don't tell me about any police shootings of unarmed black people. I just can't deal with it anymore", and obtain support for self-enforced ignorance, securing temporary relief from anxiety but at the potential cost of disabling my ability to respond to such atrocities by peaceful protest and petition. When enough people opt for peace of mind over awareness injustice thrives, and democracy is threatened. This is one of the most destructive consequences of self deprivation. Another powerfully effective tactic is the appeal to authority, convention or tradition in defense of continued unknowing. Donald Trump and the governors of Texas and Florida are skilled at this maneuver. Their evasions are modes of *holding-off* by appeal to one or more of the *facilitating groups* that support them. Creating, cultivating and nurturing such groups has become the hallmark of reactionary politics in America. Their leaders have grasped the truth that livable, defendable and aggressively imperial worlds can be constructed by group consensus and solidarity by closing horizons and legislating such closure into law, such as banning critical race theory in schools, whenever possible. Underlying all such groups is the fear that white supremacy, and its species of extreme individual autonomy, together with the particular kind of freedom it proclaims as a birthright, is in danger of being overthrown, and the determination to protect them by destroying or disempowering its enemies. In other words, *white supremacy thrives on confirming and protecting deprivations, even those not directly related to white supremacy, for fear their interrogation might foster an attitude of critical inquiry that could threaten its specious claims.* Hostility to science, in strong evidence among Donald Trump supporters during the covid 19 pandemic, is a manifestation of this reflex.

The affirmation of deprivations is connected to the strong national cult of "positive thinking" and the avoidance of "negative thinking", which,

238   BEING-IN-AMERICA

although it may affect Americans of any race or ethnicity, is a particularly pronounced characteristic of whites. It is a manifestation of the WSCU working to forestall the possibility of whites falling into moods, such as self-doubt, profound sympathy for the victims of injustice and inequality, social altruism, generosity, and, perhaps most worrisome of all, actively receptive curiosity that could promote the uncovering of aspects of the Shadow, and even of the WSCU itself. The WSCU works to forestall such mood shifts by fostering the pervasive countervailing mood of unreasoning optimism that beleaguers Americans, and makes them feel that "dwelling" on catastrophic national acts such as the Vietnam War, or the 2003 invasion of Iraq and subsequent war, or slavery, is "negative thinking" and "divisive", which is why "critical race theory" is so vociferously attacked by conservative Republicans. They are correct in sensing that such initiatives, if allowed to flourish, could change the national mood from brash, optimistic national glorification, that helps to conceal the fundamental oppressing power of white supremacy, to one of active-questioning and self-doubt in search of new personal and national identities.

Notes

1   Schopenhauer posited that the "normal" person had sufficient knowledge to pursue their purposes in life but insufficient knowledge or intellect to contemplate the world objectively *"without a purpose"*-apparently, he did not consider contemplating the world "objectively" as a purposeful act-while genius "consists in an abnormal excess of intellect which can find its use only by being employed on the universal [sic] of existence." Arthur Schopenhauer, *The World as Will and Representation*, translated by E.F. J. Payne (New York: Dover Publications, Inc. 2014),2 vols., 2:377,370,372; 1:194-195. He argued that the superior intellect of "man", his ability to silence the will and contemplate life objectively accounted for the increase of pain he experiences compared to animals who, he asserted, lack concepts. Arthur Schopenhauer, "On the Suffering of the World", in *Essays and Aphorisms*, Selected and Translated by R. J. Hollingdale (London: Penguin Books, 2004), pp. 45-46. However, if we accept the development of our humanity as indispensable to developing a new kind of self that will promote, rather than retard, the survival and welfare of all beings on earth, and of the earth itself, what once seemed excessive consciousness turns out to be our needed ability to challenge the insurmountability of horizons in order to develop our humanity, in other words, to evolve. It only appears excessive when it gets in the way of our attempts to narrow our awareness in support of our current way of being, which is grounded on closed horizons.

2   I am influenced in the concept of predispositional reflex by Antonio Damasio's discussion of dispositional representations in *Descartes' Error, Emotion, Reason, And the Human Brain* (New York: Penguin Books, 1994), pp.102-105, 136-138.

ELECTIVE DEPRIVATIONS 239

3 Symbolic thought is considered by anthropologists to be the hallmark of modern humans, distinguishing them from all other living beings. However, it should be pointed out that this judgement seems a homocentric assumption that draws its criteria for the possession of the phenomenon it asserts exists only in homo sapiens on behavior characteristic only of modern humans, and seems to ignore the possibility that other beings may possess symbolic thought and imagination but manifest it in ways that we do not recognize and may be incapable of recognizing within our ontological and species horizons at the present time.

· 34 ·

SET BEING AS FOUNDATION FOR ARTIFICIAL INTELLIGENCE, OR THE OBJECT TRIUMPHANT

Artificial Intelligence is a product of a way of being that predisposes us to surrender our freedom of choice in small, incremental and seemingly harmless matters such as finding our way by GPS. We think of this as achieving convenience rather than surrendering freedom. In any event one can always turn off the GPS and do it the old way. On the other hand, we are so constituted, presently, as to seek our convenience whenever possible. This is such a commonplace and seemingly banal characteristic that we rarely think of choosing convenience as a choice at all. People say "use your smart phone to pay" or "use your phone to download this app." We no longer ask first "Do you have a smart phone". It will soon be impossible to navigate the socio-economic world without one. Seeking more convenient ways of doing things seems a natural response to a complex world in which we are overtaxed. In this sense, AI is a manifestation of *set being*. We have already set our being by *holding-off* awareness of what might interfere with our focus on what we deem most necessary to our livelihood, to being mindful. This operation restricts, and may even foreclose, the exploration of alternative interpretations of the Given Circumstances we live in, and forestall our awareness and development of intuitions that feel threatening to our settled world view. Artificial Intelligence feels comfortable and natural because it is an extension of our

242   BEING-IN-AMERICA: WHITE SUPREMACY AND THE AMERICAN

customary search for convenience and convenience is simply a euphemism for *Set Being*.

Holding off, *forestalling* and *foreclosing* are low tech modes of setting our being. AI allows us to automatically set ourselves on a predetermined developmental path. With GPS, for example, we can go directly to our destination without getting lost and without even thinking about how to get there. At the same time, we are involuntarily directed away from the kinds of chance encounters and accidental discoveries that occur when we take the wrong turn, or simply travel the most leisurely route or the route dictated by intuition. We easily ignore the possibility that our dependence on GPS may erode our memory of the routes we travel and our ability to navigate on our own, possibly even weakening or undermining our native sense of direction. Such outcomes could leave us totally dependent on GPS and helpless without it. When we rely on the "contacts" file on a smart phone rather than recall phone numbers on our own we soon forget them. If the phone breaks or we lose it we may be socially stranded. The sensible retort to these flaws is that they are fixable. One can imagine a smart phone that never breaks down, and a cloud storage system, independent of particular locations that is invulnerable to failures or cyber attacks, perhaps situated in the brain. Of course, such systems would deepen our dependence on AI.

In exchange for overlooking unpleasant possibilities, AI makes us feel more secure. We exchange a degree of freedom in what seem harmless areas of our lives for the certainty that something we need to be done or want to be done will be done without our conscious intervention. This reveals the hidden reason for our seeming obliviousness to the dangers of AI. Except for a very tiny minority we seek the sense of completeness which comes from being *set*. One may say, it is only about convenience, but what is convenience if not the state of not having to go out of one's way, not having to bother with things, not having to decide which route to take to our destination. In short, not lacking the means to obtain what we need or want amounts to being *set* automatically, the way an animal is set by instinct, in other words completed. I simply say go to 146 West Drive and the computer plots a course. Soon I will not have to drive the car myself but only give it orders and sit back. One can imagine a distant future when all I need do is think "San Francisco" to find myself there. I am more complete now because I lack less. I am more complete now because even time and space can be overcome.

In short, AI allows us to do many things at once by dividing our consciousness into an automatic mode, represented by the machine, and our own

SET BEING AS FOUNDATION FOR ARTIFICIAL INTELLIGENCE, 243

active, intervening consciousness, which we have already made partially autonomic, which is still capable for the time being of switching off the GPS and navigating on our own. Thus, our major rationale for accepting AI is that it allows us to use our time to do more important or more interesting things, while less important and boring things are taken care of automatically by machines. This function is analogous to the operation of the autonomic nervous system that allows us to do many things necessary to staying alive and well, such as breathing, while doing other things at the same time. We can read a book or bake a cake and still breathe. In short, AI allows us to overcome at least some of the limitations imposed by our temporal nature, so that we need not choose between one option and another. At least in some circumstance we can actually do two things at the same time, for what is AI if not our current *humanbeing* programed into a computer. In fact, we have been conditioned to accept this way of being by low technology. Taking a train instead of driving allows us to travel to our destination while reading a book or sleeping or watching a movie. Where once we had to concentrate on the journey, mindful of what we were doing as we traveled, now we can sit back while the machine is mindful for us, freeing us for other activities. AI does this on a much more sophisticated scale. It is the solution to one of our fundamental dilemmas as humans, the temporal constraint or horizon that forces us to choose between one project and another. And as AI becomes increasingly powerful and complex we will be less and less dominated by time and space, eventually transforming into a different kind of being, one less temporal and more objective than subjective.

Fundamentally, AI is a mode of overcoming the present temporal limits of humanbeing by creating a complex and dependent relationship with a species of objects to which we surrender a quantity of freedom in exchange for the opportunity to use our time differently. Its logical extension is the creation of a set of objects that manifest their agency through self-conscious thought, eventually claiming fundamental rights as conscious beings with agency. In this way, increasingly, objects will come to demonstrate their agency which will change from *assertorial* to *willful* agency. The logical development of humanbeing, and in particular, our attempt to transcend our temporal limits, created in the first place by our relationship with objects, is the creation of a shadow being, a double who performs acts for us simultaneously with our performance of other acts that would be impossible for us to do without it, simply because we cannot do two things precisely at the same time. Because of its ability to think and act infinitely faster than any human could without being bioengineered to do so, we will likely become completely dependent on the double, leading, once it has attained self-conscious thought, to its domination of humanbeing. That occurrence would be nothing more than making visible our always-already existing dependence on objects. And even if our brains were bioengineered to perform the functions now executed by external AI apparatuses, that would only shift the engagement between human and object to an internal rather than an external ground. Our relationship with objects develops towards increasing interdependence in which objects become more humanlike while humans become more objective. We will surrender to machines at an ever accelerating rate because it is more convenient to be objects than subjects.

· 3 5 ·

THE ÜBERMENSCH

Towards the end of the nineteenth century, Friedrich Nietzsche proclaimed the coming of the Übermensch, the Overman, a kind of human being far above the common person. One can debate the merits of such an advent, but it seems certain that the day of the Overman is at hand, and its coming will render all of our current notions of race obsolete. Ushered in by genetic and bioengineering and accelerating developments in artificial intelligence and robotics, in the context of the enormous concentration and inequality of wealth and political power in America, the time will soon be upon us when some human beings, predictably the more wealthy and politically powerful, will be able to do with their bodies what they now do with their wealth, to alter the terms of engagement, the way life is imagined and lived, passing on to their children wonders denied to the great mass of human kind. If it becomes possible to alter our biological inheritance, increase our brain power exponentially, modify our bodies, making them tremendously durable and powerful, immune to disease and resistant to aging, when these developments reach the stage of practical application, no doubt at a price beyond the reach of most people, those who can afford the change will transform into supermen and women, hoarding the benefits for their children, creating a race of superhumans. Once this occurs we will no longer share the same biology, undercutting at once the centuries old basis for arguing the equality of races. Engineered humans will open the possibility of master and slave races, based not on crackpot theories that fly in the face of scientific evidence, but on actual, verifiable fact. We must also face the nearly certain creation of androids that would be far superior to us by any criteria of performance, who will eventually demand equal if not superior rights to some if not all human beings. We will become completely dependent on them because of our demonstrated willingness to exchange freedom of choice for convenience, indeterminate being for *set being*.

And the future I am predicting will be a further development of our historical and existing preoccupation with race, which has frustrated the development of a deep and overarching identity as human beings regardless of nation, ethnicity, religion or gender. Instead, it has exacerbated our sense of difference, together with the feeling and conviction that we are in a life and death competition for resources and markets. This socio-cultural environment was bound to generate the ambition to engineer superior races of humans, manifested in the Nazi movement, Hitler's rise to power, the march into the Second World War and the Holocaust, as well as Japan's counter white supremacist war, itself a variant of white supremacy. Given our bloody history as a nation, the demonization and genocidal treatment of Native Americans, the enslavement and exploitation of blacks and the contemporary wedding of tremendous wealth with political power, letting the genies of Artificial Intelligence, genetic engineering and robotics out of their bottles, could easily, and probably will, tremendously enhance the dominance of the power elite, perhaps leading to an Armageddon pitting a master race allied with androids, or hybrid android-humans against the rest of us inferior, unmodified people. This coming transformation represents a potential threat to human equality and human rights that exceeds any threat that exists today in white supremacist America, because it would finally entrench white supremacy in biological superiority, banishing the argument that we're all the same under the skin which powered the abolitionist movements in Europe and the United States and the American Civil Rights Movement.[1]

Notes

1 Jürgen Habermas has made a similar argument about common biology and human rights in *The Future of Human Nature* (Cambridge, UK: Polity Press, 2003).

EPILOGUE

My eldest daughter had pressed me for some years to have my DNA analyzed. She was eager to discover her ancestral roots. Recently, I gave in. The results were exactly as expected, with one surprise. The man I'd known as daddy was not my biological father. Many things began to fall into place: his nearly constant anger, the strange words that flew from his mouth in combat with my mother, all came into focus. He certainly knew, yet he raised me as his own. I felt a great sense of appreciation, added to the love I'd always held for him, despite the way he'd scarred us all, even those who fear to admit it or refuse to know it. My intuition, always good, had detected what science now confirmed. I was an outsider, incomplete in more ways than one. Incompleteness is the tragedy of American civilization and I was more American than I had suspected.

Seeking to restore parts of myself that had gone missing, my enterprising daughter extensively, and ingeniously, researched my biological father, and presented me with a large scrap book of his life. As I poured over its pages, thick with news clippings and photos from the 1930s and 1940s, I was amazed by the affinities that seemed to exist between me and the father I'd never met. A graduate of a historically Black seminary college in Virginia, he spent most of his later adult life as a Baptist minister. There was certainly no link

248   EPILOGUE

there. Religion would have been a bone of contention between us. His career as a preacher came later. First, and foremost, it seems, was the theater. He started out in Cleveland, Ohio acting in the Gilpin Players theater company. Relocated to New York he was a member of the Harlem Experimental Theater, where he directed and acted in several productions. He also performed on air in the cast of the African American John Henry Radio programs. Later, in Mt. Vernon, he directed the West Side YMCA for Negro youth. There he produced and directed plays for young people, found time to run for the local Board of Education and was active in the anti-lynching movement. As I read of his political campaign, I wondered what mommy must have thought, when in 1993 I ran for the Worcester, Massachusetts School Committee.

It was at the YMCA that my mother and the reverend met. Together they produced me, and a story that I may never know. Six months after my birth he moved to South Carolina, eventually becoming minister of a large Baptist congregation, while finding time to host a radio gospel hour. His younger brother, my biological uncle, was a successful actor with an extensive list of film and TV credits, including *Cocoon*, and the role of bartender Tiger on the 1980s TV Program *Frank's Place*.

As I read the pages of the scrapbook, I could not help wondering if the hidden existence of these creative and talented brothers was the deprivation I had always lamented. As my daughter had hoped, discovery helped make belated sense of my life; but, as if in a Greek tragedy, discovery was accompanied by loss. The day we obtained DNA proof of the identity of my biological father, I found two new wonderful brothers, one a retired psychiatrist, the other the founding director of the largest radio station in the Bahamas. Sadly, on the evening of that same day my brother Charles suffered a massive stroke at his Martha's Vineyard home. Late that night he was flown to Brigham and Women's hospital in Boston. I arrived an hour later to find him in deep shock. He never regained consciousness and passed away at mid-morning. Within the space of sixteen hours, I had recovered a lost father, found two new brothers and said goodbye to the brother I'd known since Fourth Street. Once again, with dramatic intensity, I was given a glimpse of the gossamer thread that weaves us all together in a hidden web.

INDEX

A

absence 10, 11, 18, 28, 39, 50, 69, 135, 159, 161, 162, 197, 221, 227, 229–30
A Christmas Story 57
acts of omission 210–11, 220
A Discourse on Inequality 198, 214
The Adventures of Wild Bill Hickok 50–1
affinity horizons 201, 202
Affirmative Action 208
African American John Henry Radio programs 248
African Genesis 127
AI 3, 224, 241–4
The Alabama Christian Movement for Human Rights 211
Aldean, Jason 203–4
allusion 59, 118, 157, 158, 177, 180, 182
alternate parents 78
American Autonomous individualism 208, 233
American Civil Rights Movement 200, 246
American colonization 194, 200

American individual autonomy 210–11
American individualism 28
American Museum of Natural History 117
American racism 66
American savages 198–9
American society 76–7
American style individual autonomy 100
American tradition of parenting 91
American way of being 2, 37, 219
Amos n Andy 50
Ancien Régime of Identity 199
androids 246
Annie Oakley 50–1
Anti-Asian racism 206
Anti-Black racism 206
anti-black stereotypes 72
anticipatory connectivity 215, 219–25, 233
antidemocratic, authoritarian and demagogic behavior 43
Anti-Hispanic racism 206
anti-racism 211
anxiety 22, 86, 92, 130, 134, 148, 160, 169, 209, 217, 232, 233, 237

250 INDEX

apodictically 148, 188
Archaic Man 205, 216
Ardrey, Robert 127
Army Doctor of Chinese ancestry 170
art 28, 69, 78–80, 92, 96, 125, 134, 157
artificial intelligence 241–4
assertorial agency 188
atom bomb 115
Attica prison riots of 1971 155
Audubon for black people 169
The Autobiography of a Yogi 106
autoethnography 1, 2
autonomic narrowing reflex 236
autonomous individualism 191
a very sad case 131

B

babbling 10
"The Ballot or the Bullet" 170
barbarian hordes 40
Bash Bish Falls 117
basketball 9, 10, 33, 93, 159, 161–2, 222
Beechwood cemetery 45
Behn, Aphra 201, 215
Belgian Congo 202
Bennett, Lerone 172
Berkshires 117, 141
"Big Apple" 6
The Big Bang 106
big barrels 14
"Big Headö," 63, 146
Binghamton 5–8, 39, 138, 144, 154, 156
bioengineering 224, 243–5
biological father 247, 248
biological horizon 230–1
biological superiority 230–1
bio-racist construct 197
Blackamoors 201–2
black community 61
*The Black Jacobins: Toussaint L'Ouverture and
the San. Domingo Revolution* 73
Black liberation 66, 109

Black Nationalism 40
black/Negroes/Africans 202
Black Power Movement 108, 131, 154
Black Skin White Masks 205
black superheroes 181
Black University 172
The Bomb 115, 116, 171
border wall 204
Boy Scout camp 144, 183
Boy Scout Jamboree 41
Boy Scout meeting 55, 56
Boy scouts of America 113
The bravest man 110
the brightest meteor 143
British Subject 83
Buddhism, Zen and Yoga 106
Burt the Turtle 116

C

the call of the wild 21, 96, 113–18, 129
canteen 9, 10, 33, 93, 178
Cape Cod 150
Capstone of Negro Education 169
Carmichael, Stokely 131, 170
Carnegie, Andrew 105
Cartesian moment 160
cat's eyes 31–4
Central park 96, 152, 154
cerebral Trojan Horse 115
Charles 62, 92, 94, 97, 196, 202, 213, 248
Che Guevara 170
chestnuts 31–4
Cheyanne 95
childhood play 37–8
childhood vocations 33–4
Choate, Henry 203
Christian morality 74
Church and Sunday School 116
civil defense 116
civilized Europeans 198
Civil Rights Movement 35, 54, 79, 211
Clarissa 194

INDEX 251

coffin 138, 153
Cold War 115
Cold Warriors 116
collective racial identity 199
"colored" boy 65
colored people 56, 57
coloreds 65
comet 142
Commager, Henry Steele 168
commission 197, 210, 211, 220, 222–3
communal self-defense 25
concentration and inequality of wealth 245
concept of culture 128
"The Concept of the Collective
    Unconscious" 204
Confessions and Julie 194
Congress of Racial Equality 6
the connectivity 201, 215, 219–25, 233
conspiracy of happiness 196, 203
cosmic event horizon 78, 227, 228
coziness of the booth 178
creative imagination 94
creativity 67, 76, 79–80, 82, 92–4
crew team 133
culture concept 128
culture of fierce individualism 148

D

daily bullied 71
Davis, David Brion 193
The Day the Earth Stood Still 96
Debray, Régis 170, 172
demonic 18, 76, 150, 155, 164, 209–11
depression 53, 148, 159
deprivations 227–33
developing our humanity 222–3
diorama 117
discursive comprehension 219
"the disenchantment of the world" 195
diversity and inclusion movement 3, 77,
    192, 211
Dorothy 152

drafted 66, 92, 170
Duck and Cover 115–16

E

Eagle's Nest 117
Earl of Shaftesbury 201
early childhood and adolescence 3
early home life 14
earthquakes 142
East Coast Native Americans 200
Eastern techniques of spiritual
    enlightenment 129
Eddy 97, 99
education in whiteness 49–51
eldest brother 103–11
elective affinities 201
elective deprivations 235–8
Ellenberger, Henri 206
Emile 199
encouraging creativity 94
engine 9, 10, 33, 51, 74, 81, 83, 87,
    135, 142, 145, 149, 160, 161, 224,
    225, 243–6
The English boy 154
enormous eels 20
enslaved people 197
episcopal congregation 16
ethnography 2
Euro-Americans 198
Euro-centric philosophers 187
European civilization 205
European colonialism 194, 200
Eurydice 143

F

facilitating group 78, 237
fallout shelters 116
Fanon, Frantz 205
fatalistic thinking 88–9
Feynman 165

252 INDEX

Filter Queen vacuum cleaners 104
Fish Avenue in the Bronx 97
Flexible Flyer, small wooden platform 32
foreclosing 207–8, 241–2
forestalling 207–8, 223–4, 241–2
fortieth anniversary 146
foundation 92–3
Founding Fathers 202
Fourth Avenue, shopping 14
Fourth Street 24
Frost, Robert 157
Fulton, Robert 54
Fun With Dick and Jane 50, 62

G

Galileo 229
genocidal 193, 246
genocide 193, 200, 206
Gilpin Players Theater Company 248
Given Circumstances 36, 37, 66, 77–9, 88, 100, 229, 236, 241
Glen Island Lagoon in New Rochelle 19–20
"the God Man" 104, 108
Goethe 194
good will 28, 168, 198, 214
Governor DeSantis 203, 232
Governors Abbott and DeSantis 229
GPS 241–3
Grandma 19
"The Grand Opening of the Doctor's Office" 145
Grandpa 19
Great Apes 127
Great Books of the Western World 105
the great Shawnee 141–2
Greenwich Village coffeehouse 92, 108
The Growth of the American Republic 168
guns 33
gymnastics center 23–4

H

Habermas 246
Halloween pumpkins 9
Hamlet 164
hand ax 86, 114, 185–7, 189
Harlem Experimental Theater 248
Harriman State Park 96
The Harvard Classics 105
Harvard-MIT Electron Accelerator project 149
Henson, Matthew 117
Hobbes 33, 93, 194–5, 201, 212
holding-off, self-limiting exercises 134, 210, 241–2
Holocaust 246
Hopalong Cassidy 50–1
horizons 37, 54, 65, 72–3, 77–80, 91, 92, 94, 132, 134, 135, 142, 168, 173, 178, 181, 187, 192, 198, 199, 201, 202, 223, 225, 227–33, 236–9, 243
Hottentots 198, 214
Howard University 7, 73, 127, 153, 169, 170
human agency 184, 188
humanbeing 1, 2, 37–8, 97, 134, 136, 185, 188, 191–2, 196, 222–3, 225, 227, 229, 231–3, 243, 244
human interconnections 5
human-made objects 185
Hume 213
Hunter College 96

I

Iago 201
Ibram X. Kendi 193, 212
identicality 199
identity-as-self 199
imagination 19, 24, 29, 54, 72, 77, 79, 94, 113, 115, 118, 134, 158, 160, 165, 180, 201, 216, 236, 239
imperialism 194, 200
inclosedness 210

INDEX

inclosing reserve 210
income inequality 225
incomplete being 232
individual entities 10–11
interiority 194, 198–200, 202, 207
inuit 117
The Invasion of the Body Snatchers 96

J

Jackson, Andrew 66
James, C. L. R. 73
Jefferson, Alison 1, 191
Jewish Bakery 14–15
John Stuart Mill's philosophy of liberty 46
Jordan, Winthrop 195
Jung, Carl 204, 216

K

Kant, Immanuel 99, 187–8, 190, 198, 201,
    213–15, 225, 228, 230, 233
Kant's humanity 99
Karenga, Ron 170
katabasis 109
Kennedy, Bobby 132
Kierkegaard, Soren 209, 221
King, Martin Luther Jr. 67
Korea 116
Korean War 66
Ku Klux Klan 99
Kundalini/serpent fire yoga 107, 130

L

Lake St. Pierre 158
language, gift of memory 10
large buck 114
Leave it to Beaver
    neighborhoods 54
    television series 35

The Leviathan 201
LGBTQ communities 198
life in many worlds 161–165
light skinned people 62
Little Black Sambo 51, 72
Little Folk of Many Lands 13
little Jew 63, 146
Locke, John 195
Loman, Willy 104
Looney Tunes 95
L'Ouverture, Toussaint 73

M

Malcolm X 66, 108
manmade 77
"the man-woman thing" 108
marbles 33, 34, 105
Marie, Anne 56, 95, 139
Martha's Vineyard 150
Marxist and Black nationalist 39–40
master race 246
materfamilias 71–80
math tutorials 23–4
Maury County Courthouse 203
McKissick, Floyd 6
McPherson, C. B. 194
The Medieval Catholic Church's censorship
    of Galileo 229
memory palace 177–81
"Message to the Grassroots" 170
meteors 141–3
Metropolitan Museum of Art 96
Mills, Charles 202
Milky Way 117
Missouri territory 142
model building 67
modern neuroscience 40
Morrison, Samuel Eliot 168
Mount Vernon hospital 139
Mount Vernon Public Library 105
Mr. Foster 27
Mrs. Foster 24–9

254 INDEX

Mt. Vernon of 1953 49
Mt. Vernon's West Side YMCA 75
Muhammad, Elijah 108
Muhammad Speaks 108
music lessons 23–4

N

Nana's, Italian butcher's shop 15
National Museum of Natural History 127
Native Americans 193, 195–6, 203
Native and African American ancestry 18
natural objects 185
Nazi movement 246
Nazi philosophers 159
Negroes 75–6, 167
   excellence 181
   features 62
   firsts 181
"Negro" strain 96
Neocons 77
New Haven Railroad train roaring 45
Newtonian cosmos 132
Newtonian universe 228
New Worlds 196
New York City 138, 144, 154
Nietzsche, Friedrich 108, 245
1970s public performance, black solidarity 6
1950s shopping 14
Nixon, Richard 6, 144
"non-human" ancestors 186
Nostrand Avenue in Brooklyn 149
Noumena 232
nuclear war 115–17
NYU 138, 146, 154

O

Obeah Women 137
objective resignation 230
objects 189–90
Oedipus at Colonus 139

ontogenesis 205
ontological horizon 79, 223, 227–8, 230
ontology 1
Orangutans 127
organic chemistry 144–6
Original Intent 202
Oroonoko: or, the Royal Slave 201
Orpheus 143
Othello 193, 201
other up-building 23–4
Overman 245

P

pandemic 200, 237
pan Native unity 142
parental fears 81–9
participant observer 2
Peek-a-boo's a child's initiation 18
people of color 99, 192, 198, 203, 204
periodic pilgrimages 45–7
period of summoning 141
"person of color", white supremacist
   America 98
pervasive sense of doom 147
phenomena 115, 141, 185, 227–8, 230, 232
phylogenesis 205
physical anthropology 127
Plato's demiurge 180
poor Jack 125–6
Port Authority 6, 7, 149
Porter, Bernard 193
positive attitudes 82
positive encouragement 147
positive thinking 74–5
possessive individualism 194
post traumatic shock 104
Powell, Adele 75
Powell, James Oris Jr. 73
Powell, James Oris Sr. 73, 74
pragmatic sanctions 231, 232
Pratt Institute in New York City 40
prehistoric ancestors 141

INDEX 255

"Prehistoric Origins", 129
"Primeval Beginnings", 129
primitive peoples 204
professional counseling services 92
psychology professor 138
Pueblo Indians 205
pursuit of happiness 196, 213

R

race-bred self-hatred 66
race man 73
Racial Contract 196
racial fortification 171
radical interiority 194, 199, 202, 207
Red Light/Green Light 131–2
Red Stick Creeks 142
reflexivity 198, 199
relentless individualism 93
religious foundations 148, 197
religious people 122
remembering 177, 182
rental income 53
Reveries of the Solitary Walker 158
"Report on an Investigation of the Peasant
    Movement in Hunan" 170
repossession 41
Richardson, Ernest W., 23, 56, 73, 83, 110,
    194, 212, 214, 215
Richardson, Ethel Toussaint 73
Richardson's *Clarissa* 194
right of self possession 194
rival armies 26
Rockefeller, Nelson 6
root problem 91–4
Rousseau 108, 158, 194, 198–9, 215

S

Sartre 108
Scottish School of moral philosophers 201
Second World War 246

self and anticipatory connectivity 219–25
self-censorship 79
self-consciously transformative living is
    the fundamental political act of our
    time 220
self-dissolution 158
self-doubt 148, 238
self-forgetfulness of play 25
self-reconstruction 134
self-reliant Negroes 181
self repression 41, 81
self retention 41
senior year in high school 168
sense of self-loathing 68
service drawing scoldings 16–17
set being 44, 232, 241–4, 246
The Shadow 36, 56, 85, 117, 158, 173, 206,
    217, 238
Shakespeare 193, 201
Sheep's Head Bay in Brooklyn 19
Shirley 80, 97, 139
shivering uncontrollably 150
shooters 33
shooting star 117, 141–3, 148, 156
"short-ages" 108
The Sickness Unto Death 221
Sidney 24–5
signs and portents 21, 141–56, 164
singularity 225, 225
Skippy 93, 95–100
slave trade 200
sledding 32, 33, 144
smallpox 200
Smith, Adam 198, 201, 214–15
Snake Hill 32–3, 146
"The So-Called Negro Problem" 73
socially autonomous individualism 208
socially autonomous self 220–5
Socrates 105
Socratic nuisances 122
The Sorrows of Young Werther 194
Southern Christian Leadership
    Conference 211
speech 10

256 INDEX

State University of New York at
 Binghamton 5, 39
St. Clement's Church 16–17
Stevenson, Robert Louis 162
The stutter 39–44, 113, 115, 126, 169
The Subtle Essence 106
the sudden 209
Sugar Foot 95
superhumans 245
Super Intelligence 224
supermen 245
Supreme Court 202
sympathetic horizons 202
systemic racism 210–11

T

Tarsiers 127
Tecumseh 141–2, 156
teenage gangs 57
10 East 39th Street in Manhattan 81
The Tempest 193
temporality 189, 190, 223, 236
tenth grade English teacher 78
The Territorial Imperative 127
Theory of Moral Sentiments 201
The Range Rider 50–1
Thermopylae, British clipper ship 67
things in themselves 228, 230
Things like this don't happen here!, 173
tiger butter 51
the tiles would rise 18
Titus Andronicus 193
Train Cake 9
Tree Shrews 127
Tuberville, Tommy 192, 211–12
Twin Lakes in New Rochelle 54

U

Übermensch 233, 245–6
unbewusstheit 206

Uncle Bill 149, 150
Uncle Louis 151
The unconscious 152, 165, 197, 199, 204–6,
 211, 216, 217, 222
University Of Ibadan College Of Medicine
 in Nigeria 97
university's prison program 6
US Army 131

V

vague feelings 10–11
value of willful unknowing 121–3
Veteran's Administration Hospital 110
Vietnam 33, 116, 144, 171, 172, 202, 238
Vietnam War 202, 238
Vivian 152
Voltaire 213

W

Wahrman, Dror 199
Washington, George 66
Watt, Ian 194
Weber, Max 195
western civilization 40
West Indian Job 82
West Side YMCA 75, 248
white Americans 75, 99, 169, 173, 191, 193,
 206, 208, 216
white Americans are sleepwalkers 173
White Episcopal Church 84
White exceptionalism 198
White First Avenue war 26
white race 197, 199, 202
white rat 9, 24
White Sands Proving Grounds 149
White Stone Bridge Drive-in 95
White supremacist collective unconscious
 (WSCU) 191, 235–6, 238
white-supremacist-individual-autonomy 91,
 94, 100, 196, 198, 233, 236

White supremacist environment 77
White supremacy 191
whores and whore masters 91
wicked witch of *The Wizard of Oz* 27–9
The Wild North 114
willful agency 188
The Wisdom of China and India 105
The Wisdom of Laotse 105, 128–9

Worcester, Massachusetts School
    Committee 248
Wyatt Earp 95

Z

Zedong, Mao 170

Milton Keynes UK
Ingram Content Group UK Ltd.
UKHW021809140724
445460UK00007BA/67